THE VILLAGE ⌐K

A DI BARTON MYSTERY

ROSS GREENWOOD

Boldwood

First published in Great Britain in 2024 by Boldwood Books Ltd.

Copyright © Ross Greenwood, 2024

Cover Design by Head Design Ltd

Cover Images: Adobe Stock

A CIP catalogue record for this book is available from the British Library.

Paperback ISBN 978-1-80549-691-5

Large Print ISBN 978-1-80549-692-2

Hardback ISBN 978-1-80549-690-8

Ebook ISBN 978-1-80549-693-9

Kindle ISBN 978-1-80549-694-6

Audio CD ISBN 978-1-80549-685-4

MP3 CD ISBN 978-1-80549-686-1

Digital audio download ISBN 978-1-80549-689-2

This book is printed on certified sustainable paper. Boldwood Books is dedicated to putting sustainability at the heart of our business. For more information please visit https://www.boldwoodbooks.com/about-us/sustainability/

Boldwood Books Ltd, 23 Bowerdean Street, London, SW6 3TN

www.boldwoodbooks.com

Dedicated in memory of Gail Stidolph

Too much love will kill you,
   In the end

— QUEEN

1

THE VILLAGE KILLER

After the headlights die, my only company is the idle growl of the engine. The tension ratchets up, like a noose around a neck, but not my neck. I won't need to wait long. Sandy remains a creature of predictable routine, even though she has secrets now. Her recent metamorphosis was a profound surprise to me, but, thinking back, it shouldn't have been. She always was a star, so this is merely a phoenix rising from the ashes.

I reach over to the passenger seat and grab a tin of Monster Energy. I should stop guzzling these. My blood sugar blasts through the roof afterwards, adding fuel to the unending roller coaster I seem to be on. No doubt it echoes the rush drug addicts chase, when the chemicals first race through their veins. We all have our poisons. Recent times have proven they are a personal thing.

A familiar figure comes into view at the top of Love's Hill. Castor is a village of soft edges. Here, the streetlights don't burn; they glow. Sandy, draped in affluence, appears to possess it all, but it's merely a cloak. All is not as it seems.

The façade is crumbling under the unbearable weight of those secrets and lies, for even heaven can soon become hell.

Her silhouette emerges, ponytail swaying in rhythm with her stride. An effortless beauty, almost gliding. Posh holidays, pampering, and bundles of money have beaten back time, but destiny's whims are unpredictable. Her future remains uncertain.

When there's a hundred metres separating us, I kill the engine. A streetlight becomes a spotlight, and, under its ephemeral beam, Sandy is frozen for a second. No, a lifetime, an image for eternity. She is everything. Beauty and vulnerability. Available yet elusive. Distant but close.

Memories of past infatuations resurface in my head. I chose the quiet one from a famous band. In my mind, that was an attainable dream. Sandy weaves through those thoughts, scattering them like leaves. The inebriation of extreme emotions has spilled beyond my imagination. These are not dreams. Tonight, the drama is no longer in the recesses of my mind. It will unravel before my eyes.

I sit in the dark, dry-mouthed, even though Sandy will swing into her fancy house before she reaches me. The gate's opening mechanism is broken, so she'll use the horrible little door in it. Then safety, or at least the illusion of it.

These are strange times. Society folds in on itself and insanity ensues. Once, we watched the world's news as onlookers, but with social media's relentless gaze, the only topic is our favourite and most important subject. Us. We are the spectacle.

My attention is drawn back to Sandy. Her breathing is ragged. Her face a grim mask. She thinks she runs alone, but she does not. Capricious lady luck is on one shoulder, me lurking on the other, perhaps others waiting to be revealed, for we have all gone mad.

The stakes are high. Love, survival, and the intoxicating danger of the unknown, but this is not our moment. The stage is set. Performance time has to be soon, before life loses all lustre. Without Sandy, it's a pointless journey. She'd leave a void I could not endure.

Sandy pauses before she slips through the small entrance. She glances in my direction. A fantastic smile, teeth like beacons. Eyes sharp as diamonds. They pierce the gloom. She won't recognise the neighbour's car. Then she's gone.

Questions lurk in the still air. Who will claim the girl? Who escapes unscathed? The answers, like the night, are masked in shadows, but soon will be the unwinding of fate, and none of us will emerge unchanged.

2

INSPECTOR BARTON

At home the previous evening, Inspector John Barton had taken a call from Chief Superintendent Troughton to arrange a meeting in Barton's office at nine sharp the next day. It was that time now. Barton glanced at the clock with boredom. As a front-line officer, he'd regularly had morning butterflies in his stomach, in anticipation of the day ahead. These days, his belly would more likely contain a bacon sandwich. Troughton's visit wasn't even registering a tremor.

Barton rose from his chair, which groaned with relief, and flicked on the kettle. He grabbed the tin of Azera and tipped big spoonfuls into two mugs. His friend, Shawn Zander, had given him a lovely Nespresso coffee machine the previous Christmas. Barton had been using it as a cap stand since February. The mugs were also from Zander. They were a joke set with *Cops* written on one, and *Joggers* on the other.

Troughton appeared in the doorway and breezed in.

'Excellent timing,' said Troughton, with a smile at the kettle.

'Morning, sir. Coffee?'

'Perfect.'

They shook hands, then Barton swiftly made their drinks. He kept the cup with the picture of the fleet-footed burglar making his escape and gave the one with the wheezing overweight PC on it to Troughton.

'Let's take a seat,' said Troughton.

Barton sat in his chair, which complained loudly.

'Your chair's ready for retirement, John. The question is, are you?'

Barton's smile fell away. His role in the Divisional Development Unit was ending. The department was closing at Christmas. Some of the team were being absorbed by other training departments, but most would be moving to pastures new. Barton included.

Troughton was in full dress uniform and looked the part of the professional police politician and a smooth operator. He was intelligent and shrewd, and he could manipulate with the best of them. Barton liked him though. Troughton didn't take life too seriously and knew when he was being spoken to in confidence.

'Going anywhere nice?' asked Barton.

'London, glad-handing with our commissioner. You'd hate it.' Troughton studied Barton's face. 'So, what thoughts have you had about the future? Are you planning to hang up your pocket notebook and get your fishing tackle out?'

Barton chuckled. 'I don't think the world's prepared for that, never mind me.'

'There are a variety of openings available.'

Barton was unsure whether he was joking or not. 'I wasn't expecting to make a decision yet, but I have been considering options.'

'Is retirement one of them?'

'No, I've got five more years until my thirty is up. It makes sense to stay until then for my pension.'

At fifty-four, Troughton was five years older. He gave Barton a wry look.

'It's a bit depressing when we start thinking like that, isn't it? You still have interesting alternatives, though, don't you? Did you research the ones I sent over?'

Barton leaned forward and tapped the space bar on his computer, bringing it to life. He entered his password, and the screen unlocked to show the list Troughton had emailed him a few weeks back. Barton cleared his throat theatrically.

'Force Profiling Directorate.'

'Exciting role, that.'

'Divisional Assets Bureau.'

'Challenging position.'

'Policy Reporting Bureau.'

'I don't know much about that one. It's the commander's pet project, though, so a decent budget is guaranteed. It'll keep you busy.'

'Deposit Analysis Facility.'

'Sorry, my knowledge is light there, too.'

'That's because I made the last one up. Even though it sounds as if I'd be hunting through shite, it's still the most appealing.'

Troughton laughed. 'Excellent. I must admit, the rest sound more like medical conditions than career opportunities.' He paused, then took his cap off. 'Ah, I see what's going on here.'

'You do?'

'Yes. How long have you been behind this desk?'

'Three years.'

'Time flies.'

'Sure does.'

'The thought of another similar five years is far from scintillating.'

'Got it in one.'

'It's what happens, John.'

'I feel like a stranger in my own life. I'm too young to be put out to pasture.'

Troughton relaxed in his seat. 'I felt the same way when I left the front line.'

'How did you cope?'

'I spent the extra wages on a better car and warmer holidays. Paid for golf lessons and new clubs. In time, I learned to manage.'

'That's inspiring.'

Troughton gestured to Barton's computer. 'John, those are interesting roles. You could make a real difference.'

'I know, but I've got a big birthday coming up, and it's made me realise I want to do something exciting again, before my knees won't let me.'

Troughton nodded. Barton hadn't been able to work out why Troughton wanted to see him about all this well before the year ended. Then Barton sighed. Sitting in an executive chair must have taken his edge away. He had been played like a fiddle.

Troughton leaned forward.

'It's funny you should say that, John, because I have an interesting proposition. Might be right up your street.'

3

INSPECTOR BARTON

Barton smiled.

'Give it to me straight, sir.'

'Who was your old boss back in Peterborough for Major Crimes?'

'DCI Sarah Cox.'

'I assume you've heard she's taken up a role in London.'

'Something to do with social media and conviction rates across all sentencing areas.'

'Spot on. She's working with that prodigy, Hector Fade. We have high hopes for his future. Cox was selected to run the unit, but she has a young family and wasn't overly keen on the commute. She finally agreed to set it up and make it work for a year, but after that, she wants her old job back.'

Barton's eyebrows headed for the skies. 'You want me to be acting DCI while Cox is away?'

'It's an option. Didn't you cover for her once?'

'Yes.'

'Wasn't it around the time of The Ice Killer case?'

'It was.'

'Your team went down in folklore for that one, John.'

Barton almost laughed out loud. Troughton was a man who did his research. He knew exactly when Barton had covered for Cox.

To Barton's surprise, those long-missing butterflies returned.

'Just for a year?'

'Yes, although a lot can happen in twelve months. Let's face it, you'll only be winding down behind that desk from now on. You'd have until Friday to close everything off and pass on any workload. HR will do a Zoom call and talk you through the specifics. I think you'd be a brave man to take it on though.'

'Why is that?'

'You know, being in the thick of it again. Life and death.'

Barton reined back his rising excitement.

'To be honest, sir, I don't think I can return to the irregular hours. My wife carried the family for decades while I pursued my career. She put her ambitions on hold. I was constantly letting her down, absent at parents' evenings, skipping kids' taxi duties, and missed celebrating wedding anniversaries and birthdays. I couldn't subject her to it again.'

'You said you wanted exciting. And as I said, it is only for a year.'

'Twelve months could feel like forever if my wife was unhappy.'

Troughton nodded. 'I agree, but so could five years behind a desk if you're unfulfilled.'

Sneaky fucker, thought Barton, but he had a point. 'Look, I'll have a word with her, but I doubt she'll go for it.'

'That's all I can ask.'

'I'll bring it up this evening.'

'You'd be able to help your friend out, too.'

'Which friend?'

'Detective Inspector Zander.'

Barton hadn't seen Zander for a few weeks. His team were investigating reports over the past few months of an older man making inappropriate comments to youngsters near libraries. Three incidents outside the one at Bretton, which was an area of Peterborough. It had been dealt with by CID without success, but a young female who spent time near that library had vanished about a week ago. All hands would be at the pumps in the major crimes unit.

Barton recalled the local news, which he'd watched a few days back. The police and crime commissioner was up for re-election. A missing fourteen-year-old girl on his patch was a terrible advert for the campaign.

Troughton grinned at Barton as though reading his mind.

'High-profile case, John. All the resources you need. Get those brain cells going again.'

'I'll talk to Holly tonight.'

'Good man.'

'Wait. Won't Zander be interested in covering Cox's role? It would be a natural progression for him.'

Troughton's eyes narrowed as he sipped at his drink.

'Zander's record has been patchy of late. I think he'd appreciate your help.'

Troughton pushed his seat back, grabbed his cap, and shook Barton's hand again.

'Thanks for the coffee, John. Ring me in the morning.'

At the door, Troughton paused, then turned around.

'Last week, I met a friend I've known for decades. He's seen me do many different jobs in the force and asked me how I'd reply, after I'd retired, if someone asked me what I used to do for a living.'

'Would you simply say you were a police officer?'

'No, I'd say I was a chief superintendent.'

Troughton put his cap back on, gave Barton the briefest of

winks, and strode from the office. Barton shook his head. If someone had asked Barton what he'd done with his life, he'd have said he had been a detective. That was the difference between the two men.

Which Troughton, the wily old fox, already knew.

4

INSPECTOR BARTON

Barton drove home from Huntingdon HQ at six thirty, deep in thought. He was later than usual, having spent the afternoon staring out of his window considering exactly what would make him happy. He'd taken his office-based position to be more involved in family life. It was now Holly's time to have some freedom. She'd been a teaching assistant for decades, so she could work and still be able to look after the children while he pursued Cambridgeshire's most wanted. She enjoyed the job, but he knew there were other things she'd rather have been doing.

Barton had found it fabulous attending sports days after missing so many. Luke had won his running race the final year of junior school. Barton grinned at the memory of his youngest son sprinting back along the track, flushed with success, beaming at his proud father.

Luke had insisted he go in the dads' race that year, seeing as he'd never run it before. Barton had lined up with a bunch of whippersnappers in their twenties and early thirties, but Luke and Holly, and, to be fair, most of the other parents, had given him the biggest cheer when he'd thundered home in last place.

Luke was at senior school now. The little boy from the juniors had vanished, at least most of the time. Lawrence, his eldest, had finished university then moved to Norwich to be with his girlfriend. Barton had seen him only three times all year. Layla, who'd started her A levels, hadn't developed, she'd mutated, into something volatile and scary. Her biting comments and shrieks had been anticipated, but they still came as an abrupt shock. A procession of spotty boys had come calling and appeared to be the source of Layla's wild moods. At least Barton got to enjoy some fun with the nervous lads when they came knocking.

He bumped his car onto the drive, took a deep breath, and got out of the vehicle. It was one of those mild November evenings that seemed to be a regular occurrence of late. Peterborough was on the edge of the fens and enjoyed little rain. Barton had put the central heating on twice so far this winter, although Holly said that was down to miserliness, rather than there being a higher-than-average seasonal temperature.

Barton chuckled because one of Layla's courting fools had arrived at the same time as him and was standing at the front door. Barton marched over and stopped a touch too close to him. At well over six feet, he towered over the boy.

'Are you collecting a penny for the guy?'

The kid shrank away from him. 'What?'

'Pardon is politer.'

Barton had seen this particular confused urchin before. Chao might have been his name. He was on Peterborough United's youth books. Barton knew the trainee football players were warned they represented their team even when they weren't in their tracksuits, so they should always be on their best behaviour. This made Chao cannon fodder.

'Are you after Layla?'

'Yes, is she in?'

'I think some hunk took her out in a red convertible.'

Chao's face darkened as the door opened in front of them. Holly appeared.

'I hope you're not winding him up, John.'

Before Barton had a chance to reply, Layla flounced out of the house. Ignoring her mother, she grabbed her friend's hand and pulled him inside.

'Thanks for coming, Kai.'

Layla glared at Barton and prodded a finger at him.

'So embarrassing.'

'Why?'

Layla's eyes flashed. 'Because you're weird. And gross. And old!'

Holly almost stifled a laugh, but failed. Layla's glare turned on her.

'And you're as bad.'

'Hey!'

Barton entered the house triumphantly.

'What are you grinning at?' asked Holly.

'I never get to win, so I'll take a draw.'

Holly shook her head at him, then reached up to give him a kiss on the cheek. At not much over five feet, she had to stand on the bottom stair. Holly was no fool. She noticed straight away something was on his mind.

'Do we need a chat?' she asked.

'Later. Zander should be here soon.'

Holly's face lit up. 'Excellent.'

Barton slung his jacket on the back of a kitchen chair and strolled to their rear garden, where he made another chair groan. It was peaceful and the first stars were appearing. He often went there for a think.

'Can I sense a disturbance in the force?' asked Holly, who had followed him.

Barton grinned, realising later was going to be now, but his smile drained away. Holly pulled up a seat.

'Cheer up, John. You've got it all. What could you possibly need in your life that you don't have right now?'

'I don't have a bar of Dairy Milk.'

Holly playfully slapped him on the arm. 'Spit it out.'

Barton gave her Troughton's news, after which she remained silent for a full minute.

'Do you want to take it?'

'I want what's best for us, so I'm going to say no. I love being around for the kids. It takes some of the weight off your shoulders.'

Holly made an unusual choking sound. 'Looks like I need a glass of something cold. Unpeg those towels, please, while I nip inside.'

Barton's mind wandered for a moment after she'd gone, but his wife soon returned wearing a jumper and holding a bottle of wine and two glasses. She poured one for each of them, then sat in a seat next to him.

'Are you happy?' she asked.

'Without my Dairy Milk?'

She slapped his arm again.

'I'm okay.'

'Are you worried about your usefulness?'

'Kind of.'

'Well, I'm concerned with your uselessness. Have you unpegged the washing?'

'Oh, sorry, I forgot.'

'John. Let me see,' said Holly, slowly. 'How can I explain it best?'

'Explain what?'

She reached over and squeezed his hand.

'The time you're talking about has gone, but it has been great having you clutter up the place.'

'Thanks.'

'Lawrence has left home. Luke is at senior school. From now on, he'll be in his room or cruising the streets on his bike with his friends. The days of him following us from room to room asking questions are over, and Layla will be circling the roof on her broomstick for the next few years. You're off the hook where the kids are concerned.'

'What about you?'

'For the first time in nearly two decades, I don't have to do the school run. No more making packed lunches, except yours, which admittedly is a big job. I was going to talk to you about me quitting as a teaching assistant.'

'And get your old career back?'

'Hell, no. That's long past as well. I'd like a position in a café or restaurant with little or no responsibility. Maybe running a small eatery one day might be nice, but not now. I want to work part-time, join a yoga class, do some leisurely clothes shopping. Go to the swimming pool. All on my own!'

Barton took a sip of his drink. 'Are you saying I'm surplus to requirements?'

Holly giggled. Perhaps it wasn't her first wine.

'How much shuttling of the children have you actually done? Who still does all the washing and ironing?'

'Ironing makes me hot, and not in a good way.'

'Who does all the food shopping and cooking?'

'I went to Lidl last week.'

'And I went back two days later to get the items you forgot. I couldn't return the beer you bought instead because you'd drunk it all.'

'Ah.'

'Take your old job back, John. It's only twelve months. At least if you're doing long hours again, you'll have less time to make a mess here. We've loved having you around for three years, but I can tell doing office work is gradually diminishing you. It's not who you are.'

Barton leaned over and gave her a lingering kiss. 'Thank you.'

'Ooh, it's given me a nice idea for a birthday celebration though. You said most of the guys are still there. We should have your team over.'

'No, I've been gone too long. I need to get a feel for the department before anything like that. A lot can change in a stressful environment, and I'm looking forward to you and me having a steak together on the Saturday, just the two of us. Then, on Sunday, a takeaway with Layla and Luke. Keep my birthday for family. Perhaps do something with the guys around Christmas.'

They heard the doorbell ring. Gizmo the greyhound half-heartedly woofed a few seconds later.

'There is potentially one issue,' said Barton.

Holly was already on her way to answer the door. Her face fell.

'Oh, God,' she said, turning back to him. As usual, Holly saw straight to the nub of the matter. 'You'll be taking Zander's promotion.'

5

INSPECTOR BARTON

Barton heard Holly and Zander laughing in the kitchen and stood to greet his former colleague from Peterborough Police Station. Detective Inspector Shawn Zander was also his closest friend. They'd joined the force within months of each other and moved through a variety of departments at similar times, finally progressing through CID to Major Crimes. When Barton had left for his desk job, Sergeant Zander had stepped up temporarily to DI and was soon made permanent. That was getting on for three years ago.

It had surprised Barton when Troughton implied Zander had been struggling of late, but Zander and his girlfriend had two-and-a-half-year-old twin boys. Barton knew from raising his own family that Zander was fighting a war of attrition on two fronts.

Holly and Zander came out to the garden. Zander gave him one of his huge grins, but Barton spotted the hollowed eyes of a man who hadn't been getting enough rest for quite some time. He pulled him into a Barton bear hug.

'Great to see you, Zander.'

'You too, mate. I was going to bring beer, but Holly said you aren't allowed any.'

'She's not the boss of me.'

Holly shot Barton a scowl as she unpegged the washing.

'You look well, Shawn,' she said.

'No, I don't. I'm developing a dad bod.'

Barton chuckled as Zander sat and his stomach spilled a little over his belt. Zander had always kept in great shape, seemingly without doing much exercise.

'It's lovely you're so involved,' said Holly. 'You show me a man with a six-pack who has kids in nappies, and I'll show you a man who isn't pulling his weight.'

'Did I have a six-pack?' asked Barton innocently.

'Most weekends, if I recall. Do you want a glass of wine, Zander?'

'God, no. I wouldn't wake up 'til New Year. John said he wanted a quick chat, then I'll shoot home and catch bedtime.'

'I need to put the dishwasher on.'

Barton and Zander shared a smile as Holly diplomatically made an excuse to leave them to it.

'So, Cox is leaving,' said Barton.

'Yes, this Friday.'

'Did they announce interviews for her replacement?'

'Even the news of her leaving was fairly sudden, so what's happening next is still up in the air. In true police style, I suspect they'll just ask someone to cover. She might only be gone a year.'

'It's a terrific opportunity to step up. Get experience of a higher rank.'

'Yeah, I hope her replacement isn't too green. We're struggling at the moment.'

'I thought everything was going okay.'

Zander puffed out his cheeks. 'We lost our latest sergeant to long Covid. You know Zelensky scared the previous one off.'

'Is Kelly still not bothered about coming back?'

DS Kelly Strange had arrived from London over six years earlier. After some skirmishes, she and Zander had finally got together. The twins had come quickly, and she was on extended maternity leave.

'Nope. She's planning to return when the kids start play school next September, but it's great we can afford to have her at home.'

'What's the problem at work?'

'All year we've had scrappy stuff. No clear evidence to go on. Witnesses vanishing. Suspects fleeing to countries where we don't have extradition.'

'Have you been getting some heat?'

Zander raised a tired eyebrow. 'What do you think, with the commissioner up for re-election?'

'And now a young girl has disappeared.'

'Yep. We're short-staffed, as are CID, who have been involved with this latest case.'

'So, the new DCI will need to be on the ball. Don't you fancy it?'

'No, I do not. I'm pooped as it is.'

'They should get someone young and dynamic. With a cracking track record of solving complex and intricate crimes. A person respected by both top brass and those pounding the pavements.'

'Exactly. The last thing we need is a career politician.'

'It would be a bonus if they knew most of the team already. A handsome, charming man, maybe. Bring a bit of swagger to the department. A guy full of ideas and drive, combined with street smarts, but who still has a conscience.'

'I told you. I don't want it. They'll probably drag a dinosaur out from behind his jam-covered desk.'

Barton's head swivelled towards Zander, who, judging by his grin, had perked up.

'You guessed, then?' asked Barton.

'I'm exhausted, not brain dead. Your position was ending, and it's clear we need someone with experience. I suspected they'd ask you a while ago.'

'But you still thought you'd let me worry about treading on your toes.'

Zander smiled and stood with purpose, looking more like his old self. 'Do I need to call you sir again?'

'You didn't call me sir before.'

'Excellent. Welcome back.'

'I'll get Holly and tell her the exciting news.'

'It's okay, she told me you'd be accepting it in the kitchen. Said you'd fanny around all night otherwise, skirting the subject.'

Barton tutted. 'Of course she did.'

Holly came out at that moment and gave Zander a glass of water, which he downed in one. She beamed at Barton, then at Zander.

'Just like old times,' she said.

'Yeah, me and John can do some exercise together again. Badminton and tennis, become fit, trim up.'

Holly groaned.

'It will be like old times if you do it once, become injured, then knock it on the head. Although John does need to get fitter. Desk jobs don't suit men who are permanently hungry.'

'Hey, I was only eighteen stones last week. The scales do not lie.'

'John, those scales have been knackered for months. They told Layla she was four stones five pounds yesterday. She almost had a heart attack.'

'Old times.' Zander smiled, raising his glass.

Barton took a swig from his glass and grimaced. 'This tastes weird.'

'It's low cal,' said Holly.

'Doesn't that mean low alcohol?'

'Sacrifices have to be made as we age.'

Zander chuckled. 'It's John's big day on Saturday. Are you still having a romantic meal? We should fit in a night out soon, or at least a lunch.'

'Even though it's a bit late in the day, I was thinking about throwing John a surprise birthday party,' said Holly.

Zander frowned. 'It won't be very surprising for him now he's heard you mention it.'

'No, the surprise is that he's made it this far.'

Barton sat back down as Holly walked Zander to the front door with both of them laughing their heads off.

Barton sipped his wine and relaxed. It was great to see Zander smiling. Holly would be giving him another ring-us-at-any-time speech. She was a brilliant wife and a dependable friend. Barton reckoned he had an excellent chance she'd return with a chocolate bar.

6

THE VILLAGE KILLER

The oppressive weight of a Sunday night fills the air. I've parked on the other side of Sandy's property this time, so when she comes up the hill, she will pass me. There's always tension in her house, so she'll have escaped for her regular run. I silence the engine but leave the headlights on for a moment to enjoy autumn entering its final throes.

I reflect upon my youth. Funny how the seasons used to bore me. I wanted it to be high summer or snowing every day. Now, I appreciate the changes. They are necessary. For some things to live, others must die.

I glance behind to check if she's coming, and flinch. My shoulder twinges from a gardening accident. I need to be more careful. My thoughts slither towards other concerns, to money and my future, as they regularly do, but I'm saved from those worries when I detect movement in the rear-view mirror.

A ghostly figure navigates the contours of the hill. I observe for a few seconds. It looks like it's arduous work tonight. Do heated arguments drive the energy out of most women, or do they kindle a raging flame? Sandy stumbles. It's a fleeting moment of vulnerability before she grits her teeth and runs on. Her head goes back for one last effort. Why do these fitness bunnies do it? They must want to live forever.

The darkness intensifies as I extinguish the headlights. Now should be the calm before the storm, but adrenaline courses through my veins. I need to keep control. It is my lifeline; a single mistake could unwind the delicate weave of this dark tapestry. My heart steadies, a solitary beat in my car's cavernous silence. The most important thing is to get away unseen. If another vehicle arrives, I will abort. There'll be other nights.

Sandy, driven by unseen urges, pounds past, rolling, not gliding, stirring the leaves in her wake. The streetlight ahead adorns her with a halo.

After a last check, I see we're alone on this quiet road and press the ignition button. I flick the headlights back on. Full beam. Perfect Sandy stands out like running women often do on book covers. She looks over her shoulder with concern, but her beauty remains untouched.

I ram the gearstick into first, release the clutch, then inch forward. Instead of pulling over to the correct side of the road, I carry on with the driver's side wheels on the pavement. My body leans with the angle. Eyes like a predator. My pulse quickens when Sandy peers around again, but there's still some distance between us. She has a hundred metres to her gate. She's probably not too worried.

I change gear. Low beam, full beam, low beam, full beam. I depress the clutch and rev hard. She stops, twists and stares. Now she suspects. Her eyes widen, she turns and runs. But I am coming.

Even at this moment, I'm drawn to her figure. In particular, to the part where the bumper will hit. I'm close now. She takes a final slow glance. Leaves pirouette and dance in the surrounding air. I imagine those drifting leaves are fallen souls. Victims of another's battle howl.

Sandy looks right at the row of thick impenetrable hedges and looming gates. There's no escape that way, darling. Home is her only chance, and it doesn't look like she'll make it.

Her form is ragged. Arms flailing. Lungs burning. Heart pounding. Muscles aching. Skin tingling. How much does she yearn to survive? Her idle fears have become irrelevant. She won't be cursing her luck. In a sense, she should thank me. Only like this, in moments between life and death, are we truly alive.

My slowing pulse is a thing of the past. Blood roars in my ears. My foot stamps down. The engine snarls with enthusiasm.

It's clear Sandy knows how to run. Now, let's see if she can sprint.

7

DCI BARTON

On Monday, Barton said goodbye to his family, who for a change were eating breakfast together at the kitchen table, and walked to the front door. They'd enjoyed a great weekend. A perfect steak with Holly at Middletons on Saturday night, and an Aroma take-away with Layla and Luke on Sunday night. Barton had drunk only four beers all weekend without thinking too much about it. He wanted to remember every moment.

'Don't forget to wash your hands!' shouted Holly.

'Be nice to the other kids,' hollered Layla.

'Farts aren't supposed to have chunks in them,' bellowed Luke.

Barton shook his head but chuckled. Holly was right. The children had changed. Barton felt different, too, and it wasn't first-day nerves. It was anticipation.

He stepped into his Land Rover and set off for Thorpe Wood police station. Living in Peterborough meant his drive to work now took less than five minutes, as opposed to the half-hour journey to HQ. He could even start walking in again.

When he arrived, he noted the drab, brown, boxy building hadn't changed, with its views of the business park and a busy parkway. The Huntingdon one wasn't much better, he mused, but he didn't come to work for the scenery. It was well before eight, so the office was dark when he arrived. He headed to DCI Cox's office, which was empty, both of people and things, except for a desk and chair. On the desk was a Post-it note.

Dear John. Sorry, not even a handshake this time. If you need anything, email me. Cheers, Sarah.

There was nothing like being brought up to speed, although it would be Zander who had his finger on the pulse of the department. Barton plugged his laptop in and placed his briefcase on the table. He had a morning of settling in ahead of him. Barton's passwords for the necessary databases had expired, and the helpline was engaged. He was rubbing his temples when Zander arrived next.

'Like you've never been away,' he said.

'Yep. Anything urgent for me to face?'

'Not right now. The team is still chasing their tails with this missing girl, Poppy.'

'I saw it on the news. Cute kid. The mother said it's completely out of character, and there's nothing on Poppy's mobile phone, which she strangely had left at home.'

'It's worrying. We've seen CCTV of her walking past the entrance to Sainsbury's, but she doesn't catch a bus because we checked a security camera at Domino's, which looks out on the stop. The CCTV has been checked at the central bus and train stations, and she's not been seen entering either of those, either.'

'So,' said Barton. 'It's going to be a new boyfriend. Someone unsuitable. Big age gap. Car owner. If she walked, he probably picked her up nearby. If he's not on her mobile phone, he may well have given her a burner phone. They're likely to have been in regular contact.'

'Yep. We're with you all the way. The traffic on her usual phone slows in the last month. She may well have been using another one.'

'That's concerning. That suggests significant pre-planning on the boyfriend's part.'

'Yeah, we suspect he got her to run away with false promises. It could be love. More likely infatuation. She took a bag, and her mother said make-up and clothes are missing.'

'Hmmm,' said Barton. 'Let me read the file once I've got settled. Do you think this is linked to the guy who's been approaching teenagers near libraries?'

'The missing girl, full name Poppy Madden, lives in Bretton. Her group of friends occasionally hang out near the Sainsbury's nearby. She gets her hair cut at the Cresset centre over the road, which has the library inside. The kids try to purchase vapes from Martin's or ask adults to buy them. Poppy's friend remembers coming to meet her the weekend before she disappeared and seeing her with a bloke in an ill-fitting suit, but he left before she got close. Poppy had a new watermelon vape, and she was sketchy about how she'd got it.'

'I hate these bloody vapes. CCTV in Martin's?'

'We checked the whole morning, and while they sold a lot of vapes, none were to a guy in an oversized suit.'

'Shit. So perhaps he bought the vape elsewhere and used it as an icebreaker.'

'Yeah. We're checking the recordings from retailers nearby. Sainsbury's is the big one, but you can imagine how much tape there is to check.'

'Excellent. Nice to see you're on the ball. I read there was already a report of predatory behaviour around that time near to the Cresset centre?'

'Yes, a week before. Two young boys an hour apart said an over-friendly man approached them outside the library. Offered to buy them a vape. Guy in a suit. Middle-aged. Dapper. We have him on CCTV from a distance.'

'Description?'

'Guy in a suit. Middle-aged. Dapper.'

Barton laughed. 'Could it *be* the same guy?'

'Details are on the file,' said Zander. 'Same MO that's been happening all over the city these last six months.'

'I should have it wrapped up by lunchtime.'

Zander smiled.

'I hope so. It's a PR disaster with Poppy's pretty face staring out of the newspapers.'

'Are her parents kicking up a stink?'

'Not as much as I would be doing. I think the mother, Audrey Madden, isn't taking it seriously enough. Poppy lives with her.'

'Maybe involved?'

'Nah. Kind of unfriendly and a bit rude. She sent the liaison officers away. Told them to spend their time looking for her child, not putting her on edge.'

'Anything else?'

'One call this morning regarding another matter. Rang the station instead of 999, which is a little odd. A response vehicle is attending, but they'll pass the case to us if it's what they suspect.'

'Anything interesting?'

'Attempted murder.'

8

DCI BARTON

Once Barton could log in, he found the morning zipped by. He emailed Zander and his team to meet up at 5 p.m., not wanting to disturb them as they ploughed through hours of CCTV. He read the file on Poppy Madden while he ate his lunch. There was a surprise when he saw her social media images, and a phrase in one of the witness statements concerning the dapper man pulled at the tendrils of a long-distant memory.

Barton was giving himself a headache trying to drag a connection from the dusty attics of his brain, when Zander appeared.

'That investigation is ours,' he said.

'The attempted murder?'

'Yes. It's—'

'Wait. You might as well tell me in front of the rest of the guys. I called a meeting for later, but we can do it now and run through the details of this case, and I've got a distant bell tolling for this abduction.'

'No time like the present.'

The team soon congregated in a meeting room and Zander said he'd introduce everyone.

'Malik, Leicester and Zelensky, you know. Not much has changed there. Malik has since got married, and Leicester has taken up triathlons. Obviously, it's now DS Maria Zelensky. Hoffman had just started when you were here, and plenty has changed with him, but only on the outside.'

Barton smiled at Kevin Hoffman, who'd resembled a young Barton the last time he'd seen him, but he'd lost a lot of weight, and his arms were covered in tattoos. He'd been balding too, but now sported shoulder-length hair.

Zander scratched his head.

'Unfortunately, we have two long-term sick. I'll email you about those later. The other team member here is Mini. Caroline Minton. She's been with us six months and has slotted in nicely.'

Even though she was sitting down, Barton could tell Mini was one of those ironic nicknames.

She gave him a quick smile. 'I'm looking forward to working with you, sir. Heard lots of good things.'

'Heard any excellent things?'

'Not from Zander.'

'Sounds about right.' He looked around the faces. 'I had a fantastic, motivating speech prepared, but seeing as you all pretty much know me, let's get down to business. I've been going through the details of your predatory cases and read most of the interviews of the five kids who were approached. Three boys. Two girls. Two of the boys and one girl said that the weirdo, as they all called him, said the same thing. "Do you want to be mates? Good mates." That line registered with me from way back. I heard a youngster say similar over twenty-five years ago, and I just remembered who.'

Zander perked up. 'Brilliant.'

'It was Frank Bone,' said Barton.

Zander's expression didn't change.

'He went by Frannie. We nicknamed him Funny Bone.'

Barton imagined a furnace firing up behind Zander's eyes as his face reanimated.

'Yes! I do recall him. He had unusual features. Prominent forehead and chin.'

'And you called him Funny Bone?' asked a scowling Mini.

'Not to his face,' said Zander.

Mini shook her head. 'Rude!'

Barton wasn't sure if she was pulling their leg or not. 'It was over two decades ago and different times. We were in uniform. It was a similar scenario. I suppose it was my beat, not yours, Zander. What do you remember of him?'

'Mr Frannie Bone wasn't the full ticket, for want of a better phrase. He had a habit of approaching children and asking them to be pals.'

'That's right. He used to say, "let's be friends, best friends".'

There were a few comments around the room until Zander continued.

'The other kids clocked him for being different, but he went under our radar for a long time. There was no CCTV back then, and he looked young himself. It probably wasn't a priority. I can't think what happened to him.'

'A member of the public recognised him from a newspaper article and then rang the police, which led to him being caught,' said Barton. 'Some of their neighbours threw stones and painted on his door when it all got out. I arrested Frannie a few times afterwards. There were restraining orders, which he breached, but I'm pretty sure his dad took Frannie when he moved out of the area. That's the last I heard of him.'

'Malik, have a quick look on the PNC, please,' said Zander.

PNC stood for Police National Computer.

'While he's doing that, what's the score with this attempted murder?' asked Barton.

'Sandy Faversham went out for a jog yesterday evening in Castor, and a car chased her along the top of Love's Hill. She lives there and managed to get through her gate in time.'

'But she didn't report it until today?' said Barton.

'Not 'til this morning. She was shaken up and unsure what to do. Her best friend convinced her to ring us.'

He'd only been back for little more than half a day, but the Barton belly began to rumble.

'That sounds interesting. I'd have been on the phone straight away in case whoever was responsible tried to enter my house. The properties on Love's Hill are huge. There's a serious amount of wealth along that road. We know how money drives people to distraction. Any evidence apart from what she said?'

'Uniform attended immediately to check for any present danger. There are no tyre tracks on the grass or skid marks on the pavement. No CCTV looking out of the property, but they said it sounds concerning. She escaped by inches. If she hadn't reached her gate, we could have had a murder inquiry on our hands.'

Zander gave them the rest of the sparse details as they waited for Malik. When Malik returned, he was stony-faced.

'Frannie Bone, AKA Francis Bone and Frank Bone, aged forty-three. He's been to prison seven times.'

9

DCI BARTON

Barton noticed Zander tense his jaw and frown, no doubt irritated at not having made the connection earlier. It was Barton who asked the pertinent questions, though.

'Are those stays for relatively low-level crimes?'

'They're nearly all breaches. Criminal and antisocial behaviour orders, and a restraining order.'

'Sexual offences or kidnap?'

'I've only had a glimpse of what is a long record. He was on the sex offender register for seven years, but no violence.'

'Sounds like he's a guy of interest. Seven years on the register would mean a custodial stay of less than six months for the sexual conviction, so it won't have been a high-tariff offence such as rape.' Most of Barton's team would be aware of that, but some of the newer members might not. 'I assume our impressive computer system gave you a current address, assuming he isn't at His Majesty's pleasure as we speak.'

'No, that's the thing. There's been no criminality for fifteen years.'

'Interesting. Last known abode?'

'Harmony Farm, close to Newport in Wales.'

'Excellent. I love it when they're nearby. I'll head to this Castor case. DC Minton and DS Zelensky can come with me. It will help get me back in the detective's mindset. Seems as if you guys have some investigating to do of our Mr Bone. There's nothing like a manhunt with a cold trail.'

'No worries,' said Zander. 'We'll soon chase him down.'

'Minton,' said Barton. 'Book a car out. I'll be down in five minutes. Zelensky, meet us there in another vehicle, please.'

Barton waited for her and the rest of the team to filter out before taking a seat beside Zander.

'Should I have remembered Frannie Bone?' muttered Zander.

Barton was tempted to make a joke but didn't.

'No, I don't think so. Bone never struck me as the type to abduct anyone, and he wasn't someone you were directly involved with. Anyway, it was yonks ago.'

'These men escalate, John. Who knows what kind of monster he's grown into?'

Barton rose from his seat and shrugged.

'You know what these investigations are like. They're dominos. He might well be the first one and the others will fall.'

'That's why I'm annoyed,' said Zander, rubbing his temples.

Barton squeezed Zander's shoulder, then he grabbed his suit jacket and left the room, knowing his friend was near to burning out.

He met Minton downstairs. They got in the car, and she drove them confidently out of the station. It was a bright day, and she slipped a pair of Oakley sunglasses on.

Barton casually took in her appearance. He deliberately hadn't asked about her, so he could make his own judgement. Other than the sunglasses, her wardrobe style was smart and sensible. Shoulder-length brown hair pulled into a tight ponytail.

Barton was hardly an expert on make-up, but she didn't appear to be wearing much. Her shoes appeared more functional than showy.

'How are you enjoying the job?' he asked. 'I assume you came from CID.'

'I did. To be honest, it's not been great.'

Barton chuckled. 'How so?'

'We had a murder case where the culprit fled to Kashmir, and another kidnapping where the people we wanted to speak to simply vanished. The other investigations haven't been exciting.'

'You thought Major Crimes would be pacier than CID, but it's actually been slower.'

Minton gave him a brief glance. 'Precisely.'

'That's because the cases are relatively minor in CID, so they quickly go on the back burner if there's little or no progress. It's a conveyor belt.'

'Yes, and I knew that Major Crimes didn't have that luxury until much further down the line, which means checking and double-checking. I expected it to be meticulous work. I just didn't realise how meticulous.'

'So, no speeding cars or foot pursuits yet?'

'None at all.'

'Except at home time.'

Minton took off her sunglasses and grinned and Barton witnessed a transformation. Her face lit up, which made her seem younger than her approximately thirty years. It was disarming when the rest of her appeared so unflamboyant. Zander had told him she was a brilliant interviewer back when she first joined his team. A beaming smile like that would be a handy asset when dealing with male or female suspects.

Two miles later, she took the slip road off the A47 and turned left onto Love's Hill. The road ran on for a few hundred metres, then had a steep dip into the village proper. Along the top rise, there were large plots housing grand properties.

Minton whistled. 'It's been a while since I was up here. It's a bit different from where I grew up.'

'Are you a Peterborian?'

'Paston.'

Barton nodded. Paston was a mostly working-class area. 'My parents raised me on a similar estate.'

'Some complained about Paston, but I didn't. It was fine.'

'If everyone more or less has the same, then you're all just kids growing up.'

Minton smiled again.

'This is the one,' said Barton a few seconds later. 'Paddock Green. Nice name.'

A short drive led to a solid six-feet-high wooden gate, which was obviously the entrance for vehicles to the property. Minton parked in front of it. There were fence panels a similar height joining both neighbouring homes, with conifers growing behind them. It was a formidable entrance.

They left the vehicle and approached the gate just as Zelensky pulled in behind them and walked over. A throaty lawnmower was operating nearby, but otherwise it was peaceful. Barton could see over the gate easily enough on tiptoes. Minton could peer over, too.

'Now you know why I wear flats.' She glanced down at Zelensky, who was a foot shorter than her. 'Do you want a leg-up, Sarge?'

Zelensky nodded imperceptibly. Barton frowned. The Zelensky he knew would have laughed and come back with something witty or, more likely, abusive. Not disinterest. She'd never been a flashy dresser, but her black suit and white blouse were crumpled.

They checked behind them as a silver car cruised by. It braked, slowed further, then, indicator blinking, turned into the next drive. Barton watched the driver, a grey-haired man in business attire, raise his hand. He held what looked like a remote control. After a few seconds, the sleek Bentley coasted out of sight.

Barton turned back to admire the building at the centre of Paddock Green.

'Not bad,' he said.

They searched for a state-of-the-art doorbell but failed to find one of any kind. Taped-up wires stuck out of a hole in one of the door posts. Barton knocked loudly on the wood.

'I love this village,' said Zelensky as they waited.

'What about it?' asked Minton.

Zelensky gestured to the rolling countryside that stretched off into the distance behind them.

'This is how life should be. Quiet streets, small primary school, friendly local shop, a couple of brilliant restaurants, beautiful individual old stone houses, and the River Nene runs along the back of it. My friend married a guy who grew up here and they moved into his family's farmhouse. She's massively smug.'

Barton laughed.

'Perhaps a bit boring for the children,' said Minton.

'I suppose it depends on the type of kids,' said Barton. 'Remember, a lot of them now socialise virtually, so it doesn't matter where they are. Then when they do step outside, they're surrounded by miles of woodland and riverside. There's a lot of money here, so there's riding, fishing, and shooting for those who want it, and cosy pubs for those who don't.'

'Didn't the A47 go through here once?' asked Zelensky as she knocked again.

'Yeah, the bypass killed no end of businesses off when they lost the passing trade, but that's got to be over thirty years ago. The village actually dates back to Roman times. The church is one of the finest Norman churches in England. Rebuilt in that style after the Vikings destroyed it.'

Barton gave them his smuggest look. 'Impressed?'

'Kind of,' said Minton.

'My eldest son did a GCSE project on the village, so I kept having to drive him here. I was forced to spend a lot of time in the cosy pubs. It was a real hardship.'

Barton was too old for hurdling high gates, but there was a small pedestrian entrance in the main body of the door with a latch, which, to his surprise, opened when he tried it. Even so, he only just fitted through. It led directly to a driveway.

There were four cars parked outside a triple garage. A white van with Steele Garden Services on the bonnet, a battered black truck, a brand-new white Lexus, and a ten-year-old red Mini Cooper.

A man with a tanned head and a circle of grey hair was kneeling at the side of the right-hand post. His overalls appeared well used. He had the cover off a rectangular box, which Barton suspected was the mechanism for the electric gate. A screen on a stand had also been dismantled next to him. The man looked up and smiled. He pointed down the driveway with his screwdriver and returned to his task.

The officers strode down the block-paved drive that narrowed into a path, which split a large lawn. The lawn was empty except for two young oak trees, which guided the approaching officers' vision towards the stone house before them. As they approached, Barton realised the bricks were relatively new. It was the dead ivy over them that had fooled him.

A chugging ride-on lawnmower trundled around the side of the property and headed in their direction. It conked out a few metres away and a man in scruffy jeans and a worn denim jacket dismounted it and shook his head. He had unkempt, shoulder-length hair and a short beard, which reminded Barton of Jared Leto, who he'd seen in the film *Morbius* recently.

'The maintenance guy only fixed this yesterday,' he said to nobody in particular.

Barton strode forward and showed his warrant card. 'DCI John Barton. My colleagues, DC Minton and DS Zelensky. Lovely place.'

The man barely glanced at it.

'It is beautiful here. Six acres, too. What I would call a substantial detached property within six acres of wonderfully landscaped south-facing formal gardens, all maintained by me. That includes the woodland and paddocks at the back, and there's a swimming pool.'

'All in an attractive edge-of-village setting,' said Minton with a little smile.

'Exactly.'

'It's certainly striking,' said Barton.

'I wish it were mine.'

'You aren't the owner, then?'

'No, I'm Timothy Steele. I work here.'

'Sounds like you're proud of the place.'

'I am. This is one of the many properties along this road where I'm the horticulturalist. When I promote my company to other homeowners nearby, they need reassurance that I can maintain the high standards they insist upon. Knowledge of the area and pride in my work is important.'

Barton assumed those well-rehearsed lines meant he was the local gardener. Up close, he could see Timothy's beard was wispy. He put his age at mid-twenties.

The front door in the middle of the grand house opened behind Timothy, and a stern-faced woman appeared in the doorway. She seemed overdressed for a Monday morning, unless she was heading to a posh business dinner. Her clothes were a touch on the tight side.

'At long last!' she shouted. 'Come in.'

Barton had expected a cut-glass accent, and his eyes widened at the rough voice. He supposed it wasn't a time for pleasantries. The woman disappeared, leaving the door open. He was about to follow her in when he noticed the expressions on his team's faces. Mouths had fallen open.

'What is it?' he asked.

'We've met her before,' said Minton, recovering first.

'Who is it?'

Zelensky marched past him. 'Audrey. She's the mother of the missing girl.'

10

THE VILLAGE KILLER

So, the police are taking it seriously. The first responders treated the situation with all the urgency of a reported stolen bicycle, but these three in suits exude an air of focus and determination.

If Sandy had called 999 immediately after it happened yesterday, all flustered and 'I'm gonna die', then there would have been flashing blue lights and blaring sirens, but she didn't. Even though her concerns must have festered overnight, she was still resistant to having the police here. That is interesting. She could have died last night.

Time, a relentless adversary, will now play its hand because delay dulls our memories. Births, deaths, shocks, scares, you name it. Eventually, everything fades and curls at the edges. The once sharp contours blur, and doubt creeps in like an eager shadow. I suppose that feeling of incredible vulnerability would have dissipated. Adrenaline spikes cause tunnel vision. Her brain panicked. Perhaps she was mistaken after all.

And Sandy is under a lot of stress.

Time is the defence lawyer's greatest asset. Can you be sure the car in question was black? Your first statement said it was blue. Are you certain it was 9 p.m.? You mentioned the lights blinded your vision, so would you say you are more or less confident than fifty per cent?

I recall a programme I watched long ago, which explained that every time you relive an experience, your brain subtly alters it. Details shift, fragments rearrange, others are inserted. When you next retrieve that moment, it may be the latest distortion you recollect, not the original event. Memories grow so imprecise they reach the point of being totally false. I've often wondered since that show whether my favourite reminiscences, the ones from school, occurred as I recall.

I suspect the truth of the matter, and the reason for Sandy's tardy call to the authorities, is that last night's incident wasn't such a surprise. She will have had a foreboding sense of doom lingering within her, long before yesterday.

She'll know nobody escapes scot-free. Her secrets are simply truths yet to be discovered.

11

DCI BARTON

Minton strode up to Barton while he took a moment to consider the ramifications of the missing girl's mother being present at this house. He swiftly decided there were too many.

'CID told us that the mum, Audrey, is a cold fish,' she whispered as he followed her inside.

When they reached an impressively large lounge, Barton spotted a striking man in chinos and a blazer. He turned once to acknowledge the new arrivals with a nod, then stared back out of the window. Barton estimated him to be around sixty. The woman who had answered the door stood next to another groomed lady, who held her head with shaky hands. Zelensky was scowling at Audrey and clearly waiting for an answer. The other woman lowered herself to perch on the sofa.

Audrey's chin rose before she spoke.

'Sandy Faversham is my best friend. When she told me what happened, I came straight away.'

'Didn't you want to be at home in case your daughter returned?' asked Zelensky.

Audrey's eyes narrowed.

'Poppy has my number. She can ring me any time.'

Barton analysed Audrey's stance and expression. She leaned towards Zelensky as she talked, which might indicate hostility or a plea for help, but her shoulders were down, hands open, and her mouth was relaxed. It was not the typical demeanour of a terrified or desperate parent.

Still, there was nothing to be gained by aggressively grilling the mother of a missing child, and Zelensky should know that. Barton introduced himself.

'A chief?' said Audrey. 'I'm glad you lot are at last seeing this for what it was. My friend could be in hospital or worse.'

Barton smiled at her. 'Can I have a quick word with you in the kitchen?'

Audrey held his stare, then nodded. 'Follow me.'

They headed through a set of French doors, which led to a grand kitchen with an eye-catching island.

'What is it?'

Barton suspected Audrey was no stranger to arguments.

'I've been doing this job a long time so forgive me for being frank,' said Barton, calmly. 'I see a woman who's not worried about her missing daughter.'

'I am concerned.'

'But you're not terrified.'

Audrey stared at the floor, then through the back window into the vast garden. She didn't comment.

'I expect you know where she is,' said Barton. 'Or at least you believe Poppy's safe, or safeish. She's not been abducted against her will.' Audrey remained quiet. Barton was onto something. 'Has she been in touch recently?'

Audrey returned her gaze to Barton and shook her head. Barton waited.

Audrey sighed. 'But she has been home since I reported her missing.'

'What? You saw her?'

'No.'

'When was she back?'

'Maybe yesterday.'

'Why do you suspect that?'

'I'm pretty sure more of her clothes and another couple of pairs of shoes have gone.'

'I see.' Barton reflected on why she'd kept the news to herself, but he still thought Audrey should be more concerned. Then it dawned on him. 'Was that the first time she's returned?'

Audrey tipped her head. 'Possibly once before that.'

'Don't you think we'd like to have been informed?'

Audrey's jaw bunched. Her reply was almost a snarl.

'How would it have helped? You would have taken her case less seriously. Scaled down the hunt, maybe. She's still fourteen, and she remains nowhere to be found. I want you—' she jabbed a finger at him '—believing the worst, so you—' another jab '—try your best.'

Barton considered her response. He never judged folk harshly in these kinds of situations. People could act in any number of ways under pressure, and to a certain degree she was right. Stolen child grabbed more headlines than runaway girl.

'Okay. I'm in charge now. Her priority is as high as it was previously, but we may take a different approach. Don't worry, I'll get your child back.'

A tear welled in Audrey's eye, but she blinked it away. Barton took out his notebook.

'Can you tell me about your relationship with Sandy?'

'Sandy's my closest friend. We've known each other since senior school. I ring her or pop over most days if I can. Usually, I work part-time, but they've given me compassionate leave. When Sandy said today that someone tried to run her over last night, I was like, oh my God, what did the police say? But she hadn't told anyone.'

'Not even her husband?'

'Nope.'

'Why do you think that was?'

Audrey shrugged. 'Shock.'

'Okay. I'm going to talk to her now. I'd like you to stay here and give the tall detective, DC Minton, all the latest news on your daughter. We need you to cooperate fully. That gives us the best chance of locating Poppy.'

Audrey let out a deep breath and fiddled with the ends of her highlighted hair. 'Okay.'

'I assume that gent at the window is Sandy's husband.'

'Yes, Charles Albert Faversham, and he's a dickhead. That's probably why she didn't tell him.'

Barton gave her a tight smile and returned to the lounge. He had a brief chat with Minton, who said she had been talking to Sandy. Minton left for the kitchen, and Barton sat opposite Sandy Faversham, who now had her hands over her face, but they had stopped shaking. Zelensky had her notebook out and was standing next to Charles.

'Exactly my point,' shouted Charles. 'It's not normal Castor behaviour, at least not at this end of the village. We get the odd joyrider here. No speed cameras, you see.'

'So, you've seen nothing suspicious lately?'

'Nothing.'

'We saw the front gate was damaged. Might someone have tampered with it?'

'Jerry said the motor burned out. They're damned expensive.'

'Can we have a look at your CCTV?'

Charles grimaced. 'That's been on the blink, too. It's all

connected. The gate kept triggering the alarm. In the end, I turned it all off six months ago. The part needed for repair had to come from China, but it arrived faulty, so they've sent another replacement. Bloody nightmare. I'm not paying for a new gate. I can wait. After all, nothing ever happens here.'

'Something happened to your wife.'

'I'm sure she... I don't know... misconstrued events. Perhaps someone lost control for a bit and veered over the road.'

'Sandy appears shaken up. Is there anyone who might want to cause her harm?'

Charles rolled his eyes. 'Of course not. That's the thing. Who could she upset if she does nothing?'

Barton's head twirled towards the diminutive figure sitting on the sofa. Sandy had lowered her hands and was glaring straight ahead. Barton realised she hadn't been shaking with fear. It was anger.

12

DCI BARTON

Barton cleared his throat as he stood.

'Could you give us a minute, please, Charles?'

'I'd like to stay.'

'The sergeant will talk to you outside.'

Barton waited for Zelensky to usher Charles out of the front door before he took the armchair opposite his wife.

'How are you feeling, Sandy?' asked Barton.

'Like I wish I hadn't mentioned it.'

'It's important we know if someone's driving dangerously, never mind if they were trying to run a person down.'

'He's got me doubting myself, as usual.'

'Talk me through what happened.'

Sandy's face relaxed, and she smiled. She reminded Barton of when Minton had smiled earlier, but this was like feeling the strength of the sun as it broke the clouds on a spring morning. Now he saw her clearly, her beauty shone. As Sandy talked, she spoke with grace and poise. She was certainly the type of woman who drove others to act out of character.

'I'd had a hectic day and was looking forward to my jog. I do the same route of five miles three times a week to keep in shape. I came up the hill, which is a great finish, because it's so steep, and approached home. Then I was lit up. I glanced around and saw a car with its full beam on. I hadn't even noticed the vehicle, what with focusing on my burning calves, so I carried on running. When they pulled away, I heard the engine revs pick up.'

'When was this?'

'Around 9 p.m.'

'What side of the street were they on?'

'The side next to the houses. They had parked up, half on the road, half on the pavement, away from the driveways. People do that when they don't want to block the gates.'

'So, normally they'd pull away, then move into the correct lane.'

'Yes, it's a quiet place at night nowadays due to the bypass, and it's a wide road.'

'But this vehicle continued driving on the wrong side, which brought them up behind you.'

'Yes, I think so.'

'You only think so?'

She clenched her fists.

'I was tired. The headlights were right in my eyes. It just felt aggressive, but I suppose my husband's right. If they'd wished me dead, I would be. They could have caught me if they wanted. I was already flat out.'

'Who would want to scare you?'

Sandy threw her hands up in the air and rose from her seat. Barton couldn't see her expression until she turned around. It was blank.

'He's correct there, too. If I do nothing, then how would I possibly upset anyone?'

'We can investigate this, but it sounds like you aren't certain. We'd need to use a considerable amount of resources.'

'What would be involved in an investigation?'

It was a strange question for a victim to ask.

'If you're reasonably sure an attempt was made on your life, then we'd delve into the potential reasons why. Look at everyone close to you. It could be someone in your circle, whether that's work, family, friends, or neighbours. They would all go under the magnifying glass. We'd try to trace the car from various traffic sources. It's worth our effort if you are concerned.'

Barton watched Sandy run her tongue across her teeth. There was something odd occurring, and that was without the drama around her best friend's daughter.

'Can we just forget I rang?'

'That isn't how it works, I'm afraid.'

'Shame. What are you going to do?'

'I'll have a word with your husband before I go.'

'He won't be pleased.'

'That's what I'm counting on. Is your relationship tense?'

'Do you mean, does he wish me dead?'

'I wouldn't want to put words in your mouth.'

Again, the megawatt smile.

'I am his porcelain doll. He'd hate to see me broken.'

'I see. Anything else I should be aware of?'

'No. I'm safe here.'

'I thought the CCTV and the alarm weren't functioning.'

'They aren't, but there's usually someone about during the day. My husband would never allow any harm to come to me at night. Let's hope it was a one-off. You know, high jinks. Kids messing around.'

Barton made another entry in his notebook. He hadn't expected to be doing that as acting DCI, but he wanted to give Zander some free time in the office. It also showed the team he wasn't afraid to get his hands dirty. He gave Sandy his business card.

'Think it over. Ring me tomorrow and we'll talk again. If you have somewhere else to stay, caution never hurt.'

'Understood, Inspector. Thank you for coming.'

Barton stepped outside the house and found Zelensky putting her pen in her pocket. Charles glowered next to her.

'Can I have a word, please, Charles?' asked Barton.

'I've talked to your officer.'

'Humour me. Is everything fine here?'

It was a blunt question, but Barton was leaving, and there was something out of kilter. To his surprise, Charles grinned.

'Relationships are complicated, but love can't all be roses and champagne, can it?'

Barton didn't smile back. What was he missing? He wouldn't be amused if there had been the slightest hint of an attempt on Holly's life. 'Where were you last night?'

'Here. On this side of the gates.'

'It's a pity the CCTV doesn't work to confirm that.'

'I love my wife. More than anything, or anyone.'

Barton studied his face.

'Keep an eye out, Charles. Get in touch at any point if you want to talk, or if you think of something, or spot any suspicious behaviour. Please, take this seriously.'

Charles sneered. 'If it was an attempt to run her down, they were far from successful.'

'Perhaps,' said Barton sternly, 'but practice makes perfect.'

13

DCI BARTON

Minton and Audrey left the house as Charles marched back inside.

'Audrey's heading home,' said Minton, 'in case her daughter appears again. I've rung Social Services. They're going to meet her there.'

'Okay, great. Can you and Zelensky have a word with that neighbour we saw turning up, and see who's on the other side? Just a friendly chat.'

Minton gave the quickest of nods. 'Sure, boss.'

Barton smiled as the two women left. He could already tell that with time and experience Minton would be a real asset. He walked with Audrey down the drive. The Mini Cooper was her car. Before she got in, she turned back to Barton.

'Are you concerned about Sandy's safety?'

'Of course, but resources are stretched. It's hard for us to commit them if she's so vague about any potential threat. Don't worry. We'll be in touch again shortly.'

'I'll talk to her.' Audrey scowled. 'You know, I come here all the time, and he's horrible to me as well. He's so stupid. It doesn't have to be that way. I'm her best mate. I am not going anywhere.'

'If he's so awful to her, why does she stay?'

Audrey gestured around her. Barton was nonplussed.

'Luxury isn't worth unhappiness,' he said.

Audrey opened her mouth to make a quick retort, then closed it. She visibly deflated. 'They were infatuated with each other to begin with, but weren't we all?'

Barton kept quiet as Audrey stared off at nothing. She resisted the silence for a while, until her anger resurfaced.

'He was charming and rich. They had a wonderful time. Holidays, meals, a fucking horse in the paddock. But as he got older, he became possessive. He started to restrict the money, block her friends, even sold the nag without telling her. Said he couldn't afford the vet's bills.'

'But you stuck by her.'

'Damn right. The rest of her mates gave up, but he's never getting rid of me.'

Barton pondered what he'd read on the file of her daughter.

'I'm up to speed with Poppy's disappearance. I've seen the pictures of her. She's a pretty girl. Looks all grown up. It's a tough stage.'

Audrey chuckled.

'She's fourteen, going on forty. She's a sexual person. Even when she was a child, she'd insist on dressing provocatively.'

It was another unusual comment. Why bring that up?

'Isn't she still a child?'

'Absolutely, but she doesn't think so. She knows it all, knows her worth. Our life isn't enough for her. Poppy trawls through TikTok and YouTube watching all those women seemingly making money for sitting around looking pretty. She thinks that's a desirable existence. The kids nowadays want a future of excitement and glamour, not minimum wage as a trainee receptionist.'

'Aren't you concerned somebody out there is going to take advantage of her?'

Audrey barked out a laugh.

'To a certain degree, if she has been taken, I feel sorry for whoever took her.'

She astonished Barton again by holding out her hand. Barton took it, then watched her get in her car. She trundled towards the front gate. Barton didn't have an ear for engines, but even he could tell something was awry under the bonnet. The old guy slid the big gate back for her. Barton ambled over and introduced himself. They shook hands.

'My name's Gerald Cann. Caretaker. Everyone calls me Jerry, for obvious reasons. Do I get to know why you're here?'

'There was an incident outside the front of the property last night.'

'Oh, what kind?'

'Maybe joyriders, perhaps something else.'

Jerry pulled a face. 'Should I be worried?'

'That depends on whether you did it.'

Jerry tipped his head back and guffawed.

'Nice one. I'm getting a bit long in the tooth for incidents. I usually do early afternoons here. Just a few hours. I occasionally work at both of the neighbours' properties too, and the odd job down the road.'

Jerry gestured to the house where Barton had watched the car pull in, then pointed at the other side.

'Keeps me busy.'

'Are you in Castor all week?'

'Yep.'

'Is there that much maintenance needed?'

'You'd be surprised. They're massive houses and some are quite old. Replacing a door handle and changing a tap can use up a few hours. I help the gardener if I've got any spare time. He's a reliable lad, and the grounds here are a big job. He does the neighbours, too, which is just as well.'

'Why?'

'We're worried we might be out of work here soon.'

'How so?'

'Charles has been a brilliant payer, but he's been a little late for the last few months. Only a few days. Cash flow, he said, but we reckon it's more serious.'

'Go on.'

'Like this gate. They're expensive to fix. The parts take ages to arrive, but he could get an engineer out for a few thousand. Recondition the whole thing.'

'You think he can't afford that?'

'I reckon money's tight, so seeing as the repair isn't essential, he'll leave it for the moment. There are loads of issues. The lawnmower's on its last legs. The roof needs serious maintenance, and the electrics throughout aren't great. Don't touch anything metal or the hairs on...' Jerry paused and looked up at Barton's bald head '... your arms will stand up.'

'Excellent recovery.'

'Thanks. Sandy uses the pool a lot, but that's crying out for a complete overhaul as well.'

'Why hasn't he released one of you already if money's tight?'

'I'm not sure. I fixed the washing machine twice last month. If I left, the place would cease to function. These grounds are extensive. If he sacked Timothy, the gardens would swiftly go wild. You know rich people. They're all about appearance. I suspect he's delaying the big purchases and keeping their finances ticking over. Maybe he's hiding the fact from his wife, that all is not tickety-boo.'

Barton stared at the vast lawn and imagined how different it would appear with no attention for a month.

'Have you worked here long, Jerry?'

'Years.'

'That's your thing, is it? Maintenance.'

'All my life, I've enjoyed seeing how things work. It fascinates me. How they interact. The knock-on from one action against another. Cause and effect.'

For a moment, Barton wondered if he was talking about people.

'I guess,' said Jerry, 'you might call it a passion.'

14

DCI BARTON

Barton convened a meeting as soon as they returned, so he could bring the team in the office up to speed. The detectives filtering in appeared to have more vigour in them, now they had a lead to chase in the form of Frannie Bone. Barton kept quiet to see if Zander would take charge. It was, after all, his team, but he sat staring into the distance.

'Okay,' said Barton. 'Malik. Tell us about Mr Bone.'

'His record in Peterborough is only juvenile, and details are pretty light with it being so long ago. Sounds as if he moved away prior to being eighteen, because the magistrates in Blackpool dealt with his next offence. It seems he carried on doing there what he was in trouble for doing here.'

'Which was?'

'Odd behaviour. Stalking. Harassment without violence. We're well aware these offences have custody as an option under the sentencing guidelines, but they usually lead to fines and community orders, then restraining orders. Breaches of these can then progress to multiple short stays under lock and key, and that's what they did for Frannie. Strangeways became a regular vacation spot.'

Barton nodded. HMP Manchester used to be called Strangeways, but they rebuilt the place after a riot in 1990 and renamed it. Little else changed. Most people still referred to it by its original name.

'Didn't you say there was a sex crime?'

'Yes. Indecent exposure, for which he got six months' custody, and seven years on the sex offenders register. That's his latest offence, unless, of course, he's responsible for these crimes, too.'

'When was the last conviction?' asked Zelensky.

'Fifteen years ago.'

'That's unusual. I wonder why he stopped?'

'Must have been nice on the farm,' said Hoffman. 'Maybe he was away from temptation, or perhaps he found the sheep didn't report him.'

That got a laugh from the room, but Barton suspected the temptation bit would be the truth.

'Perhaps something happened there recently,' said Minton. 'He did something he shouldn't and got thrown out. Then he made his way to Peterborough.'

'I like what you're saying, Mini,' said Hoffman. 'Now he's back here, he returns to form. Except he's been in jail multiple times and has progressed to more serious offences. Abduction might be the next logical step for him. If the kids he merely talked to reported him, he could have decided to sod it and take one home.'

Barton waited for Zander to comment, but he was rubbing his eyes.

'That's obviously a major concern,' said Barton. 'The Frannie Bone I remember was a reasonably large child. Stick three decades on him, he may well be huge and could easily overpower a girl. It's worth stating here that Poppy's mum, Audrey, mentioned her daughter's a handful. It sounds like she'd fight, which is also concerning.'

'Yeah, that is worrying,' said Leicester. 'He might feel inclined to shut her up. Permanently.'

Barton drummed his fingers on the table.

'Let's consider the other victims. The ones who weren't taken. They are all of a similar age, but if you check the file, they look young. The other girl doesn't appear to wear make-up. Even if she did, she is short and has braces. Those children come across as exactly that. Poppy, on the other hand, vanished on a Saturday in full drag. They were her mum's words.'

'Nowadays, there are online tutorials on everything from smoky eyeshadow to luminous nail varnish,' said Zelensky.

'Right,' said Barton, recalling Layla watching them in what she thought was secret, but her web visits were tracked by Microsoft. 'Kids often experimented with make-up in my day but ended up looking like Coco the Clown.'

'You told me you were on the rugby team,' said Zander to laughter.

Barton chuckled. Most of his previous DCIs would have hated that kind of banter, but Barton didn't mind. Humour was the strongest shield when you were a detective and regularly had to stare into the abyss of dangerous minds. It was also proof that, like Zander said, he was tired, not brain dead. He was struggling, though.

Barton thought back to where he was.

'What I'm saying is that if a child was taken, why take the one who looked least like a kid?'

'Maybe Frannie prefers them older now?' asked Hoffman.

'Maybe. There are quite a few puzzles at the moment.'

Barton gave them an update on the possible attempted murder, saving the juiciest part until last, which was met with stunned silence.

'You're saying the missing girl's mother is the best friend of a woman who thinks someone was trying to run her down?' said Malik.

'More or less, although it seems from what Sandy herself said, if the driver had wanted to hit her, they had time. I suspect the intention was to scare her.'

'Did she have any idea why anyone would want to harm or scare her?' asked Leicester.

'No, she didn't. Minton, what was your feel for Sandy?'

'I liked her. She seemed a sweet person.'

'Nothing dubious about her?'

'Hell, yeah. There's something fishy going on between husband and wife, but I didn't get the impression he would do anything to put her in danger. It's interesting he may have money issues. Let's hope he hasn't recently taken out life insurance on his wife.'

A few present chuckled, but Barton had investigated a case where that had happened.

'I got the impression he was shrewd and intelligent, so that's unlikely.'

Leicester raised his hand. He had a habit of doing so, even in informal settings, which Barton found endearing.

'Is it possible any of the people you spoke to today are involved somehow with the missing kid?'

'Excellent,' replied Barton. 'I was hoping someone would ask that. Seeing as Audrey and Sandy are close mates, Poppy must have visited Paddock Green.'

'Damn, I should have thought of that,' said Minton. 'There's a swimming pool. Maybe she was there in a bikini and the husband noticed. The mother indicated the girl was sexually aware.'

'And he was driven insane with lust like in *Lolita*,' said Hoffman. 'She's probably chained up in his garage right now.'

'I hope not,' said Barton, 'because I walked past their garage and didn't look inside. They have a regular gardener and maintenance guy, so that's a lot of traffic coming in and out for any one of them to bring and keep a kidnapped girl on the grounds.'

'Maybe they're all in on it,' said Hoffman.

'I can see your imagination has improved since I left, Mr Hoffman. Plausible, of course, but Audrey suggested her daughter had returned home twice for clothes.'

'How do you know it was Poppy who came back?' said Hoffman. 'She could be in restraints somewhere, and the abductor took the key to fetch a dressing-up kit for her.'

'You sure she's not in your garage?' asked Zelensky.

Hoffman laughed. 'No, I'm having a month off that sort of thing.'

'Surely, there'd be too much of a risk of the snatcher getting caught for just a few items of clothing,' said Leicester.

'Agreed, unless they were daft,' said Barton. 'Zelensky, what was your take on the neighbour with the silver Bentley?'

'His name's Henry Bancroft. Rich, old, handsome, charismatic. He only came to the door, but I could see his place was like something you see on *Selling Super Houses*.'

'I assume that means top-end. Any vibes from him?'

'No, he told me his wife died over a year ago. When I asked if he'd seen anything the previous night, he just shook his head. He seemed pretty sad and half asleep, but he was still sort of flirty.'

'Lonely, and horny,' said Leicester with a raised eyebrow. 'Very dangerous.'

'No, he was charming. Now I know he's rich and single, I might go back in a little black dress. Make a change from dating unreliable skint coppers.'

Barton picked up on the jibe immediately. Zelensky studied her nails. Barton scanned the room. Ah ha. Leicester's face had gone as red as his hair.

Barton smiled. 'And the other neighbour?'

'Nobody home. We could see through the gates, but it had a deserted air about it. The windscreen of the car outside was covered in leaves.'

'Okay. Social Services will look into the fact Poppy has probably been home a few times, so we can leave that to them. We received plenty of information today, which could be helpful, or a distraction. Let's get the PNC and the databases updated. Consider everything we've heard and think about what to focus on. We'll meet at nine tomorrow morning.'

Minton was frowning.

'Paddock Green needs another visit.'

'Agreed. We'll return and take full statements from the couple, the gardener, the handyman and the neighbour, even if it's a bit of an arse-covering exercise. When a minor is missing, Joe Public expects no stone unturned. Our presence today will have worried anyone with anything to hide, but they might think they've brushed us off. They won't like it if we turn up tomorrow mob-handed. Any questions?'

'I've got the complete file on Frannie Bone, but it'll take all evening to read,' said Malik.

'Ah, you're after overtime. I can give you something much, much sweeter.'

Malik's face lit up. 'Yes?'

'My eternal gratitude.'

Malik chuckled. 'It's a deal.'

'Do you reckon there's any ongoing risk to Sandy?' asked Hoffman.

'That's another decent question,' said Barton. 'I'm not sure. I'll get Uniform to do a house check this evening, but she jogs on Sundays, Tuesdays, and Thursdays, so if the person knew her routine, they may well wait for tomorrow.'

'She promised to knock the running on the head for the moment,' said Minton.

'Perfect, although that indicates she's taking it more seriously than she let on. Anything else?'

Hoffman stood and folded his arms. 'Are we all allowed to sleep in meetings or is that just for inspector level upwards?'

Barton turned to Zander, who had nodded off.

When the rest of the team had left, Barton nudged Zander awake. He stared blearily up at Barton.

'Sorry, what did I miss?'

'Zander, I'm going to have to let you go.'

15

DCI BARTON

Zander yawned.

'Did I nod off?'

'Come on, mate, dozing on the job's not a good look. I respect you having a relaxed nature with the team, but that's taking it too far. You'll soon lose their respect.'

'I know, I know.'

'Is there an issue with the kids, and you, being a stupid man, haven't told anyone?'

Zander nodded glumly. 'It's Zane. He's running a temperature and has a horrible hacking cough, so he's not sleeping. Kelly has him in next to her, and that's unsettled Zack, because he's used to being next to his brother.'

Barton's jaw dropped open. He rested his hand on Zander's arm.

'Oh my God, I'm so sorry.'

Zander nodded once more. His son with a previous partner died of carbon monoxide poisoning from a neighbour's boiler. It destroyed Zander's relationship, and he had been close to the edge. Now, one of his children was ill. How could you rest when your fevered child coughed next to you when you'd already had a child who went to sleep, then never woke up?

Barton spoke gently.

'I'm going to have to relieve you of duty.'

Zander jerked back. 'Say what?'

'On the hush-hush. You need a holiday.'

Zander's brow crumpled. 'I've got nothing booked.'

'You told me you had a week in the diary four months ago, but never took it.'

'I was swept up in The Tandoori Killer case.'

'Yes, I remember you saying it was a hot one.'

The sides of Zander's mouth twitched. Barton suspected that particular joke had paled with familiarity.

'It feels like I haven't slept all week.'

'Zander, you and I, on song, are the best in the business. The stats don't lie, but you're running at eighty per cent because you're exhausted. Your team feeds off you, so they'll struggle, too. Malik and Leicester are fine detectives. They're consistent and effective, and, eventually, they'll take our jobs and be brilliant at them. But right now, they need us at one hundred per cent because then they can operate at that level, too. Zelensky is all at sea because she's trying to bridge the twenty per cent herself. It's making her too aggressive, too driven.'

'There was nobody to take over if I disappeared.'

'I'm here now. A fully functioning Zander is what we need. Get rested and come back reinvigorated.'

Zander ran a hand over his bald head. A little smile crept out.

'Are you trying to curry favour with me?'

Barton chuckled. 'That's the spirit.'

Zander's shoulders dropped.

'You're right. It's like I can't get a break. At work, or at home.'

'That's because you need a break. Go home for a week. Do nothing. Drive the kids to one of those horrific play-area things, tire them out, then nap when they nap. Visit Waitrose, buy organic meat and fresh pesticide-free vegetables. Relax. Exercise. Doze. Watch documentaries. Take a walk in the park.'

'I keep thinking they're only two-year-olds, how can we be so tired?'

'Kids are relentless, and you have two in nappies. My mum, brutally rude as she was, used to say if you wish someone ill, wish them twins because they won't know what's hit them. Raising children, in all its glory, is draining. They keep going, exhaust you and them, then they sleep for thirteen hours if you're lucky, and get up primed to go again. It chips away at your resilience until you fray at the edges.'

'I suppose I wasn't much involved with my first son because I was working full-time and doing overtime. Now, because of what happened, I can't help being hypervigilant whenever they're sick.'

'Which is totally understandable but you'll make yourself ill. Don't keep things like that to yourself again. Holly will be mad at you. She'll want to help. We can help.'

'Agreed.'

'If you fancy a game of tennis on Wednesday night, that should get the old endorphins flowing. I need to trim down a few pounds, too, now I'm back in the detecting business.'

'A few?'

'A few pounds per day, for six months.'

Zander smiled.

'You're right. Kicking your ass at tennis would perk me up.'

'Game on, then, son. Recharge your and Kelly's batteries for a week. She'll be feeling the same. Holly and I will babysit at yours on Saturday night, so you can go to the cinema, chill over pasta and wine somewhere, or relax on a bench in a quiet wood. Whatever it takes. We'll see you back here next Monday, firing on all cylinders. We'll be unstoppable.'

Zander stood and gave Barton a brief hug. He dragged his jacket off the chair and trudged to the door, where he turned and waved. He looked incredibly relieved.

'Amen to that.'

16

THE VILLAGE KILLER

I've had time to process the last few years, and I've changed. I'm definitely more heartless. Perhaps because my world is tilting off its axis, and I'm slowly going around the bend.

I visited the seaside for the day a few months back, to clear my head. After a long queue at an ice-cream van, the lad said he couldn't take cards. I didn't have any cash on me, so the little git threw my flake ninety-nine into the bin instead. At that moment, I'd happily have donated a kidney for a hand grenade.

That aside, the main issue is Sandy. I find it hard to fathom where we've ended up. If someone had asked me five years ago if anything like this could happen, I'd have laughed in their face and assumed they were deranged. Yet here we are. I suppose it's love, in all its myriad ways, and we are all capable of giving love a bad name.

My sickness is something that began at the start of senior school. The distant adoration of another student who didn't know I existed, or at least didn't care. I tried to become closer to them, to mimic them, but passions hurt at that age. The fairy tale that dies.

Then the later teenage years. The heady thrills of the physical stage. Bodies writhing, twisting, glistening. We were all so beautiful. Love seemed so simple, but it's not. Kindness turns into resentment, communication into control, and commitment to ownership.

Now Sandy is in my life, I just can't let her go. She must not leave. I need her in my world, and I'm prepared to do anything to make that happen. Even kill.

The police didn't appear to be fools today, so they'll be back. That's perfect. It's part of the plan.

I expect we'll be seeing a lot of those officers over the next few weeks.

17

DCI BARTON

Barton left the office at 6 p.m. in an upbeat mood and drove to his house. He felt motivated, but he was also drained. His brain was churning away in the background, trying to unravel the twisted strands, but he didn't have all the information to do that. Before he left his desk job, he could usually turn off those thoughts when he got home. He suspected it might take a while to get back in the groove.

He made himself a cheese sandwich with slices from a sourdough bloomer he found on a chopping board. It was rye bread, but mayonnaise would sort that out. For once, he noticed the dishwasher needed emptying and filling, so he did that, confident he would get a prize for being such a good boy. It took a while as he was distracted by the newspaper and the depressing news within it.

Barton found Holly sitting in the lounge and chuckling at *Married at First Sight*, where contestants married strangers on the day they met them. He flopped down next to her.

'Are you still watching this guff?' he asked.

'I love it. Makes me laugh so much. It's sweet as well.'

'But they don't actually get married. It's pretend.'

'Stop ruining my programme. Do I criticise the rubbish you like?'

'I don't watch crap.'

'You don't watch anything. You come in here, put a show on, then, boom, off to the land of nod. Koalas sleep less than you. Even greyhounds.'

Barton's eyes flicked over to their greyhound, Gizmo, who was upside down on an armchair and quietly snoring.

'You two really are a dream team,' said Holly. 'Now, is this a social call, or a sexual one?'

'I'm keeping my options open.'

'In the spirit of upfront communication, I'm not inclined for either. I'm shattered, enjoying this, and I've still got another load to put in the machine when the current one's finished, unless you're going to assist.'

'I see a deal coming, but I need to tell you about Zander.'

Barton told her his news and she gave him a sad smile.

'It'll get easier when they're older and can communicate better. I'll ring and offer our services.'

'Zander's taking the week off to recharge. I said we'll babysit Saturday.'

'Great idea.'

'Zander and I are planning to play tennis on Wednesday night. Are those shorts I wore this summer still floating around?'

'The shorts you accused me of shrinking?'

'You did shrink them.'

'Everyone's washing is done together, but you seem to be the only one having issues with tight clothes.'

'Perhaps mine have a higher cotton count.'

Holly shook her head. 'Promise me you'll take it easy. No limping through the front door afterwards.'

'We'll warm up.'

'Right. Let me finish this, and I'll put the load on. Then maybe we can have an early night, assuming you don't conk out.'

'Never!' declared Barton as he stifled a yawn.

18

DCI BARTON

Barton woke at 5 a.m., still sitting on the sofa in his suit. Holly had draped a crocheted blanket over him, which made him feel like a geriatric. He'd slept well, though, so it wasn't all bad. He walked past the dog, who seemed to grin at him.

After a quick shower, Barton joined Holly for breakfast, where he endured Greek yoghurt, nuts and milled linseed. Fibre was her latest thing. Barton felt full but unsatisfied, so he drove to the office with enthusiasm, knowing he was about to re-familiarise himself with the vending machine.

The team joined him in a meeting room at nine, after a Mars bar had perked him up.

'Okay, guys, quick update from me. There were no emergency calls last night from Castor, and there have been no sightings of the missing girl from North Bretton. DI Zander has taken the rest of the week as holiday after he had his break cancelled four months ago, so I'll be acting as your DI, as well as being your DCI. I'm heading to the Favershams' as planned. Has anyone had any eureka moments overnight?'

'I'd like to look more into the Frannie Bone angle,' said Malik. 'His record isn't a serious one. It's more sad.'

'I suspect his victims would beg to differ,' replied Barton.

'True. I'll try to trace friends or relatives from his time here. I'll liaise with Social Services and the guys from CID who investigated before we got involved. If I delve deeper into his past crimes, I might get a sense of where he's heading next. Frannie's a bit of a ghost now. No driving licence, no council record. No social media that I can find.'

'Great idea. To a certain degree, it doesn't matter whether or not he's responsible for Poppy's disappearance. The reality is we haven't found him, so who's to say he isn't involved in the other approaches? It's also possible Poppy is dead and buried, and he's thinking about his next victim. Did you have any joy with his previous address?'

'No. There was a telephone number listed for the farm, which doesn't connect.'

Barton pursed his lips.

'Maybe the business folded. Try local police. The Internet. Perhaps another farm nearby might know something, or the closest post office. Or even a pub. Otherwise, you're going to have to cycle down there.'

Barton's phone ringing interrupted the laughter. It was from one of the Social Services Missing Persons team and he listened intently. After explaining someone would be in touch with them, he cut the call.

'Leicester, you link up with Social Services. Malik can assist. They've just told me they spoke to Poppy's neighbours last night about the possibility of her having returned to the house and collected personal items. Next door but one spotted a guy approximately in his forties, who she didn't know by name, but she's noticed him a few times in the area. There's a path to the bins at the back of the fences. She saw him down there.'

'Does the description match the guy from the libraries?' asked Hoffman.

'No. She said he was dishevelled. Right, Minton, you come with me. We'll take statements from Sandy and Charles. Zelensky and Hoffman, can you interview Poppy's mother, Audrey, if she's there, about her relationship with Sandy, but probe into how often Poppy has been over?'

Zelensky nodded. 'Having spoken to the three of them already, I've got the feeling this might turn into an Agatha Christie novel, where nobody tells the complete truth.'

Barton knew how she felt.

'Have a word with the gardener and handyman, too. The tradesmen may have picked up any tension between their bosses, and it sounds like they'd recall this Poppy being at the property.'

'Will do.'

'Remember, there are two angles at play. One is we have a possessive husband with a beautiful wife, and the other is the money situation.'

'The more I thought about it before I went to sleep,' said Hoffman, 'the more troubled I was by Audrey being present when we got there.'

'Coincidences do happen,' said Leicester.

'True,' replied Barton, looking unconvinced.

'It's also plausible someone was just pulling away from the road and Sandy panicked,' said Malik. 'After all, she talked down the danger after you arrived. Was she highly strung?'

'Yes, she was,' said Minton. 'I'd say Sandy seemed scared and worried.'

'Aren't they the same thing?'

'No. I think the incident scared her, but I reckon she was already troubled by something else.'

19

DCI BARTON

Barton finished the meeting and sent Zelensky and Hoffman in one car, while Minton booked another out for the two of them. He asked her to drive. People often spoke freely when they were concentrating on something else.

The parkways that circled Peterborough were built specifically to promote swift access in and around the city. They had been landscaped with a wide variety of trees to keep the traffic noise from the surrounding estates, so the view was like a dual carriageway through a country estate. At this time of the year, the branches were dressed in their finest autumn clothing.

'So,' said Barton. 'Where do you see yourself in a few years?'

Minton's cheek twitched. 'Ooh, sneaky. Grill me while I'm driving.'

Barton laughed out loud.

'It appears I'll need to get up early to catch you out. What were you hoping for when you left uniform?'

'I guess what all detectives hope for.'

'Ah, the career-defining case. One you're asked about at dinner parties in years to come.'

'Yes. I want the challenge of a hugely complex investigation. A real skull-crusher.' She gave him a wistful glance. 'I suppose I shouldn't hope for the arrival of a Moriarty or Ted Bundy type character.'

'No, let's hope we don't have one of them, but you'll get those cases, eventually. I'll warn you, they often don't feel exciting at the time. Success is usually the result of painstaking work, which includes hundreds of interviews. The careful elimination of suspects and retrieval of evidence. How many people have we already talked to over this missing girl? Think of the CCTV that's been trawled through, gardens searched, and backgrounds checked.'

'Yeah, and now Poppy's mum has hinted she's probably just at a boyfriend's house, and he's most likely regretting it.'

'A lot of serial-killer cases start with a missing person.'

'Yeah, I know, although those victims are often poor old prostitutes.'

'True.'

'Let's hope Poppy hasn't really gone off the rails.'

Barton chuckled. 'Audrey did say she was a handful.'

When they arrived at the Paddock Green property, the sun had begun its slow ascent and cast long shadows from the trees over their cars. Barton and Minton stepped from the vehicle and walked towards the small entrance door in the gate. Barton pulled in the crisp, invigorating air, tinged with the earthy scent of fallen leaves, which marked the transition from autumn to winter. It was a season of change, which included Barton, and, he ruefully suspected, the Favershams as well.

As Zelensky and Hoffman strode over to join them, what sounded like a chainsaw started up on the other side of the gate. Barton recalled the case of The Cold Killer. He shared a look with Zelensky, who was the only one of the three who had been on the team when that unpleasant incident occurred. She raised an eyebrow.

'Let me guess,' said Barton. 'Age before beauty?'

'If you insist,' she said, holding out her hand.

Barton knocked, but suspected, with the racket, he was wasting his time. When he pushed the small door open, he was relieved to see the gardener, Timothy, trimming an oak tree with what smelled like a petrol hedge trimmer. Timothy had a helmet, goggles and ear defenders on, but he noticed the officers appear and clambered down his stepladder onto a blanket of branches and russet-brown leaves.

'Sorry, I didn't hear you,' said Timothy.

'That's okay,' said Barton. 'Or is doorman part of your services?'

'We all kind of muck in. I told Jerry I'd have a look at the gate, but I don't know much about electrics.'

'He'll be here this afternoon, won't he?' asked Barton.

'Not today. He texted me to say he's poorly, but he should be better tomorrow.'

Barton caught Zelensky and Hoffman share a glance at that news.

'That's a shame,' said Hoffman, cynically. He gestured at the oak tree. 'Aren't you a little early with the pruning?'

Timothy smiled. 'Are you a keen gardener?'

'My dad was. He never pruned anything until December.'

'Me neither, but Charles wants the approach to the house to be perfect. He'd have me trimming all year, but I've said this is the earliest to prune or he risks disease.'

'Is Charles in?' asked Barton.

'You've missed him, although he said he'll be back in an hour. Charles has a best friend in the village who had a stroke a few months ago, so he regularly walks down to give him some company. He's got carers, but nobody else.'

'That's nice of Charles,' said Barton.

'Yes. Maybe he's just keen to get out of the house.'

Barton checked Timothy's face to see if he was implying something, but he couldn't detect anything. Perhaps he meant with Charles working from home.

'Sandy's in the back garden,' said Timothy.

This time Barton detected a crinkle around Timothy's eyes.

'Is Audrey here?'

'I haven't seen her.'

'Is it okay if DS Zelensky and DC Hoffman take a statement from you? We'd like some background after the worrying incident outside the gates.'

Timothy nodded. 'Sure. We can talk in the games room. That's where I have my breaks. It's almost coffee time, anyway. Charles mentioned Sandy's scare. Sounds as if it could have been nasty.'

'Was he worried?'

'Yes. He told me to keep an eye out for visitors.'

Barton pondered whether that meant Charles was being less blasé about the danger to his wife than he'd first appeared or was concerned for his own safety. He gestured for Minton to follow him, and they headed around the side of the property, through a stiff iron gate, then down a path in the centre of the rear lawn, which led between two thick hedges. The gentle sound of water lapping sounded ominous instead of peaceful.

Barton and Minton reached a pool area where they both stopped dead. A body floated in the water.

20

DCI BARTON

Barton strode forward. Sandy was floating on her back, motionless, arms spread, with a cascade of hair fanning out like a veil of silk. She wore only a pair of gold bikini bottoms.

Barton's gaze ran over her body, but there was no obvious sign of injury. After tugging off his suit jacket and slipping out of his shoes, he was poised to leap in. Then Sandy's eyes opened. She glanced over at him and grinned.

'I can lend you a pair of Charles's Speedos if you like, although they might be a touch snug.'

Barton heard Minton choking back a laugh behind him. Sandy dropped her feet down and swam to the edge of the pool, where she crossed her arms on the side to cover her modesty.

'It's kind of you to look in on me, but everything's fine.'

'We need to take a written statement from you.'

'What for?'

'To have a proper record of what happened, and I wanted a chat about Audrey's daughter, Poppy.'

'Have they found her?'

'No, so we need to check every angle. I assume with Audrey being your closest friend, you know Poppy well.'

'Yes, mostly from seeing her at Audrey's, but she started coming here and we spent some lazy days together. Audrey's one of the few people my husband hasn't scared off, and when Poppy heard about the pool, she loved coming over.'

'So, Poppy was here recently?'

'Yes. June was a bit of a washout, but we had plenty of warm days after, just the three of us. Charles said he didn't want a holiday this year. He was too busy, apparently, and he wouldn't pay for me to go away with Audrey, so we hung around here over the summer. There are worse places.'

Barton nodded as he glanced at the beautiful lawns and manicured hedges.

'We'll talk to you inside, if that's okay?'

'Of course. Could you pass me my robe?'

Barton walked over to a lounger and grabbed the large white terry-towelling bath robe on it. When he turned back, Sandy had pulled herself from the water and was holding out her arm. Barton noticed a birthmark at the bottom of Sandy's neck near her left collarbone. He fixed his gaze upon it. He passed Sandy her clothing, then turned to look at the house. The mature trees along the sides of the garden concealed the pool from the neighbour's properties, except for one window on Henry Bancroft's side.

Barton saw the curtain move.

21

DCI BARTON

Barton and Minton followed a robed Sandy back towards the house. She seemed a different person from the one he'd met the previous day. He supposed she could have still been in shock yesterday, but this woman swaggered. The word vampish sprang to his mind. Barton cast another eye up at Henry's window. There was nobody there. He was wondering how to ask Sandy a personal question when Minton did it for him.

'Do you always go topless in the pool?'

'Yes. I like the feeling of freedom.'

'Even with the workmen around?'

'They're only breasts. We're all adults here.'

'Except for Poppy.'

'Yes, but she's also a woman.'

Minton smiled. 'You mean a girl.'

'I mean, her body shouldn't embarrass her.'

'Did she bathe topless here?'

Sandy stopped walking. 'No. That wouldn't have been appropriate with, as you say, the workmen around.'

'Your neighbour could watch as well.'

Minton had also clocked next door's property overlooked the pool area.

'Henry? I don't think so, and who cares? Visit any beach and you'll see women sunbathing.'

'I suppose,' said Minton. 'Are you friendly with the neighbours?'

'Henry waves. The other side has a villa in Spain so we rarely set eyes on him.'

'I hope you don't mind me saying you're in great shape.'

Barton smiled. It had been many years since he'd have got away with a comment like that.

'For a lady of my age?' asked Sandy, with the hint of a smile to Minton.

'For a lady of any age.'

'Let me tell you, it doesn't get any easier, especially after the rigours of childbirth. If I'm honest, I haven't worked since the pandemic, so that helps with finding the time to exercise. My husband didn't like me working. He accused me of sleeping with my colleagues, despite the fact I was employed in an all-female office.'

Sandy carried on walking and let them into the kitchen. They all took a seat at the large table. Minton had brought her laptop, and she began tapping away as Barton confirmed Sandy's personal information.

'You never mentioned any children before,' said Barton.

'You never asked. We have a boy called Roger. Terrible name. It was Charles's father's name, and he insisted. All his friends call him Dodge.'

'Are you close?'

'We were when he was growing up. Charles preferred me to be a stay-at-home mum, so it was just me and my son for years. A united front fighting against the world. Well, if you can describe private school and holidays in the Seychelles as a battle.'

'Does he live here?'

'No, he studied at the University of St Andrews in Scotland, then left for a summer job, which Charles found for him with one of his friends who owns a vineyard in France. I reckon Charles did it deliberately so he could keep me to himself. They took him on as an assistant, and now he's a trainee manager. He had huge rows with Charles once he became a teenager. He doesn't return much, but why would he?'

Barton nodded. He thought of how little Lawrence stayed in touch now he'd become an adult, but that was the way of young men. They had their own lives to lead. Barton had been in his late twenties himself before it had dawned on him his parents would like more contact. Even a regular phone call would have been an improvement.

Sandy had nothing else to offer about the incident. In fact, she downplayed it, her answers curt.

'You can't think of anyone who might wish you harm?' asked Minton. 'Physically or mentally?'

'Nope.'

'How about Charles?'

'I reckon a lot of people would like to hurt him.'

Barton knew Minton was asking whether Charles might be responsible, but she switched tack gracefully.

'Why is that?'

'Actually, I'm being unfair. He was a decent father, and they were pretty close until Dodge started pushing the boundaries, as all young lads do. Sadly for us, when our son headed off to Scotland, Charles and I couldn't find our way back to each other.'

Barton thought carefully about his next question.

'Does Charles have enemies?'

'I believe Charles has money trouble. He thinks I don't know, but the signs are there.'

'Perhaps someone set out to frighten you as a warning to him.'

Sandy's lips puckered as she considered what he'd said. Even with no make-up on and her hair hanging damp on her shoulders, she was an incredibly attractive woman.

'Charles adores me, so that's a possibility.'

'Aren't you worried about the money situation?'

'I've had enough of this marriage. Charles can see me slipping away, which is making him try and hold me closer. He used to give me money, but everything goes on a credit card now, which he pays, then he grills me on the details. We haven't been physical for years. For some reason, I can't bear for him to touch me. I'm not sure why, so I am literally fading away here. There's no stimulation, romance, or fun, but I have a plan.'

Barton waited for it.

'Sorry, Inspector. It's a secret, so I can't tell you too much. I will say that in a few more months, he'll come home to an empty house.'

Barton gestured around him at the marble work surfaces and shiny units.

'There must be loads of equity in this property. Are you going to give all that up, or fight for your share?'

'I'm leaving it all behind. This house is a Faversham family asset, anyway.'

'What does that mean?'

'It's all bound up in complicated trusts. My son will inherit when Charles dies. I won't get a penny out of the estate, and I've no idea what other assets he has. I suspect Charles has stripped his investments and pensions to keep us afloat.'

'You've made it clear he's controlling,' said Minton. 'So do you really think he'll let you slip away?'

'He won't know where I've gone to start with, so he won't have that choice.'

'Regarding Poppy's disappearance,' said Barton. 'Could she have talked to anyone here?'

'Visitors are rare. Charles scared everyone off apart from Audrey.'

'What about Timothy or Jerry?'

Sandy blanched. 'You're wondering if they grabbed her?'

'I understand they're difficult questions.'

'Timothy and Jerry are busy men. Charles lets them use the games room as a base, so they keep out of our way.'

The sound of a door opening and closing distracted them. Then they heard the stomp of approaching feet. Charles marched into the kitchen. His eyes scanned the people present.

'What the hell is going on here?'

22

DCI BARTON

Barton rose from his chair and held out his hand, which Charles took after a delay.

'Excellent timing, Charles. We've just taken a statement from your wife about the incident and a few other matters. We'd like to talk to you now.'

Sandy stood from her seat, gave her husband a cool smile, and walked towards the back door.

'I'll continue my swim and give you some peace.'

Charles stared after his wife. It was hard to discern exactly what Charles's expression said, but it didn't seem to be love.

'Sit down, please,' said Barton.

For a man who had money troubles, Charles was highly groomed. A gold watch sparkled on his wrist, and his shoes shone.

'You're wasting your time talking to me.'

Barton decided he didn't much like Charles, but he suspected he was the type of person who needed his ego massaging.

'You appear to be a man of the world, so you know how it is.'

'I didn't get to my age without learning a few things.'

'You'll know when a wife rings the police, we often start with the husband.'

Charles's hands, which were resting on the table in front of him, involuntarily closed.

'Of course.'

Barton watched Charles as Minton asked for his date of birth. There was a light sheen of sweat on his forehead, and he fidgeted with his mobile phone.

'You have a lovely home and a beautiful wife,' said Minton.

'I do.'

'You must run a successful business to pay for it all,' said Barton with a smile.

'Yes, but both the house and Sandy eat up the funds,' replied Charles without malice, which surprised Barton. 'She's not working at the moment.'

'Some men like their wives out grafting. Others prefer them nearby.'

'Oh, I enjoy having Sandy at home, where I can see her. She doesn't need to work. I prefer her to be here when I return.'

'I thought you worked from your home office.'

'I meant when I go out, or away on business.'

'And if she isn't home?' asked Minton.

Barton winced. It was blunt.

'Are you implying we have marital problems?'

Barton smiled at Charles. Whatever he was, he wasn't a fool.

'My wife has a fantastic house and a limitless credit card, which I clear every month for her. No questions asked. We're happy. In fact, the only thing we argue about is that grubby friend of hers.'

'Audrey.'

'Yes. She's a shit-stirrer. The crazy bint wants Sandy all to herself.'

'I hear she visited a lot over the summer.'

'Yes. She even brought her vile daughter.'

Barton studied Charles's mannerisms intently, but there was no real change in his demeanour.

'I've seen pictures of Poppy,' said Barton. 'She's a striking girl. I imagine she'll grow into an attractive woman, so vile isn't a word I'd have used.'

'Vile personality. She's poison.'

'Did something happen to upset you?'

'I know the type. She's dangerous. I keep well away from her, which is why I wish she and her mother would clear off. Has she been found?'

'No, not yet. One final thing, Charles. I obviously noticed the front gate wasn't working, and it appears a few other areas need looking at.'

'Yes.'

'Do you have cash-flow problems?'

For the first time, Charles's eyes met Barton's and remained there. Seconds drew out.

'I've been forced to move funds around. These interest rate rises are making the pips squeak somewhat.'

'Okay. Well, everyone needs to be vigilant after what happened. It's a shame the CCTV and alarms don't function.'

'They both work in the house. The ones outside haven't worked for six months.' Charles waggled his phone at Barton. 'I'd know if anyone broke in.'

Barton peered around the kitchen and spotted the camera above the back door.

'Those record in every room,' said Charles.

'I had the impression your wife thought they weren't working. It would give her peace of mind if she understood they were.'

'Does she seem hugely concerned about intruders?'

'I suppose not. She's probably forgotten how scared she was. Her initial suspicions were probably right.'

'I'll be sure to tell her.' Charles gestured to the camera in the corner of the room. 'After all, the eye is all-seeing.'

23

THE VILLAGE KILLER

I often ponder what causes marriages to unravel. When two people are so deeply in love at the beginning that they joyfully walk down the aisle, isn't it perplexing how everything can deteriorate so drastically? Surely, most of what was there still remains.

I suppose foundations crack and crumble until somebody declares enough. It's tough on the other one if they don't notice it coming, or maybe it's worse knowing but being powerless to stop the axe from falling. If there's an air of inevitability about it, surely striking first makes sense. Be the aggressor, not the victim, before it's too late. Take control. Manipulate. Win.

It's plain to see Sandy is planning to leave. Her behaviour has changed. She's gone from a woman on death row, who had accepted her fate, to a lady with a mission. We can all tell. She has a solution that she is sure is the right one, and that breeds confidence. Perhaps even overconfidence.

What would her reaction be if she were aware of how obvious it all was? If she understood what we know? Would it make her pause for thought? Would it make her immediately flee?

I want her to stay so much that I'm capable of anything, but it's not just me who can't be without her. Everyone adores her. The thought of her living another life elsewhere is enough for me to bite my tongue. A heavy, grey, dusty drape would fall on my landscape. Forever. I'd rather die than let that happen.

So, no, she won't be going anywhere. I'll make sure of that.

24

DCI BARTON

Barton nodded at Minton that it was time to leave. When they reached the front of the property, Hoffman was laughing next to a straight-faced Zelensky.

'What's so funny?' asked Barton.

'Hoffman's incredibly pleased with his little joke.'

'Go on, Hoffman, hit me?'

'What do you call Hugh Jackman when he's sunburned?'

'No idea.'

'Tangerine.'

Barton groaned. 'Did you make that up all by yourself?'

'Yeah, I did, then I found the joke was already on Pinterest. It's hard to be original nowadays.'

Barton shook his head.

'How was Timothy?'

'He was a talker, and I don't reckon I've ever met anyone so motivated by money.'

'Any concerns?'

He scratched his jaw. 'I'll have a think when I write up my notes. But I'd describe him as obsessed.'

'Okay, Hoffman. Why don't you take Minton back to the office and start on your paperwork? Zelensky and I will have a chat with Henry next door. FYI, Sandy is confident of her body and happy to sunbathe with little or no clothing.'

'Typical. You get the topless stunner, while we get the hairy gardener.'

'It seems the neighbour had a bird's-eye view.'

'You caught him perving at the window?'

'I definitely saw movement, and it wasn't the breeze because the window was closed. Looking out of his house isn't a crime, and Sandy didn't seem bothered, but there's something off here at Paddock Green. For a start, we've heard conflicting stories about the money situation.'

'Timothy said he'd been paid late, but only by a few days,' said Zelensky.

'Jerry mentioned the same thing.'

'Charles told Timothy he had to wait for a new lawnmower, but it wouldn't be long.'

'I'm beginning to suspect there is no cash-flow issue. If his finances were so stretched, would he keep a gardener on? I think it's part of Charles's controlling behaviour. Sandy believes the CCTV has been broken for ages, but Charles said to us it works inside. I bet it feeds through to his phone. In a nutshell, he's restricting who she sees, where she goes, her access to money, and, if he wanted to, he could watch what she's up to in the house.'

Nobody needed to mention they were all classic signs of domestic abuse. Barton exhaled.

'What did Timothy say about whether he'd seen Poppy?'

'She came over once or twice, but he had nothing to do with her.'

'Was he believable?'

'Yeah, I think so. He's super focused on building his business up.'

Barton rubbed his chin. 'Sandy gave me the impression Poppy visited a lot over the summer, which would mean he would have met her more than a few times. Where is he now?'

'There,' said Hoffman, pointing at Timothy, who'd walked into view with a pair of shears in one hand and operating his mobile in the other.

'I'll have a quick word with him.'

Barton wandered over.

'Hi, Timothy. We were leaving, but an anomaly has cropped up.'

'Hang on.' He finished with his phone and slipped it into his front trouser pocket. 'Just texting Jerry.'

'What for?'

'The pool water's not as warm as it should be. I told him you guys had returned. We let each other know what's happening all the time. I like to think we look out for each other.'

Barton tried to hold eye contact with Timothy, but he twisted so they weren't facing each other.

'You said you saw Poppy on a couple of occasions over the summer.'

'That's right.'

'Sandy said she was here frequently, so wouldn't you have seen her regularly?'

Barton watched Timothy's face redden.

'I tended to avoid the pool area when Poppy came over.'

'Why?'

'I wasn't sure of her age, but she used to lie on the recliners with next to nothing on. It felt a bit icky.'

'How old do you think she is?'

'Sixteen perhaps. Although she looked older in clothes.'

It was a strange reply, but Barton suspected Timothy was no ladies' man.

'She's fourteen.'

Timothy's mouth dropped open. He put a hand over it. 'Oh, God.'

'What?' asked Barton.

Timothy waged an internal battle. The horror spread all over his face.

'When I said she had next to nothing on, I meant nothing at all.'

25

DCI BARTON

Barton frowned at the young man in front of him, who took a step back.

'Hey, listen,' said Timothy. 'This job is important to me. That's why I was careful whenever she was about. I tried to avoid her.'

'Right.'

'No, really. Look, if I'm honest, I'm more the other way. Older women.'

'Such as Sandy?'

Timothy's face went scarlet at the mention of her name.

'Honestly, I regularly work in the garden near the pool. I apologised the first time I saw Sandy like that, but she told me not to be silly and to carry on.'

'Meaning you didn't make yourself scarce when Sandy was around?'

'Not always, no. Can you blame me?'

Barton supposed not. 'I have the feeling we'll be talking again.'

Timothy didn't seem concerned at that, so Barton said goodbye and trudged back to his team.

'Today is not going how I expected it. You guys set off. Come on, Zelensky, I almost daren't imagine what we'll hear next door.'

Barton and Zelensky left the Favershams' property and strolled to the entrance of Henry Bancroft's. There was an intercom, which Zelensky pressed.

'Bancroft's,' said a male voice that sounded younger than Barton expected.

'We're here to talk to Henry.'

'Who is it?'

'DS Zelensky and DCI Barton.'

The solid gate clicked, then sedately swung away from them.

'That wasn't the man I spoke to yesterday,' said Zelensky.

Again, the lawn was large. The Favershams' seemed more modern and landscaped, whereas this one had different trees dotted around, and they were mature. Barton recognised a silver birch and possibly an ash but couldn't name the others. A gravel drive led up to a grand stone house, which to Barton's inexperienced eye appeared centuries old.

He knocked on a large ornate wooden door, which reminded him of the one at the church he got married in. It opened to reveal a short man, who Barton guessed would be mid-fifties.

'How can I help?'

'We'd like to speak to Henry Bancroft, please,' said Zelensky. 'I had a brief word with him yesterday.'

'And you are?'

She and Barton showed their warrant cards.

'He's dozing in an armchair at the moment.'

'Are you a relative, or...?' asked Zelensky, hunting for the correct term.

'The butler? I prefer manservant.'

Zelensky nodded.

'Just kidding, I'm his secretary, Robert Young. Actually, manservant isn't too far from the truth, and it's more of an informal role now. I oversaw his affairs and did so for twenty years, but I still advise him and visit when I can. There's a housekeeper who cleans, cooks and shops for him, but she's on holiday this week, so I said I'd pop by.'

Robert Young was striking in a perfectly tailored suit, blue paisley tie, and designer glasses. His grey hair had receded, but his skin glowed with vitality. It appeared he had health and wealth.

'There was an incident on the street outside this property at around nine o'clock, two evenings back,' said Barton. 'Have you heard or seen anything?'

'No, I wasn't here then and Henry didn't mention anything to me when I arrived today. I can rouse him, but I'd ask you to go easy. He's not been the same of late. He is seventy-five now, so that's kind of to be expected, especially after a minor heart attack a year ago. He's been a little vague since.'

'Have you seen or heard anything out of the ordinary lately?'

Robert frowned.

'Actually, the odd thing has gone missing in the house.'

'Could they have been stolen?'

'I doubt it. Most of them have turned up again. A gold watch hasn't, though. Perhaps he hid it when he was tipsy. He loves a few cognacs at night.'

'Does he suspect anyone?'

'He hasn't said so. Henry's always been as sharp as a tack. Great with managing his investments, up with technology, and a bit of a raconteur given half the chance, but, well, I'll wake him and you can judge for yourself.'

'Please do. I only have a few questions.'

They walked into the property and Robert guided them to a huge lounge that ran the length of the building. A man was sitting in one of the armchairs, next to an eye-catching but unlit open fire, checking his mobile phone. His face was lined below snow-white hair. He looked up and smiled.

'Afternoon. I wasn't expecting visitors.'

He struggled to his feet.

'It's okay. You don't need to get up,' said Barton.

'Nonsense. Henry. Henry Bancroft. Hello again, young lady.'

Barton introduced himself, then asked Henry if he'd seen or noticed anything a few nights ago.

'No, you occasionally hear boy racers drive past, although, at my age, everything seems fast nowadays.'

'Do you get on well with your neighbours?' asked Zelensky.

'We're polite, but it's not like we live in a terrace, so you only tend to see each other outside the front every now and again, and I'm usually in my car. One side are much older than me. The chap on the other side is a bit grumpy, but the lady of his house is a beauty. Lovely woman. Often waves.'

Barton pictured her doing that from the pool area, but he kept his thoughts to himself. He was wondering what else to ask when his mobile rang. It was from an unrecognised number. He held up a finger. 'Excuse me a moment.

'DCI Barton.'

'Hi, it's Sandy Faversham. We spoke this morning at Paddock Green.'

'Yes.'

'It's about Poppy.'

Barton pressed the phone against his ear. 'What is it?'

'She's just walked out of the paddock.'

'Pardon?'

'Poppy must have climbed over a fence at the bottom of the garden. I'm looking at her now.'

26

DCI BARTON

A range of emotions rushed through Barton. Relief that the girl was alive and safe, but confusion over her turning up at the Faversham property.

'Is she okay?'

'It seems so. She asked to borrow a swimming costume.'

Barton had to be incredibly careful with Poppy as a minor. Assuming she was a victim, they'd need specialist officers to interview her, not a relic who'd spent the last three years stuck behind a desk.

'Did she say where she'd been?'

'No. I asked, but she said it was none of my business.'

'Oh,' said Barton.

'Whatever's happened, it hasn't changed her.'

'Okay. Make sure she doesn't leave. I'll be right over.'

Barton cut the call and slowly put his phone away.

'Was that what I think it was?' asked Zelensky.

'Yes. Poppy strolled into Sandy's garden as though she'd returned after an hour of blackberrying.'

'I take it you've found the young girl who's been missing?'

Barton looked over at the elderly man, who was gingerly lowering himself back into his seat.

'Yes. Do you know her?'

'No, I've been following it on the news.'

'You've probably seen her out and about. Down at next door's pool.'

Henry scrunched his eyes with confusion, but Barton suspected it was an expression to hide the blush that was spreading up from his neck.

'Tall, slim girl, long brown hair,' said Barton. 'She's the daughter of Sandy's best friend.'

'Oh, I didn't know that.'

'Yes, pretty child. Fourteen years old.'

Henry's face blossomed further.

'I wasn't aware of that, either.'

Barton kept his eye on Henry, who was suddenly interested in the fireplace. Barton didn't have time to analyse what might be going on, so he said he'd talk to him again. Then he and Zelensky left the house at speed.

'Ring Social Services,' said Barton.

'About a specialist interviewer?'

'No, don't worry about one of those for now. Social Services know what they're doing and should be along asap. We just need to ensure Poppy's still here when they arrive.'

Barton and Zelensky left Bancroft's and marched back to the pool area at Paddock Green. They found Poppy larking around in the water with Sandy. Poppy, with a face full of make-up, could have passed for twenty-five. Radiant with the power of youth, she even put Sandy in the shade.

Barton sat on a deckchair, which squeaked ominously underneath him. This was turning out to be an extremely strange day. He decided not to say anything and instead leave it to the Social

Services team who would be there in minutes. Poppy glided effort-
lessly up and down for a few lengths, then swam over to his side of
the pool.

'Are you a policeman?'

'Yes.'

'You look like you could handle some trouble.'

'Thanks.'

'I bet you'd make a big splash.'

Barton couldn't help chuckling. 'Luckily for you, it's a work day.'

'What are you doing here?'

'Looking for you.'

'That was lucky. My mum wasn't at home, so I came to Sandy's,
thinking she'd be here. I also fancied a dip.'

'It's nice to find you safe and sound.'

She gave him a languid smile.

'I bet you've been wondering where I've been. Don't worry. You
won't need to do anything.'

Barton didn't want to get into that with her. This unusual,
slightly sexualised behaviour could well be a coping mechanism. It
was also sometimes a sign of a girl who'd grown up too fast. Maybe
abuse at home, or more likely neglect.

'We'll see,' he said.

Poppy gave him another grin and returned to swimming. Barton
heard rapidly approaching traffic from the front of the property.
Then a short screech of brakes. A minute later, two women in
casual clothes strode towards him. Barton knew one of them. He
pulled himself out of his seat and spoke to her quietly away from
the others.

'Hi, Shirley.'

'John, pleasure to see you again. It's been a while. I was
informed you'd left the sharp end.'

'Major Crimes sucked me back in.'

Shirley's head bobbed but she wasn't one for small talk.

'Has she said anything?'

'Not really.'

'I assume you haven't grilled her.'

'You assume correct.'

'Sorry, I should have known that, but not everyone's on the ball nowadays.'

'I would say Poppy's acting strangely cool.'

'Understood.'

'Do you need any help?'

'No. Let me find out what's going on. I'll ring you later.'

They were interrupted by shrill shouting coming from the direction of the house. Barton stared at Sandy, who shrugged.

'Bloody hell, you silly little mare,' bellowed a voice from behind the hedge. 'Where the blazes have you been?'

Sandy had obviously rung her friend Audrey, as well as Barton. Audrey charged down the lawn, past the hedge, head down, shoulders forward, arms pumping. She reminded Barton of a squat scrum half he'd struggled to contain many years ago. She stopped at the water's edge, eyes bulging at her daughter.

'I'm fine, Mum. Sorry to have worried you.'

Audrey burst into tears, then plunged straight into the pool.

27

DCI BARTON

Ten minutes later, Barton and Zelensky were heading back to the office.

'I didn't see that coming,' said Zelensky.

'No, it'll be interesting to hear what Poppy says. Hopefully she'll tell us who was responsible for taking her away, or at least who she was staying with, and we can bring them in.'

'Sounds like she won't be saying anything.'

'The experts will find a crack somewhere to get her talking. Remember, whatever she may think and however grown-up her life may appear, Poppy's a child at heart. The person she's been staying with had to be an adult with reasonable resources, or they wouldn't have kept it together for this long. That means there's probably an imbalance of power and a crime committed.'

'I don't know. She came across as someone who'd returned from the airport after a week on an exotic beach.'

'Kids are, by definition, childlike. They're volatile and they often see life only from their point of view. I reckon, soon enough, Poppy will feel let down. Then we won't be able to stop her spilling the beans.'

Barton looked over for a response to what he considered his sage teachings, but Zelensky seemed only half present.

'Let's get a coffee,' he said. 'You can give me all the details about your chat with the gardener on the way. Did he give you much more?'

Zelensky took a left at the Thorpe Wood roundabout instead of heading back to the police station.

'A little more. I felt a bit sorry for him. The conversation repeatedly came back to money. His business was going great guns. He worked for the Favershams, both of their neighbours, and numerous other properties along this street. It sounds like he really grafted. He kept saying how he planned to grow his company and get minted. Then the pandemic hit, and his customers cut back, or did their own gardens.'

'I suppose people had more time on their hands.'

'Right, so his little empire crumbled.'

'Did he say why he's so obsessed with being rich?'

'He reckons wealthy folk have the best in life. Great houses, fast cars, and stunning women. His words.'

'I guess there's some truth in that.'

'Yes, but as his chargeable hours, as he called them, dropped off, he took a crazy risk.'

'Gambling?'

'Crypto. He had a big punt on the latest coin and lost all his savings.'

'Which presumably would have enraged him.'

'Yes, but the faceless shadows behind those companies vanish like smoke when it goes tits up. There wasn't anyone to direct his rage at, which has made him furious with himself.'

'I'd guess there are a thousand similar stories in Peterborough alone.'

'Yeah. He still has some customers. The Favershams kept him on, as did Henry.'

'Interesting. So, he's behind on his life goal of bagging himself a fortune and Miss World. Yet he continues to stare into that nirvana every working day. He may even feel like Sandy's taunting him. Parading around near naked while he tries to trim the bushes.'

Zelensky smiled but managed to resist making a joke. 'Perhaps Henry's watch ended up in Timothy's pocket.'

'Maybe. Henry just added to the strange vibe I've sensed all morning. That Robert guy, his secretary, said Henry had been acting differently, but I didn't get any hint of dementia from him. Frail on his feet, yes, but intellectually diminished, no.'

Zelensky turned into the car park opposite Sainsbury's at the Bretton Centre. It was gone two o'clock and, for the first time in years, Barton realised he'd missed lunch and not noticed.

'Do you want anything to eat, Maria?'

Zelensky held eye contact for a moment. He'd used her Christian name deliberately, so they could chat on a personal level.

'Nah, I'm fine. Just a coffee.'

'Latte?'

'No, too much dairy gives me gas, and you've got to sit in a car with me.'

Barton strolled into Costa with a smile. The sandwiches tempted him, but he resisted. A large cappuccino would hopefully see him through the afternoon. His exercise shorts would be loose again before he knew it. He returned to their vehicle and handed Zelensky her drink.

'So, how are things?'

Zelensky bared her teeth. 'So-so.'

The Ice Killer had murdered Zelensky's boyfriend. She'd naturally struggled for a while and, like many police officers before her, had used alcohol as a crutch. When she'd first joined Major Crimes, she'd been trim, peroxide blonde, fresh-faced, and keen. She'd put weight on in the three years Barton had been gone and let her hair return to a mousey blonde. There was also a world-weary air to her with the sunken eyes of someone who wasn't getting enough sleep. Or the shut-eye she was having was fevered. It was the same look Zander had.

Barton didn't want to pry, but he'd known Zelensky for over six years. She'd come to his house two Christmases in a row.

'Dating?' he asked.

'I was. I fucked it up.'

Barton took a tiny sip of his scalding coffee. 'Leicester?'

Zelensky shifted in her seat. 'You never did miss much.'

'He's a sound guy. What happened?'

'I self-destructed. Actually, no, that's not completely true. The job is messing me up at the moment. When you ran the team, it was easier. I didn't feel the weight of responsibility. It was as though the burden was across your back, not mine. The odd mistake was made, but the cases were more often than not put to bed.'

'Praise indeed.'

Zelensky shrugged. 'I'm sure you don't need me to blow smoke up your arse.'

'No, you don't want to give me gas.'

Zelensky laughed but volunteered no more. Barton put his cup on the dashboard.

'You're a sergeant now. Shouldering some of the load is part of your role.'

'I get that. It's this run of frustrating luck we've had. I'm feeling it more and more. The pressure's building. We can all sense it. Some are going sick and quitting. Others are making stupid decisions.'

'No possibility of fixing it with Leicester?'

'Not a chance. We'd gone out for a team drink to build morale. Zander had two pints and was almost asleep at the table. Leicester drove him home. Everyone else left shortly afterwards, except me and Hoffman.'

'Ah.'

'Yeah.'

'We all make mistakes.'

'Bet you're glad you came back now.'

Barton laughed along with her, but he was enjoying himself. It had been an intriguing day, and Poppy was alive and seemingly well. There was something else at play, though, and it dawned on him what it was.

'I've just worked out what's been unsettling me when we talked to these people.'

'All the lies.'

'Almost.'

Barton gave her a moment to think. She bobbed her head, then nodded firmly. 'It's secrets. Where's Poppy been? Why is Audrey so casual about her missing? We haven't learned everything about Timothy. Charles and Sandy are heading for disaster and aren't being honest with each other, never mind us. Even Henry seems an enigma.'

'Secrets tend to have a habit of not staying that way.'

'Then all hell breaks loose.'

'Yep. Let's return to the office and write all this up. I doubt we'll hear much more today.'

Barton had to grab his drink as she pulled away, but his smile gradually morphed into a frown. He'd put money on there being more dramatic events, but Sandy was the one who appeared to be in danger.

28

DCI BARTON

Barton trudged through his front door at 7 p.m. feeling tired out again. Holly was drying the dishes in the kitchen. She gave him a smile.

'You look beat.'

'You know when you covet something, and then you get it?'

'Are you talking about being careful what you wish for?'

'Yep.'

Holly chuckled. 'Don't give me that baloney. You love it. Your dinner's in the microwave. It really is like old times.'

'What am I having?'

'Gammon, chips, and peas. Luke saw the dish on a TV programme and wanted it immediately.'

'I might be too tired to eat it.'

'If you're angling at me to heat it up for you, then you are all out of luck. I've not stopped all day.'

Barton's phone rang. He looked at the screen. It was another number he didn't recognise. He glanced at Holly as if to say he still hadn't stopped. She walked out of the room, leaving the damp tea towel resting on his head.

'DCI Barton speaking.'

'Hi, John, it's Shirley. Sorry I haven't been able to call you until now.'

'No worries. What have you got?'

'To be honest, that's why I haven't called. Poppy was happy to talk to our specialist officers, but she only said she was with a friend and refused to provide an address. She came across as calm.'

'Okay, what was the specialist's opinion of her?'

'That's the concerning thing. They've spoken to hundreds of children who've been through traumatic experiences. They're trained to get them talking and relaxed. As you know, abuse and coercion are often perpetrated by clever people, so the victims don't even recognise they've been exploited. Kids are especially susceptible to this.'

'But?'

'Poppy chatted freely about her life, her hopes and dreams. She wants to live with her dad and one day be famous. When asked about where she'd been, she smiled and said it was her business, and not to worry.'

'Definitely not the father?'

'No, it was an acrimonious divorce. We've obviously talked to him a few times. Glenn admits he was verging on being an alcoholic back then, and his and Audrey's was an unhealthy relationship. The courts were involved and she was granted full custody. He only got supervised contact with Poppy for years. Glenn's cleaned himself up now and has access every other weekend and agreed nights during the week, but it took a long time for him to reach that point. Audrey made life difficult for him in the beginning, which he's bitter about.'

'It's pretty standard for kids to be used as a weapon when marriages first fall apart.'

'Yes, but Glenn's not stupid. There's no chance he'd do anything to jeopardise those visits. He reckons Audrey only relented when Poppy started to become a handful, and Audrey realised having every second weekend free was actually pretty nice.'

Barton laughed. 'As is often the way. And Glenn had no idea where she might have been?'

'No. We got the impression he's the better parent. She has a tidy room at his house with plenty of fluffy toys. They go to the cinema, take walks in the country and days out at theme parks. Normal wholesome family life.'

'Yeah, but you and I understand that it's easier being the weekend dad. They often have more money, and they can ring-fence their calendars to focus solely on their child. They make it fun. Audrey's a full-time mother, but she's working part-time as well.'

'I know, but we've been to her house on a number of occasions. It's often a mess. Typical signs of a struggling parent. Piles of washing. Dirty windows. Empty fridge. Unhealthy food in the cupboards.'

'Is there a mental health angle with her? Perhaps depression is making it hard to cope.'

'That's possible, but she could simply not give a shit.'

'But there was no real concern?'

'No, we never suspected Poppy was in any danger.'

Barton thought back to the relief on Audrey's face when she saw her child was safe. 'She was immensely relieved to see Poppy again.'

'I noticed, and her response was natural. It's a tough one. Poppy does her own washing. Mum gives her cash for personal items, and there's dinner money in abundance, so she can afford takeaways.'

'Not the healthiest diet, then.'

'That's the other odd thing. If I gave my kids free rein, they'd live at McDonald's.'

'Which would be terrible,' said Barton slowly.

Shirley laughed. 'Oh, I forgot about your addiction to Maccy Ds. My point is that Poppy isn't out of control. Her school attendance and reports are excellent. She usually makes intelligent food choices, goes jogging, but she also got her tongue pierced and has numerous tattoos.'

Barton was about to comment about the age of consent being eighteen, but Poppy could easily pass for older if she wanted to. There was the possibility of fake IDs being used if a parlour insisted on seeing proof, or people did it freelance at home nowadays.

Shirley exhaled deeply down the phone.

'She has maturity beyond her years. Poppy is a classic case of a child growing up in an environment of neglect where they become little adults.'

'That'd be my guess, too.'

'We've skirted around some tough conversations with Audrey. Finding Poppy took precedence, but we'll need to get involved now.'

'What did Audrey say when you probed about her daughter being so independent?'

'That Poppy is wilful, rude, and aggressive. She insisted on having her own money because her mum bought crap food. Audrey said Poppy demanded to clean her own clothes because her mother ruined them with her sloppy attitude to life.'

'Wow. I suppose that might be deflection, or it could be the truth.'

'Right. Poppy is physically healthy and attends school. She eats well and performs highly. There's no evidence of drug or alcohol use. The obvious indicators for an abused child are missing.'

'Apart from vaping?'

'Yes, she does vape. Sadly, that's become so common it barely registered. We asked Poppy about smoking. She reckoned it was cool. As for the tattoos, she said they looked sexy, and she laughed when we told her she was underage.'

'Do you reckon an older boyfriend coerced her?'

'Maybe, but tattoos are everywhere. Even my Facebook gets bombarded by images of stunning bronzed fitness bunnies covered in them. It's no surprise the kids think they're brilliant. I can only assume TikTok is worse.'

Barton remembered the row Holly had with Layla about getting a tattoo when she was sixteen. They were lucky Layla mentioned it to them before she did it. His stomach rumbled, so he checked the microwave and switched it on. Barton wasn't a fan of hot pineapple, but his belly didn't have time to remove it. He was so hungry he might faint!

'Are you still there, John?'

'Yes.'

'I was told you were investigating an attempted murder where Poppy turned up. Do you think there's any connection?'

'It's interesting Poppy headed there today, but we haven't found a link so far.'

'That's a shame,' said Shirley. 'Unfortunately, we're still almost totally in the dark about what's happened. I also heard you have a person of interest, Frank Bone, from way back. It'd help if you located him.'

Barton wondered who'd told her about him, but in cases like these, many agencies were involved. Social Services and CID worked together all the time because so many children went missing. He had a thought.

'Did you ask Poppy why she came home?'

'Of course. She said she didn't want to outstay her welcome.'

Barton frowned as all the information Shirley had given him slotted into place.

'Oh dear,' he said.

'Yep,' replied Shirley. 'It's only a matter of time before she disappears again.'

29

THE VILLAGE KILLER

Yesterday was a barrow full of drama, which included Poppy's sudden return to the property. A surprise, indeed. The fact that she chose to stroll over to Sandy's place with her newfound freedom adds another layer to the mystery. I didn't realise she knew about the access from the rear. I don't believe for a minute she was looking for her mum. There'll be more than one person who she has her claws in, unless she simply wanted to wash away her sins in the pool.

It was perfect timing. The police would have been worried about Poppy. I bet the connection to Sandy's property is infuriating them. They'll understand soon enough because it's time for criminal act number two.

I've walked to Milton Bridge. Autumn is dying. Last night's wind and rain stripped the trees of most of their leaves, leaving skeletal limbs reaching for the sky. The gusts whisper through the naked boughs. Thick clouds race by overhead, hurling heavy raindrops at their targets below.

Only committed dog walkers venture out when it's like this. Just two cars are in view, and one of those looks like it might have been dumped. It is only just getting light and the view from the apex of the bridge is still spectacular. Nature's beauty for all to see, for those who dare. A fish splashes in the water, a harrier hovers ahead, and the cows huddle together under a distant oak. They act on impulse, as must I. We do what is necessary to survive.

I glance around. There's nobody else in sight. I skirt along the river, squelching through the swampy ground. The wettest bit is to come. I stop and attach plastic bags to my boots and stomp on. Staring down, I see the sludge circling my ankles. The mud as needy as me.

I stand out of view at the rear of the properties, where the fences meet between Paddock Green and Bancroft's. The rhythmic splashing, from the languid strokes of someone swimming, filters through the treeline. It's peaceful, despite the distant rumble of early traffic on the A47.

I pull quality gardening gloves on and climb over the wooden fence, which is mostly draped with barbed wire. I assume Poppy climbed over the back of Paddock Green. The perimeter there is without any type of wire but stands higher and is exposed.

Both properties have paddocks at the bottom, and only a railed fence separates the two. I wander through a small orchard and stop at the last tree. Crouching low, I sneak a peek at the pool. The swimmer does a sedate front crawl, keeping their face out of the water. The skimmer net, attached to its telescopic pole, lies next to the water's edge. I pause to watch another lap. Their pace has dropped. Arms stretch slowly, the head turning from side to side. It's the perfect moment to strike.

When they turn at the end and face away from me, I tiptoe from my hiding place, crouched low. The pole feels solid in my hands, as I knew it would. Quality, as always. I edge closer, the net spreads out with the breeze when I lift it, then I hover it over the twisting head. My arms strain with the weight, but a smile creeps onto my face.

It's not a bad way to go.

30

DCI BARTON

Barton had spent Wednesday morning attending a variety of meetings at HQ in Huntingdon and was driving back to Peterborough at 2 p.m. when Control rang. He listened to the details and decided to drive straight to the scene.

After a mile of thinking, he called the office and asked for Hoffman, Leicester, Minton and Malik to meet him in Castor. There would be a lot of statements to take.

As DCI, he wouldn't get so involved in later cases when he picked up the rest of the duties the role entailed, but he had time for this. It would lift morale considerably if they solved what had been a missing girl and an attempted killing case but now could be child abuse and a murder.

Barton thought of Poppy. Was all that cocksureness yesterday a front for a child trying to be brave? They might never know. Shirley had said the team would remain in contact with Poppy and Audrey over the following week. They would need to broach any sexual angle to the crime, but they would have to tread carefully. Young minds were fragile.

Barton took the slip road off the A47 for the village, then turned left onto Love's Hill. There were two marked response vehicles present in front of the gate for Paddock Green with a top-of-the-range black BMW saloon and a sparkling white Audi Q7 SUV parked on the road outside Bancroft's. Barton stopped his car behind the BMW and stepped out.

The door to the BMW opened and Henry's secretary, Robert, appeared.

'They won't allow me in!' he shouted. 'What's going on?'

Barton walked over to him.

'If you sit down, I'll give you what I know.'

Robert got back in his car. Barton stood next to the door and rested his hand on the roof. He crouched down as far as his knees would permit.

'I'm sorry, but it sounds like Henry has passed away this morning.'

'He can't have. I only chatted to him last night.'

Barton nodded. He gave Robert time for the news to sink in.

'I understand this must be a real shock. He hasn't been found long, so there isn't any more to tell you at this point. Is there any next of kin?'

'No. He didn't have any children, and neither did his sister, who predeceased him. I can't believe it, but why are the police here?'

'I assume the person who discovered the body rang 999 for an ambulance. It's normal for officers to attend at the same time with a sudden death.'

'What do I do?' asked Robert. 'Can I follow you inside?'

'No, but my team will be here shortly. They'll take some details from you. I'll find out what happened and come back out.'

It was possible Robert had killed his boss, but unlikely. Even so, they didn't want him leaving until they'd spoken to him. The first detective to arrive was Hoffman. Barton strolled over and updated him. He left Hoffman to pass the messages on to the rest of the team when they arrived and headed over to the gate.

'What have we got?' asked Barton.

The young PC stared at him. 'Who are you?'

'Barton.'

'And your rank and surname?'

Barton felt his shoulders droop as he gave the scene guard his details and showed his warrant card. The famous quote from Marcus Aurelius sprang to his mind. '*Soon, you will have forgotten everything. Soon, everybody will have forgotten you.*'

'Apologies, sir. I think I've heard of you. The call to Control stated the cause of death was unknown. I was second on the scene. Sergeant Coehlo has set up an inner cordon, and the doctor is present. There isn't anything obvious down there. It could be natural causes.'

Barton thought back to the man he'd met the previous day. He had appeared physically frail and, as anyone who's ever worn uniform quickly discovers, sudden deaths are common.

Barton marched through the gate, which had been left open enough to allow a person through, and followed the path to the right of the house to reach the garden. Barton knew the sergeant. Coehlo used to be a policeman in Portugal when he met a Peterborian on her holidays and followed her home, although he'd been a PC when Barton last spoke to him.

Coehlo noticed Barton arrive and came straight over. Coehlo had grown a thick beard, which was flecked with grey, but it was trimmed, and he looked slim and purposeful.

'Nice to see you again, sir. I heard you were coming back.'

'Thanks. Felt like I'd never been away until your man at the gate failed to recognise me.'

'It's getting to be a thankless job. We get new trainees every week.'

'Lucky we're still here to teach them, eh? Okay. What can you tell me?'

'PC Lewis is sitting with the gardener, Timothy Steele, who came across the deceased. He didn't hear a splash or anything, just found the body floating face down. He pulled him out to try and save him, but when he got Henry on the grass the sight was already gruesome. Chalk white and eyes wide. That was Timothy Steele's description. I suspect he panicked. Young man won't have seen a sight like that before.'

Barton blew out a breath. There were no set rules on the expressions of corpses. They could be peaceful-looking or horrendous.

A woman in a crumpled light-blue suit on the other side of the pool crouched beside the lifeless figure. She walked away from it towards PC Lewis and Timothy. Lewis was standing, but Timothy had his hands over his face while he sat in a chair. She had a quick word with him and Timothy removed his hands and nodded. Barton had met her once before although her name evaded him. He wanted to say Dr Pringle but suspected that wasn't correct. She must be the owner of the Audi.

'What's her surname?' Barton asked Coehlo.

'Dr Crisp.'

Barton smiled as she walked towards him.

'Good to meet you again, Inspector Barton.'

Barton nodded. It seemed after all these years he would always be referred to as Inspector. 'You too.'

'Your star witness over there probably has a touch of shock. I recommended he see his GP, although he mirthlessly laughed at that, saying he'd be dead himself of old age before he reached first in the telephone queue.'

'That seems how it is nowadays. Anything you can tell me about the deceased?'

'He had a pacemaker fitted. I felt it in his chest wall. No obvious signs of trauma.'

'Timothy got a nasty surprise at his face.'

'Yes, which would make heart attack my guess. Perhaps Henry died gasping for air and in pain.'

'I assume estimating a time of death will be tricky.'

'I've taken a temperature, but yes, the water's heated, so that's a complicating factor. He may have been running a fever if he was feeling rough. He's been dead for a while. Probably passed during his early morning swim, but I suppose he could have fallen in.'

'Okay, thanks for coming so swiftly.'

'No problem. I live in Castor. I'd nipped home for lunch to get out of the surgery for a while. Life has become stressful for everyone. Me included.'

'This type of drama must be a rarity here.'

'Castor is a fabulous place to call home, although one of the pubs recently closed, which is a shame. It's normally peaceful. Saying that, many residents are elderly, and we don't all die warm in our beds.'

'Sadly not but I don't suppose you've seen much violence.'

'No, it's one of the reasons it's so great here. The people are friendly. They're making the most of their time. I can walk to the river in three minutes from my house and feel like I'm in the middle of nowhere.'

'Sounds idyllic.'

'I lived on a housing estate for years. What was I thinking? This is such a different way to live.'

Barton agreed it was. You needed money, though, and recent events seemed to dictate even having it didn't buy happiness. After she'd gone, Barton turned to Coehlo.

'Is CSI arriving soon?'

'Yeah, although there doesn't look like much here. Post-mortem will give you more.'

'I'm surprised old Mortis isn't here already.'

'Didn't you hear?'

The hairs rose on Barton's neck. 'Hear what?'

'His missus died. He took some time off. Last I knew, he was retiring.'

Barton recalled how Mortis felt about his wife and vowed to ring him. 'Okay, I'll get my guys to talk to the neighbours and any other workers who might have been present today. There's a handyman.'

'An older gentleman?' asked Coehlo, looking at his notebook. 'Gerald Cann. He heard Timothy hollering for assistance and came over. Apparently, it's pretty easy to slip between the two properties. That's how they move from one to the other to save going out the entrance gates.'

That was news to Barton. He filed it away.

'Okay, mention it to CSI when they arrive. Someone could have also climbed over at the bottom of the gardens.'

'I had a brief look over the fence to make sure nobody was about. There's barbed wire, but it's just about accessible. You'd get your feet wet and muddy on the other side though.'

'Let's hope they find footprints, then.'

Barton left the capable Coehlo to it and strode to the front of the house. A CSI van had arrived, as had the rest of Barton's team. Barton gave his guys instructions to take statements from those present at the Favershams'. It would be best if Timothy came back to the station to give his statement. They could have their doctor check him over in case he was in shock.

Barton decided he'd talk to Robert first. Barton saw he was still sitting in his car, so he knocked on the passenger side window.

Robert's face opened up with hope, but the shake of Barton's head put paid to that.

'Do you mind answering a few questions?' asked Barton.

'Of course not. Is his death suspicious, then?'

'He died in the pool. It's likely natural causes, but we won't know until the PM's finished. Was the pacemaker fitted because he had a weak heart?'

'He had bits and bobs wrong all over. This isn't completely unexpected. Henry was a brilliant swimmer in his prime, though. He wouldn't have minded dying that way, if today was his day.' Henry twisted in his seat to stare at Barton. 'I've been waiting and wondering, and my mind's having dark thoughts. With having met your team yesterday, I wouldn't have been surprised if you'd returned saying he was found riddled with bullets.'

'Nothing so dramatic. Is there anything else I should consider?' asked Barton.

Barton expected Robert to dismiss the question, but he frowned. His eyes closed as if waging an internal war. When he reopened them, Barton could see purpose in them. Robert took a deep breath.

'There's something I should tell you.'

31

DCI BARTON

Barton displayed his most reassuring smile. 'That sounds ominous, but I'm all ears.'

'Before I say any more, will I be able to get into Henry's house today?'

'Maybe later. As you said, with recent events here, we can't be too careful. We have to collect any evidence now and video the scene.'

'Okay. I have Henry's computer in the boot of my car. He got a virus on it, which has happened on a few occasions now. I have various cleaning programs, but they take a while, so I took his laptop back to my hotel. The system often needs to reboot multiple times so I do other work while the processes go on.'

'Oh, you don't stay here?'

'No, Henry liked his privacy as he became frailer. The time for in-house help was coming, though. I think he was resisting the intrusion for as long as possible.'

Barton detected an odd tone in Robert's comment.

'Would Henry want us seeing his computer? We need to have good cause to look at his personal information.'

'Even now he's no longer alive?'

'The dead still have rights.'

'What if he gave me power of attorney and I'm the executor of his will?'

'Then I suspect it's your call. It might be an idea for me to see the POA first. The will would help too. If Henry was killed, someone is likely to have gained from it. The most common motives for murder are money or love. It sounds unlikely to be for sex in Henry's case.'

Again, Robert was quiet. He licked his lips, clearly deep in thought.

'Can we go back to the station to talk?' he asked. 'It's a delicate situation and it might take some explaining. I'd rather not do it in view of everyone.'

'That's no problem at all.'

Barton rang Hoffman, informed him he was leaving, and gave clear instructions about what he wanted from the team if they suspected anything. He checked his watch and said they should all attend a meeting at 6 p.m. at the station.

Barton was intrigued as he drove back along the Castor bypass. Robert kept closing his eyes and mumbling. He had to be weighing something up in his head. Barton understood he could be wasting his time talking to Robert, but an opportunity like this might not come up again if the death became complicated later on.

'What's troubling you?' asked Barton.

Robert sighed. 'The easiest way to explain is to tell you about my and Henry's relationship.'

Barton's eyes switched over to his passenger. Robert grinned at him.

'No, not that kind. I joined his corporation from London Business School nearly thirty years ago. There was a group of new starters. The Protégés, he named us. Henry was a genius. He'd study a business's accounts in the morning, and by the afternoon he would know how many millions he could save the company.'

'Impressive.'

'When I started, he would then sell the advice to their board, or bring a team in, of which I was one, who could manage the change for them at a price. The fees were high, but if I offered to save your firm three million, but it'd cost you one million, you'd still do it.'

Barton puffed out his cheeks. 'Couldn't the business shop around after Henry explained what was wrong and get someone else to do it cheaper?'

'Yes, and that's what often happened. The problem was, Henry was the magician, and the other firms' accountants merely apprentices, so they'd go on to make a mess of it. Sadly that then reflected badly on Henry because it gave change management a bad name, so he needed a new plan. He didn't want to drop his fees, so he simply checked the annual accounts, spotted big opportunities, kept the knowledge to himself, then aggressively bought out the companies. Once they were back in shape, he sold them on. His reputation grew as the entrepreneurs who purchased these newly streamlined firms usually reported they'd purchased themselves real quality.'

'And success breeds more success, but didn't he get a reputation as an asset stripper?'

Robert nodded with respect. 'Well done.'

'I'm not just a pretty face.'

'A few owners got cross at losing their businesses, but most had serious problems. The financial drama after 2008 led to thousands of concerns failing, and the directors were happy to take his money.'

'Is there a sting in this tail, or did you all ride off into the sunset on golden ponies?'

'There were no dramas, and we galloped off on diamond-studded thoroughbreds. I think even back when I started, Henry was looking for a safe pair of hands to hand the company to. Remember, he had no living relatives, so his legacy was all he had. He'd already set up a trust to donate to various worthy causes the world over.'

'I understand. I take it his focus turned to the charity.'

They'd arrived at the station, so they carried on talking on the way up to the office.

'Yes, the business world is changing so rapidly that to keep on top of it all, you have to work eighteen-hour days, seven days a week, and fly around the globe. At age seventy, he stepped back and became a figurehead. Schmoozing, talks, Davos World Economic Forum, that kind of thing. Then he had his heart attack a year ago and quit any real involvement completely.'

Barton offered Robert a coffee, which he politely declined.

'We don't have great rooms for people helping us with our enquiries. It'd be easier for me if we recorded the conversation in an interview room, then I won't need to take notes.'

'Okay, but I have to know the information goes no further.'

'I can't guarantee that without knowing what it is. If it's something unlawful, then a lot of factors could come into play.'

'It's not illegal.'

They reached the office. Barton explained what was going on to Zelensky. Ten minutes later, the three of them were sitting in interview room four.

'Okay. Let me summarise before we start,' said Barton. 'Henry was a multimillionaire, who had stepped away from the limelight after putting his affairs in order. There's nobody set to gain financially from his death because it's all going to charitable organisations.'

'Correct.'

'Did he have close mates or lovers who stayed in touch?'

'Henry was friendly with thousands, but friends with few.'

'There's you.'

'I was with him ten years before I moved into what he called his inner sanctum. Henry liked to talk to me once a fortnight to keep him up to date with the business. As I said, I visited when I could. He occasionally offered advice, but I think our friendship evolved into a personal connection he looked forward to. Men like us are generally poor at maintaining relationships. Henry's passionate affair was with money. After his heart attack, he used to say he fell in love with fool's gold.'

'So, he became lonely.'

'Yes. Business is cruel. Once you leave the arena, those remaining find new gladiators to fight, and you're soon yesterday's news.'

Barton nodded ruefully. 'But you continued to visit even though you weren't being paid or contracted to.'

'Right. Everything I have, I owe to him, and that is substantial. I often fly myself here to visit him in my private jet, for example. I liked him. Henry was funny, kind, generous, but sad he'd never taken the time to create a family.'

Robert had carried a thick briefcase with him. He flipped it open and took out a slim Apple MacBook Air, which he put on the table and opened. He entered a long, complicated password, and brought up a web page.

Barton's eyes narrowed on reading its name. Robert logged into an account, clicked an icon, then edged the screen around so both Barton and Zelensky had a clear view.

'Well,' said Barton. 'I wasn't expecting that.'

32

DCI BARTON

In front of Barton was a fairly bland website called DreamViews, but the image that had been blown up was far from vanilla. A woman posed in a nurse's outfit. The poor girl had one a few sizes too small.

Robert reached over, minimised the picture, then clicked on another. This time it was a photograph of a receptionist who had also been mis-measured. It appeared to be the same person, but in both pictures her long blonde hair concealed her face.

'For want of a better phrase,' said Barton, 'who is that?'

'I've no idea, but she was his favourite.'

Barton glanced at Zelensky, who didn't appear as surprised as him.

'I assume it's a site like OnlyFans,' she said.

'Yes,' replied Robert.

'I've heard of OnlyFans, but I'm not sure how it works,' said Barton. 'Is it prostitution?'

'I was confused until Henry explained it to me. I'm divorced now, but my ex-wife would not have been pleased if she'd spotted this on the family PC's list of websites visited.'

'Or under the debits in the joint bank account,' said Barton.

'Exactly,' said Robert. 'According to the companies who own these sites, the business model assists content creators and artists to earn money from their work while building genuine relationships with their fans. They are rapidly growing social media platforms where people can upload whatever they like. That's what the companies say at least but, turns out, adult material is the most common type of content. The business model is another thing which grew exponentially during lockdowns where these pages became popular among sex workers because they couldn't meet in person.'

'So, they post pictures of themselves, many of which are naked, and charge people to look at them.' Barton scratched his head.

'They put up images of themselves provocatively dressed first. It's called a thirst trap. The punter notices, then wants to see everything.'

'Why bother when there's so much free pornography online?'

Zelensky let out a small chuckle. Barton turned to her. 'Zander told me about it.'

Robert reclined in his seat.

'That's what I said to Henry. He explained it's more than pictures and videos, the sites encourage conversations and building direct relationships.'

Barton frowned.

'So, Henry found this website and this young woman on it. She sent him racier photographs, which he paid extra for, then they started chatting online, which I assume also had a cost.'

'Yes, ten pence a reply.'

Barton smiled. 'That's how much text messages used to be, back in the day.'

Zelensky grinned at him. 'Gotta love the Jurassic age. This sort of thing is pretty common nowadays. I've got a friend who has a profile.'

'You have?'

'Yes, she pole-danced at a strip club to fund university and loved it apart from the clutching hands. When she saw this come out, she started a page and did a bit for fun. She's an exhibitionist, although her husband doesn't have a clue. It's getting to be a problem because she sometimes makes more from the side hustle than she does as a surveyor.'

'No way.'

'That certainly seems possible,' said Robert. 'I researched it because I was worried about Henry being exploited, but he knew exactly what he was doing. Henry enjoyed his chats with this woman, and it was up to him to decide what he spent his cash on.'

'How much money are we talking?' asked Barton.

'I've got access to Henry's accounts, which he obviously knows. That's likely why he explained it all to me. So, I checked. It's only a couple of grand a month.'

'That seems a lot.'

'Not for him. He'd think little of spending a thousand pounds on a day out in London. Or five grand to hire a helicopter for the afternoon. To a certain degree, it's cheap as chips, and it kept him happy. He has spent more of late, but not loads. I've seen a few of the messages from her. There's nothing overtly aggressive. His full picture isn't on his profile. He has one of him with a cowboy hat tilted over his face. Henry wanted to be upfront, knowing if anything happened to him, I'd find out and would need to understand.'

'I see,' said Barton. 'It's not illegal, but some would find it a little distasteful.'

'Isn't prostitution the oldest profession?' asked Zelensky. 'Puritans the world over have demonised the trade, despite using the services offered, giving the women who are invariably lower class no protection whatsoever. Sites like this make their jobs incredibly safe as long as they're careful.'

'It's not the same as the real thing, though, is it?' asked Barton. 'Surely they expect to meet and do the deed.'

'Henry reckoned not,' said Robert. 'He lacked the drives of a younger man. Conversation and titillation were enough. He dated women when he was younger, but whenever they sought more commitment, he would slip away. He didn't want the distraction from his business, but in his dotage, he wanted someone to chat to. She sent him nude photos and videos, which he found exciting and fun. That satisfied him.'

'It's a scam, though,' said Barton. 'She doesn't care about him. It's just her manipulating money out of a lonely man. If he stopped paying, she'd stop communicating.'

'It's like meeting my twin,' said Robert. 'I argued all that, too, but he sadly told me he had nobody else and I struggled to argue with that. A hundred thousand pounds would have been a drop in the ocean to Henry, so it's not as though he was out of control.'

Barton's mind raced at this new world.

'Wait a minute. Henry must have understood she was doing the same thing with fifty or more other men.'

Robert clicked his fingers. 'Precisely. Henry agreed. Of course he knew that, but she said he was her favourite.'

It was Barton's turn to lean back in his seat. 'Clever!'

Robert nodded. 'I guess the girls get skilled at their job. They come to know the guys who contact them. Send them the pictures they prefer. Tell them what they want to hear. Tease them in just the right way.'

Barton stared at the screen again.

'The images you've shown me are pretty soft. How does it work? Do you pay a lot extra to get the raunchy stuff?'

Robert reached over and closed the receptionist photo. He went back into the account's files, then brought up another photograph.

Barton's eyebrows shot off his head.

33

DCI BARTON

Robert reached over and shut the lid of the laptop.

'Obviously, you can understand why I don't want this information in the public domain. It wouldn't look good, even though it's not illegal. I'd hate to endanger Henry's legacy, but you need to have all the facts to check into his death. Henry would have wanted that, too.'

'Why do you think his death was caused by anything other than natural causes?' asked Zelensky.

'It's just a feeling. I often have them with business deals. I'm not always right, but it's proven beneficial to pay heed to those concerns in the past. Don't detectives have the same instincts?'

'We do,' said Barton. 'I've a meeting with my team this evening to discuss our findings from today. I'll check on the post-mortem, but it's likely to be tomorrow before we hear any results. They may be inconclusive. Of course, the pathologist could find advanced disease, poison, or any other cause of death. I'm not sure this DreamViews helps at the minute, with no suspects or evidence to point to its involvement.'

'Right, so we should wait until after the post-mortem.'

'A glance through his DreamViews account, the pictures, messages, and maybe his email correspondence and bank records, would be worth the time if the PM was inconclusive. It would be intrusive, and unlikely to get signed off without stronger reasons for seeing them.' Barton paused. Robert had been more than helpful, so he spoke plainly. 'You'd have to give them to us.'

Robert gave him a tight smile to say he understood. If Henry's death proved to be natural, then his old boss's story was over and the DreamViews' angle would be irrelevant.

'I tell you what,' said Robert. 'I'll go through everything tomorrow just to be sure. I assume I'll be allowed back in Henry's house.'

Barton nodded.

'His will and other legal documents are in the safe. I have copies, but the originals will be better. It'll take me all day and possibly some of the next to read through his email accounts, investments, the other bank statements, and this DreamViews thing. He was a wealthy man. Perhaps there are large cash withdrawals somewhere, which he just wouldn't have needed.'

'That would be beneficial,' said Barton. 'I appreciate you spending the time.'

Robert shrugged.

'It helps me, too. I need to get the ball rolling on probate and with my duties as executor.'

'There'll be a funeral to arrange as well.'

'No, he didn't want one. He thought they were a waste of money, and he'd rather give the cash to charity. He wanted cremating and me to scatter his ashes in the garden of remembrance. No fuss.'

'Sounds like this Henry was quite a guy,' said Zelensky.

'He was.'

Robert had caught a taxi as he wasn't sure of the parking at the police station, so Barton arranged a lift back to Castor for Robert, who said he was going to head to The Granary and have a pint and a meal. It was close, and he hoped to clear his head. Barton had escorted him to the entrance when he remembered a salient point.

'Did Henry always take a morning swim?'

'He did. He often swam a couple of times a day, but he took it easy because of his heart. The stretching motion helped keep his back supple.'

Barton shook Robert's hand, then spent the rest of the afternoon catching up with his emails. Six o'clock came swiftly, and the team gathered in the meeting room. Barton decided not to mention the DreamViews angle until Robert had checked his end and the PM results arrived.

'Any joy with the interviews?' asked Barton.

'I had a word with both the Favershams,' said Malik. 'Charles was in his office all morning and hadn't heard or seen anything. He seemed distracted. Sandy had been out since nine, food shopping and a visit to the dentist. She gave me the dentist's number in case I wanted to check.'

'Had Audrey or Poppy been over today?'

'No, neither.'

'And the people who live on the other side of Henry's?'

'Mr and Mrs Ashington,' said Leicester. 'Old, but very much on the ball. I got the impression they were like the others and had no contact with Henry aside from waving if they passed each other in their cars. They were polite and gave their condolences but didn't know him well. Jerry had done the odd job for them, but they have their own gardener. I only spoke to them for a few minutes because they had plans for the day at the Battle of Britain Memorial Flight Visitor Centre. There's little chance of them being involved. One of them was in a wheelchair.'

'Which leaves the workers.'

'I chatted with the maintenance guy, Jerry,' said Minton.

'I thought he wasn't about until the afternoon.'

'He came in early to catch up on what he missed the previous day when he called in sick. Said he arrived about nine thirty and worked at the Favershams' first thing, tinkering with the pool pump and the heating system, then he headed to the Bonaccorso place to prepare the outside lights. That's the other side of the Favershams' property. Bonaccorso used to light the house up at Christmas for when the grandkids came and still does it, even though he won't be back until the new year. Talk about having too much money.'

'In a way, it's a peculiar set-up,' said Leicester. 'The property owners are all rich. The houses are huge, with big fences and gates, so they barely cross paths. Yet the gardener and handyman swan around at will, climbing through fences, and one even has a gate to next door.'

'The gardener, Timothy, pulled himself together when we brought him to the station,' said Malik. 'He was happy to give a recorded statement. His story is similar to Jerry's. He spent most of the morning at the Favershams' getting their paddock grass cut for the last time before winter.'

'I don't suppose there's a horse we need to talk to?' asked Zelensky.

'There used to be,' said Barton. 'Charles sold it without telling Sandy.'

'Bastard.'

'Timothy noticed Sandy leave in the morning and return,' said Malik. 'He helped her with the shopping when she got back from Marks & Spencer.'

'So, she came back before the dentist.'

'He reckoned she was there for a couple of minutes. Then Timothy went to Henry's to fetch one of his tools and found the body.'

Barton caught Minton scowling.

'What is it?' he asked her.

'M&S is quality, but you pay for it. If I had money troubles, I'd head to Aldi.'

Barton tutted. 'You're right. Wouldn't she be antagonising Charles by splashing out? I reckon more than one person we've spoken to today has lied to us. Anyone heard when the PM will be done?'

Leicester raised a hand.

'Yep. I checked just before the meeting. Mortis will start it at midday tomorrow.'

Finally, Barton smiled at some good news. 'So, he's back?'

'Must be.'

Barton decided to head down to the mortuary to observe. It would be great to see his friend, even if there was the possibility of him suggesting there had been a murder.

34

DCI BARTON

Barton rushed out of the office at seven that evening. He was cutting it fine for his tennis match with Zander. He drove home and barged through the front door, where he almost knocked Holly flying.

'Jesus, John. Spare a thought for little people.'

'Sorry, Zander will be here in fifteen minutes. I need to get changed.'

Holly paused as she looked at his face. 'What's up with you?'

'Nothing.'

'Rubbish. You've got that expression on your face.'

'What expression?'

'Like when I catch you checking out a pretty woman.'

'Argh! Get out of my mind!'

He stomped up the stairs. Five minutes later, Barton was in the kitchen in his shorts and a Star Wars T-shirt that he'd been given for Father's Day. It had Darth Vader in a high-vis jacket on the front and the caption read 'May The Police Force Be With You'.

Holly was sitting at the table doing the crossword on the back of a newspaper. She glanced over at Barton.

'Careful how you pick the balls up in those shorts. If you bend over, it'll be like a scene from *Alien*.'

'Zander will be the one picking up the balls, after they've raced past him.'

'There's a letter for you here. It's from the surgery.'

Barton picked up the envelope. He'd finally managed to get an appointment for a well-man check-up recently, which they did for those approaching fifty. The nurse who'd taken his blood, weight and height hadn't commented on anything. Barton had assumed that was because everything was more or less fine.

Barton ripped it open. 'Shit,' he said, after reading the contents. He passed it to Holly.

'Oh, dear,' she said. 'That isn't great news.'

Barton plonked himself down on a seat.

'But not the world's biggest surprise,' said Holly.

'I suppose not.'

'And you're prediabetic, not diabetic, so consider this a shot across the bow. We can eat healthily together. I put on some lock-down pounds, and I still haven't shifted the excess from our all-inclusive holiday.'

'Rubbish. You're perfect. I like you with a bit of ballast. I could call you Jolly Holly.'

'You could call me that, but you'd regularly have a black eye.'

Barton shook his head at the letter.

'Let's do it together, then. Maybe I should go hardcore. Lose loads of weight. Perhaps even get down as low as fifteen stone.'

'Didn't you weigh that when you were born?'

'So funny. Hoffman's got tattoos and had a hair transplant. I might do the same, get a six-pack and shave my chest, start wearing eyeshadow.'

'Oh dear. It wouldn't be the same if you were thin. Young women like that metrosexual look. I want a traditional man.

Someone who can protect my children and carry eight bags of shopping at once or all of our luggage to the check-in desk. Not a tart who spends more time in the bathroom than I do.'

The doorbell rang.

'See,' said Barton, pointing at the letter, then at his belly. 'This is your fault. You're an enabler!'

'Rubbish. You could start by deleting your McDonald's app.'

Barton drew back in horror.

'What sacrilege is that? I have enough points for a free Big Mac.'

Holly chuckled as she got up. She whispered in his ear as she walked behind him.

'Answering the door burns five calories.'

35

DCI BARTON

While Holly let Zander in, Barton rose from his seat and grabbed the dog's lead. Gizmo dragged himself off the carpet in the hall and wandered after him with his tail wagging.

Zander crouched and stroked Gizmo's back.

'It'd have been easier if I'd bought a few of these instead of having kids.'

'Certainly cheaper,' said Holly, 'but your boys are at such a cute stage. I sometimes feel I could do it again for those pre-school years.'

'I think the oldest person to conceive naturally was nearly sixty, so you might still have time.'

'There's more chance of John getting pregnant than me.'

Zander gave her a cheeky smile. 'Perhaps that explains those few extra pounds he's put on.'

Barton placed a hand on a chuckling Zander's shoulder and shoved him out of the front door. 'Ready for a whooping?'

Zander's eyes dropped down to below Barton's navel.

'Are you wearing spandex shorts?'

'No. They're just tight. Holly shrank them.'

Zander smiled. 'If you say so. And why is the dog coming?'

'Gizmo loves a relaxing drive. We'll go in my Land Rover.'

'Wouldn't he prefer a run in the park?'

'Nope. He ambled around the field this morning. He's a greyhound, so that's plenty of exercise.'

'Fair enough. I can play him if you like. He'd have a better shot at winning.'

'Oh, pride before a fall. You'll probably insist on walking home afterwards. Such will be your incredible shame.'

'Bring it on.'

Zander grabbed his bag and racquet from his car and they both threw their kit in the back seats of Barton's vehicle. Gizmo rested his front paws in the boot, but Barton had to lift the rest of him in. He wasn't sure if the dog couldn't leap up on his own, or if it was merely an energy-saving tactic. Barton pulled off the drive and headed to City of Peterborough Tennis Club.

'Did you book?' asked Zander.

'Yeah.'

'I thought you had to be a member.'

'I met the bloke who manages the place at a community policing meeting. He said if I ever wanted to play, I could use a court for free, so I rang yesterday.'

'Oh, how the mighty have fallen! Big John Barton taking backhanders now.'

'You'll be witness to a few of them shortly.'

'Wow. You are on form.'

'I think he hoped I enjoyed playing and would join afterwards.'

'I won't be falling for that trap again. One of us will get injured tonight, and we'd have paid the year's membership and end up never returning.'

'Don't tempt fate. How's your week off been so far?'

'Brilliant. We've just mooched around. I've managed to turn off from work. There's been some group naps. Zane's close to normal. I'll return to the office a new man.'

'You'll come back a beaten man. I've been studying the game. Perfecting my serve.'

'I am impressed. I've not been to the courts since the last time we played.'

'To be truthful, nor have I, but I watched a YouTube tutorial last night.'

Zander didn't comment for a few seconds. An eyebrow slyly raised. 'We should have a bet. Make it interesting.'

It was dark in the car, but Barton could imagine his friend's expression.

'Sure. A bottle of Fortnum's twelve-year-old Christmas Cream Sherry to the winner.'

'That's rather specific, and more than a little weird.'

'It's Holly's favourite. She asked me to buy it last year, but I forgot. Her mum loved it, so it's nostalgic for her.'

'You forgot, or it was too expensive?'

'I'll admit to nothing, but the price seemed outrageous.'

'Okay, deal.'

They arrived and parked. When Barton opened all the windows an inch and killed the engine, the only sound was soft snoring from the boot.

Zander shook his head. 'He really is the perfect dog for you.'

They left the vehicle and walked towards the main building. Barton popped into Reception and was given court number two. A young couple stared at them wide-eyed as they strode by. Zander tutted.

'Are you worried people are thinking we're a couple again?' asked Barton.

'Maybe, but I suppose looks of surprise are to be expected with us here.'

'I know I'm going to regret this, but why?'

'It's not every day they'll see an incredibly handsome black man take his hairy pet bear to play tennis.' Zander's laugh was booming. 'Especially when the bear is in Lycra.'

Barton opened the gate to the courts. 'They really are staring. So rude. I'm almost tempted to give them the finger.'

Zander gave him a disapproving glance.

'Bad bear!'

They had a bit of a warm-up, then tossed the racquet to see who served first. It came up on Barton's side. He grabbed a ball and strolled to the serving area. After a couple of bounces, he glanced up.

'Are you ready?' he asked.

'Born ready,' was the shouted reply.

Barton threw the ball in the air. Sometimes, in a man's life, the planets lined up, and the universe itself blessed him with good fortune. It became the right moment, at the right time.

Barton hit the ball with all his strength. It zinged off his racquet, scorched through the air and ricocheted off the serving line. The only thing that moved on Zander's body were his eyes, as they briefly tracked the projectile when it flashed by. It cannoned into the wire mesh of the fence behind him. Zander's eyes flicked back to the server.

Barton swaggered to the other side of the court. After a bit of wiggling to free it, he pulled another ball from his pocket and bounced it twice. When Barton looked up to serve, he just managed to keep a straight face. His top lip formed into an impressive sneer. He barked out the score. 'Fifteen love.' Then dropped his voice to a growl.

'To Paddington.'

36

THE VILLAGE KILLER

I managed to resist checking all forms of communication until this evening, but I've poured myself a beer and turned on the TV. There's nothing on the national or local news, so I grab my phone and check online. There's a small article on the *Peterborough Telegraph* website about a man being found dead in his pool. Enquiries are ongoing. There's no reference to any suspicious circumstances.

I lean back on the sofa. Hmm. I expected the cat to be among the pigeons, but the police sound blasé. No, I'm sure they'll thoroughly investigate. I reckon I was rough enough to mark his head. That should get their attention.

I potter around, doing little. Life bores me away from Sandy. That feeling has grown and grown of late, but I don't want to freak her out by going over the top.

While the kettle boils, my thoughts stray to Henry. Was he sad to go? I may have saved him years in a home, although it would be cheeky to say I'd done him a service. He was a dirty old dog though, so he doesn't deserve too much sympathy.

It's funny how people cope with death. Will those who are left pick up on the danger? I used to wonder how the soldiers in the

World Wars could rush towards the enemy across no man's land when everyone from the previous wave had been wiped out by machine-gun fire. Perhaps it's a case of not thinking about it.

Maybe they drove themselves out of the trenches with their girl-friends from home on their minds. If I focus on Sandy, and nothing else, then I should be fine. Like those fighters, I have no choice. This is my war. Sandy cannot leave. What happens next will be a matter of life and death. For everyone.

37

DCI BARTON

Barton woke the next day feeling a little stiff in the legs, but no serious harm had been done. Any aches were well worth it. He had the pleasure of breakfast with Luke.

'Morning, Dad.'

'Morning, son. Joining me for porridge?'

'Nope. Kids don't need to eat that sort of thing. Pass me the Lion cereal.'

Barton opened the cupboard with a confused expression on his face, but then found a box with a lion on it made by Nestlé.

'What the hell is this? Mushed up Lion bars?'

'Pretty much. Don't worry, Mum only lets me have it as a treat now and again. I'll be back on the Coco Pops tomorrow.'

'That's a relief.'

Barton didn't fancy giving Luke an early lesson on nutrition when he already had a telephone meeting with Chief Superintendent Troughton booked first thing. He drove to work with a distinct lack of enthusiasm. Troughton was his boss for his previous role, not his current one, which would make for an irritating conversation. Barton already had a detective chief superintendent to harass him as and when, but he assumed professional mode when his phone rang.

'Morning, sir, DCI Barton here.'

'Morning, John. Thanks for taking the call. I wanted to say a big well done for finding the girl. Everyone's incredibly pleased.'

Barton smirked. Troughton meant the police and crime commissioner was overjoyed. Barton had almost forgotten about the grubby politics part of the role. 'It's a relief to have her back safe and sound.'

'I bet DI Zander's relieved you arrived to save his bacon. He's on leave, isn't he?'

Barton's smile slipped away. 'Yes, he's taking a well-earned break. I've found his department is in great shape, which reflects the hard work he and the team have been putting in.'

'Right. I heard you're looking into an unexplained death, and there's a loose connection to Poppy's mother. Is that correct?'

'The potential link is certainly worrying.'

'Right, let's get everything ironed out pronto. No mistakes.'

Barton briefly imagined wedging his phone handset into Troughton's mouth. 'I was about to head to an important meeting regarding that, sir. Is there anything else?'

'The county is watching, John. Good luck.'

Barton ploughed on for the rest of the morning with more administrative work and was relieved when the time came for him to drive to the mortuary for the post-mortem, which was an unusual feeling to have.

The hospital was only two miles away, so it wasn't long before he had pressed the buzzer at the entrance. A technician he didn't recognise answered the door. He showed his warrant card and she smiled at him.

'Simon mentioned you might be here today. He's doing the PM on Henry Bancroft now. He said to go straight in.'

Barton nodded and walked towards the changing room. Simon Menteith was an irascible Scotsman in his mid-sixties. His nickname was Mortis, because of his fascination with the stages of death. As Barton pulled on a gown, he considered their relationship. Were they even friends? They didn't meet socially but had worked together through many gruesome cases for over two decades. Barton didn't know his exact age, or even if he had any children.

Barton entered the room and, despite breathing through his mouth, felt his stomach roll. It seemed his constitution would need bedding back in.

'Morning, John. Just like old times.'

Barton was getting a bit sick of hearing that. He was starting to feel like an ancient slugger, past his best, trudging out to the field for his final innings. Perhaps that wasn't far from the truth.

'I prefer to think of it as a new dawn.'

'With a foul stench you probably haven't missed.'

'You can say that again. I thought you weren't beginning until twelve.'

'I'm part-time now. I play a round of golf most mornings to keep me fit, but I was keen to get going today. For troubling reasons, I was looking forward to seeing you.'

'That's the nicest thing you've ever said to me.'

'Yes, well, I've said it, so it's back to business as usual. You appear to be larger than when I last saw you.'

'It's these scrubs. They're unflattering.'

'I see.'

Barton examined Mortis and swiftly noticed he appeared smaller.

'Yes, I'm aware I should put a few pounds on.'

'It's a shame people can't lose weight by osmosis.'

'I shouldn't ask, but what?'

'I could stand next to you, then transfer a couple of stone of chub over. We'd both benefit.'

'We live in a frightening world when the scariest thing in the room isn't the cadaver on the table.'

Barton grinned, but then he rested his hand on Mortis's arm.

'I'm sorry to hear about your wife. You must miss her.'

Mortis appeared as if he was about to come back with a riposte. Instead, he sniffed.

'Yes, not totally unforeseen with her earlier cancer scare, but still so life-altering.'

'I'd have come to the funeral if I'd known.'

Mortis nodded. 'I know you would. Right, Mr Bancroft here. You'll be pleased to hear I've already removed most of his organs. Fairly typical for a man of his age. Lung pollution, heart valves appear in poor order, liver damage, prostrate growing, and there was a small tumour on his bladder, which he probably didn't know he had.'

'Heart attack?'

'The usual indicators of that are an enlarged heart, which his is, but only slightly. It kills some, others live with it for years and years, but Henry also has dilation of the heart's chambers, and the vessels responsible for blood supply to the muscle have broken down, which are both common in myocardial infarction. So yes, that's possible.'

'Okay.'

'However, I usually find a clot in the coronary artery, but there isn't one present.'

'I can guess where this is going.'

Barton couldn't see Mortis's mouth, but he suspected he was smiling.

'I thought you'd be pleased. For people in their seventies and upwards, it's not uncommon to fail to locate an exact cause of death, especially with multiple underlying conditions. Sometimes humans just die, which I can now understand on a personal level. He did not pass suddenly though.'

Barton frowned. 'Go on.'

'If he'd had a massive heart attack, that would be it. The body would have shut down, but Mr Bancroft's lungs are full of liquid. My suspicions are that he had a medical event, heart-related, perhaps a stroke, while swimming. He would have struggled to breathe, gone under, swallowed water, panicked, and thrashed around, putting more pressure on his heart. He was already in a weakened state. It wouldn't have taken long.'

'Which might explain his rictus grin.'

'Precisely. It'll be a few days to get his brain scanned for blocked arteries or burst vessels.'

'Thanks. My fears confirmed. As inconclusive as ever.'

'There is one last thing. He has grazing on the top of his head. He's not bald, but the hair's pretty thin on his crown. Faint marks are visible with the eye, so I've excised the skin and was about to peek under the microscope.'

'Interesting.'

'Pull over a stool.'

'So, how are you coping on your own?'

Mortis stopped walking towards the bench. Again, he seemed ready to make a retort, but he took a deep breath instead.

'To be honest, I'm not. My wife and I had very traditional roles. I did the cars and repairs, bins and bills. She did the cleaning, washing, shopping, cooking, and ironing. It turns out, unsurprisingly, that, without years of practice, I'm rubbish at her tasks. I seem to have spent my married life being unaware of how boring and time-consuming they are, as well as not being simple. I apologised at her graveside.'

'Why don't we meet up for a beer or a bite to eat? We've known each other for a long time. You never took up my offers before. Maybe you should now.'

Mortis's head bowed.

'I've always been content with my own company. My wife was popular. She had loads of friends and a busy social life, which she dragged me into. That was enough. Too much sometimes. I'm the type of man who needs solitude, but it appears you can have an excess of it. My wife said I'd regret not maintaining male relationships, but, being a few years older, I expected to die first.' Mortis exhaled deeply. 'How about a few whiskies beside the roaring fire in The Botolph Arms? I heard they reopened. We could get drunk, maudlin, then tell each other our sad stories, over-share, then reminisce about all the brutal murders we've been involved in, before staggering home where I can vomit in my front garden.'

Barton chuckled. 'I'm already looking forward to it.'

Mortis returned to his microscope and fiddled with the device. He froze. After half a minute of subtle moves, he took his eye away.

'There's a faint pattern on his head and a touch of bleeding. Perhaps slight bruising on his shoulders. Was there a net by the pool?'

'You mean like you have over a fishpond?'

Mortis barked out a laugh.

'Christ, I've missed your buffoonery. I meant a pole with a net on the end. They're used to pick objects out of the water. Leaves, twigs, dead pigeons, and turds, I suppose.'

Barton envisioned the pool area with Bancroft lying next to it.

'Yes, there was a long pole floating in the water. I recall it because I wondered why it hadn't sunk.'

'It probably had floats inside, so it doesn't sink when dropped. Now, it's plausible he grabbed the pole as he panicked and pulled it down onto his own head, and he possibly got the marks from netting elsewhere in the garden.'

Mortis didn't need to state the obvious, which was that in fact he thought it was far more likely that someone had used the net to drown Henry.

38

DCI BARTON

A small smile crept over Barton's face. Mortis crossed his arms.

'I thought that would cheer you up.'

'There's something unsettling me about this investigation.'

'Did you drink the pool water?'

'Not this time. There was another incident a few days back at the house next door.' Barton paused to think. 'Could a bonk with the pole have stunned him enough to drown?'

'I would say the marks are on the light side for that. He was old, so your guess is as good as mine. If there are fabric particles inside where the skin broke, we should be able to match them up. I'll contact CSI if that's the case.'

'Shall I get someone to fetch the net now?'

'No, just make certain it was bagged up. I'll push on with the remainder of the tests, and I should be in a position to report most of the results tomorrow morning.'

Barton stood to leave. 'I'll speak to you soon, then.'

'Do you play golf, John?'

'Do I look like I play golf?'

Mortis finally belly-laughed. 'We'll do that drink instead.'

'Or maybe a meal.'

'Perhaps.'

Barton chuckled to himself as he left. He had just the day in mind, and poor Mortis wouldn't stand a chance when Holly found out.

His mobile rang as he reached his car. He'd put Shirley's number in his phone, so he knew who was calling. Hopefully, they'd have managed to get more information out of Poppy.

'Hi, Shirley.'

'Hey, John. Sorry to be the bearer of rubbish news, but Poppy's gone again.'

'So soon?'

'Yeah. She had an appointment with a psychologist today and didn't show. Turns out, she hadn't been to school either.'

'Damn. We should have fitted a tracker. The one positive in this was that she had been attending class. Did the headteacher ring you, then?'

'No, the psychologist. The school was notified online through EduLink, but when we spoke to Audrey, she said she hadn't informed them. It's been a while since she used the school's system. Poppy left first thing as usual.'

Barton puffed his cheeks out. 'Which means she knows her mum's login. I suppose at least we aren't as concerned as we were before.'

'The situation is still dangerous, John.'

'Yes, of course, but last time, she just vanished. I wouldn't be surprised if she thought she'd get away with it today. She could roll in later, pretending she's been to her lessons. It doesn't sound as if Audrey's on the ball. It might not be the first occasion Poppy's logged a sick day.'

There was quiet on the line.

'You're a clever man, John. I'll check into her attendance record in more detail. Perhaps we were lucky she didn't message in on EduLink while she was missing.'

'I suppose even Audrey would still have noticed if she hadn't come home at night.'

Barton listened to silence again, then Shirley sighed.

'I hope you're right about her showing up later today.'

Barton finished the call and headed into the office. He checked his emails at his desk and found one from Robert, who'd forwarded the digital copy of Henry's lasting power of attorney and his will. Ominously, Robert said he would bring the originals in, but he should come in with Henry's laptop, anyway, because Barton needed to see something.

Barton emailed Robert back asking if he could attend at 4 p.m. He read the rest of his messages and was about to chase up Robert when he replied and agreed to the suggested time. At three thirty, Barton got a text from Shirley saying Poppy had returned home pretending she had returned from school. She refused to reveal where she'd actually been.

Barton took Hoffman to an interview room at quarter to four and explained that Robert was coming in. Hoffman was in his late twenties, so Barton asked him if he had heard of DreamViews.

'Yeah, I have. OnlyFans is the big one of that type, but I know of a few others, too.'

'I never realised it was so popular. Obviously, you don't have to tell me if you don't want to, but do you have an account with any of them?'

Hoffman fiddled with his tie. Barton couldn't help laughing.

'I don't understand,' he said. 'You're a nice-looking bloke. You've still got your hair, which I must admit I thought you were losing. Can't you get a normal girlfriend? You know, the type you can see and touch for real.'

Hoffman shrugged. 'I didn't pay for any services. One of my

friends was banging on about it, so I checked it out. My pal runs his own business and is too busy for a girlfriend, so he likes the simplicity of it. Female company, a sexual element, relationship building, all on his terms, and it's cheaper than a real partner. He doesn't have to take her for meals, buy her presents, listen to her moaning, or even remember her birthday. And there's no need to be faithful.'

'And they say romance is dead.'

'Our world is becoming a virtual one. Perhaps he's simply ahead of the game. You can also meet in person in some cases if you want.'

'Really?'

'Sure.'

'I thought the whole point of it was the women were safe behind a firewall, which gave anonymity. That way, the violence sex workers are subject to is nullified.'

'Oh, boss. You are naïve. The point is to make money.'

'I suppose so.'

'My mate's favourite girl is Czech. I saw a photo of her. She's stunning. I'm talking drop-jaw beautiful. If he sent her a grand, she would get a flight over and meet him in London. They could discuss the price of any extras he might like on the day.'

'That's not cheap. Did he agree?'

'No, he already said he was too busy for that kind of thing. Besides, she could have taken the cash and not arrived, or made up some bullshit and asked for more money. The possible ways of being ripped off are endless. In fact, it's probably a bloke doing the communicating. The girls could be models who just pose for the photos.'

'That's a charming thought. Your mate's probably been chatting to a seventeen-stone Bulgarian who has food in his beard most days.'

Hoffman laughed. 'Excellent. I'll sink that thought into his mind tonight.'

'So, your friend declined the visit.'

'Yes.'

'Did she get annoyed?'

'Nope. It's a business relationship which continues to this day. They have banal chats, which costs him a nominal fee, then she sends him photos and videos of her in various poses and outfits, doing different things, for about ten pounds a pop.'

'Without wanting to sound like a prude, it sounds kind of grubby, underhand and dishonest.'

'With respect, perhaps that's because you're pretty old. My generation isn't too fazed by it. My view is that these platforms are a positive thing, but it's another example of those with money and security having an unfair advantage over those at the bottom of the pile.'

'What do you mean?'

'To be on these sites, you need to have a home, camera equipment, and a strong Internet connection. Instead of being a sex worker, you become a content creator and you can even be lauded on social media. Get yourself on glossy porn channels. While the chaotic prostitutes, with none of the necessary, are forced to stand shivering on street corners. They still slip into the cars of angry men with foul breath. They remain participants in the most dangerous and damaging career on the planet.'

'Except soldiers.'

'I will admit to not fancying drone-dodging in Ukraine, but having sex with an aggressive seventy-year-old in a needle-strewn alleyway appeals even less.'

Barton found himself nodding. It was an interesting, if poetic, argument, but he didn't appreciate being called naïve even though in this case he was.

Barton received a call from Reception that Robert had arrived. He gave Hoffman a quick explanation of what he was planning to say during the discussion, and they waited for Robert to be brought to them.

Hoffman cleared his throat.

'I had a hair transplant in Poland.'

Barton glanced over at the officer's head. 'Not bad. Was it expensive?'

'Twelve hundred for the first session. Thousand for the second. It was worth every penny,' replied Hoffman with a grin. 'And not much more than a call girl from Prague.'

Barton touched his shaved head. 'Maybe I should consider getting one.'

'A call girl?'

'Very funny. I take it they transplant the hair from other parts of the body. I've got plenty on my back.'

Hoffman chuckled. 'I'm not sure back hair, or anything lower down, being moved to your bonce would be the look to go for. Perhaps you should just buy a wig.'

Barton was going right off Hoffman.

Thankfully for Hoffman they were interrupted by an officer escorting Robert in. Barton was immediately concerned. He gestured for the businessman to take a seat. Robert was grim-faced.

39

DCI BARTON

Robert sat down and shook his head.

'I take it you found something disconcerting,' said Barton.

'Yes, I'll cut straight to it. There's good news and bad. First off, Henry appears to be on the ball. There are no large cash withdrawals or transfers. It's the increase in the volume of communication that has caused him to spend more money.'

'All to this one woman?'

'Nearly all. He's been flitting around on the site. Checking it out, I suppose. Most have a fairly innocent picture to draw the punters in. Bikini shots. Tight gym gear. Stockings and high heels.'

'They're called thirst traps,' said Hoffman.

'Yes, I came across that term. The pictures are designed to hook your attention. If you want more, then you subscribe to their channel.'

'Which costs money,' said Barton.

'No. It seems that's all part of the lure. They know you're interested, so they communicate with you. On this level are raunchier photos. Naked with hands over their modesty. See-through underwear. Looking over their shoulders in the shower at the gym. That kind of thing. This is when the relationship starts. Henry received lots of messages at this point, from other women offering better pictures for small amounts of cash, or larger figures for videos or private viewings.'

Barton nodded for Robert to continue.

'As far as I can tell, Henry only properly engaged with three women. His favourite, the lady we know about, appeared last year. The amount of chatter between them is vast, but I'll come back to that. The other two are from last month. One, who I'd guess was in her twenties, was quite charming, then a little persistent when he didn't take the bait. Henry took the trouble to explain he had just been doing a recce and preferred older women. She bluntly tried to coax him into more, but without luck. That seems to have been the finish of it. I suppose that particular lady went away to look for other punters. The third is the concerning one.'

Robert played around with the laptop and brought up a naked image. Hoffman whistled. Barton puffed out his cheeks. This woman was something else. Some men would call her perfect in every way. Large, augmented breasts sat above a tanned six-pack. The poses indicated she could have been a gymnast. Her face was professionally made up. Long black hair pulled into a ponytail. Azure eyes accentuated by curling fake eyelashes and heavy mascara stared directly at the camera. Her features appeared Eastern-European.

'Henry had conversations with this lady and paid for extra images. They were hardcore. Men featured in some of the shots and the videos. The communication between her and Henry takes a disturbing twist. She's aggressive and wants more money. It progresses to the point of blackmail.'

'I thought it was all anonymous,' said Barton.

'I presume it is, but she demanded large transfers, or she'd expose him.'

'Why didn't he cut her off dead and block her?'

'I'm not sure. One message from her says she's tracked his IP address and knows where he lives.'

'Is that possible?'

'I don't know.'

'What did Henry say to that?'

'He asked her what she wanted to leave him alone. It was five-thousand pounds in Bitcoin to be sent to an account she'd provide. Henry insisted he knew nothing about cryptocurrencies. She told him to find out.'

Barton recalled Timothy had lost money dabbling with cryptos.

'Then what happened?'

'Henry ignored her. She chased, then came back with a final threat. Henry was informed she'd hacked into his webcam and email contacts. She had made recordings of the dirty things he liked to do to himself. If he failed to send the payment, she would email that footage and a range of still images to every single person on that contact list.'

'Blimey,' said Barton. 'I assume with viruses and malware it's possible, but wouldn't he be protected, having only communicated through the site?'

'I would have believed so,' said Robert, 'but Henry might not have known that. There are no messages from her on his personal email. Regardless, the threat would be greatly unsettling.'

'You mentioned he'd been acting oddly.'

'Yes. I thought he was losing his marbles. This must have been a terrible distraction. Perhaps he couldn't sleep. I think that's why he asked to see me. Maybe he was going to tell me everything, but then you guys appeared, and he didn't mention it.'

Barton tapped a finger on the interview table as he pondered the facts. Hoffman's thought processes were faster.

'It's clearly extortion but killing Henry wouldn't make any sense. She won't get any money out of him now.'

Barton's mind had gone on a different tack.

'What about Timothy and his connection to crypto? Perhaps it was his way of getting the cash back he'd lost during lockdown.'

'That reminds me,' said Robert. 'Henry and I discussed having a small part of his trust's reserves in Bitcoin as a hedge against inflation, but he said he didn't understand them, which made him reluctant. He also mentioned he knew someone who'd lost everything on them recently.'

Barton nodded.

'Maybe Henry suspected Timothy was responsible for the blackmail and confronted him. It's possible he told Timothy he would go to the police. Robert, you said he has a regular morning swim. Timothy would know that.'

Robert stated the obvious.

'So, Timothy waited until Henry was in the pool, then took the opportunity to secure his silence.'

40

DCI BARTON

Barton thought back to his conversations with Timothy.

'I'm not completely happy with that reasoning. What we've just heard is a complex and sophisticated attempt at extortion. Timothy doesn't strike me as being either of those things and how would he be aware Henry was on DreamViews?'

'Perhaps he had a partner,' said Hoffman. 'The bionic lady.'

'Where the hell would a hippy gardener find a woman like her?' asked Barton.

'Maybe he met her at a pub or club?'

'I haven't seen many of that sort of woman strutting around Peterborough town centre. I don't know loads about these types of schemes, but I wouldn't be surprised if the threat originated from Russia, or similar.'

'That's a decent point,' replied Hoffman. 'I doubt the person conversing with Henry was the gymnast. The scheme may be a numbers game, where they try to pull off the scam against hundreds of men at the same time. They only need a few to pay, and it's worth their while, especially if they live in a poor country.'

'It does make me wonder about that missing gold watch.'

'It's important to mention that the grammar from this black-mailer has errors,' said Robert. 'It could be they're not bright or educated, but perhaps it's someone whose English isn't perfect. Maybe a foreigner.'

'Yes, that's worth noting. Robert, you said the other missing items turned up.'

'That's what Henry told me, but I don't know for sure. I asked specifically about the Breitling watch, and he suspected it was around somewhere.'

'This is making my brain ache,' said Hoffman.

'And mine,' said Barton, scowling. 'Let's forget about the possible Russian connection. If we're simply looking for a motive for Henry's death, then Henry confronting Timothy is the strongest we have. Would Henry be confident enough to challenge a young man?'

'Henry never stepped back from a fight.'

'How much is a Breitling worth?'

'The particular model is about twenty thousand pounds.'

Hoffman whistled for a second time.

'Although an unsophisticated thief would struggle to get that for it,' said Robert. 'Who would they sell it to? They wouldn't know wealthy criminals, and a jeweller would ask for proof of purchase or ownership.'

'Which means,' said Barton, 'if Timothy took the item, he probably still has it.'

The three of them sat in silence for a few seconds.

'Do we arrest Timothy and search his house?' asked Hoffman. 'It's a decent explanation, but we don't actually have any evidence he stole the watch.'

'We know Timothy worked for Henry,' said Robert. 'I've seen

Timothy in the kitchen helping himself to a drink of water. Him and Henry did used to chat. He'd have had the opportunity to take it.'

'That's true, but unfortunately the owner of the lost piece, Henry, is dead, and he never reported the watch stolen,' said Barton. 'It's not as if we have CCTV of him taking the watch.'

'We might have,' said Robert. 'I remember Henry telling me the watch had been missing for a few days. There's CCTV in the house.'

'In every room?' asked Hoffman.

Robert looked confused. 'No, of course not, but Henry usually kept it in his safe. He wore the watch one day but forgot to return it. In effect, twenty grand was left on the windowsill. That's when it vanished. There are cameras in the kitchen, the hallways, and on the landing. I could view the footage for the days prior to him realising the piece was missing.'

'Won't that take ages?' asked Hoffman.

'Certainly a while, but I'll use fast-forward. I'm only looking for someone other than Henry to appear in shot.'

Barton blew out a long breath. 'Isn't there a housekeeper too?'

'Yes. Bushra, but she's gone back home on holiday to Turkey for a week.'

'Any possibility of her involvement?'

'Bushra? No way. She's been with him for decades, and she'd be the first person anyone investigating would suspect.'

'Yes, but that applies to Timothy, too. The only people who are allowed inside the property are Henry, Bushra, Timothy and you, Robert. Timothy would be the second suspect. While I don't suspect he's capable of cyber-crime, I also doubt he's daft enough to steal from his employer. Would he jeopardise his business? Henry was one of his best customers.'

'The handyman probably has access to the house as well,' said Hoffman.

Barton looked at Robert, who nodded. Barton felt like resting his head on the table.

'I'm going to take some time to think all this over. We've got the rest of the PM results due tomorrow morning. Unless the pathologist says it was definitely natural causes, we'll bring Timothy in. We need to be careful. Getting a search warrant for his house is going to be hit and miss, and if we miss...'

'Timothy disposes of the watch,' said Hoffman.

Barton stood, feeling all of his fifty years. Robert stayed seated.

'There's something else,' he said.

Barton plonked himself back down. 'Go on.'

'I've been through hundreds of the conversations that Henry had with his special girl. He calls her by her page name. Sweetypie. He has a whole folder with sub-files set up for their *relationship* images.' Robert did the ubiquitous rabbit ears with his fingers. 'To be fair, their messages read normally. A bit like when two people meet on a dating website. They got to know each other. She's taciturn about her personal life but gives her views on everything else from politics to world events and even local affairs.'

'Which means she lives nearby,' said Barton. 'Unless she looks up the information on the Internet.'

'Does she say where she's from?' asked Hoffman.

'No, but I reckon it's Cambridgeshire. She knows the area too well. They're so chummy and chatty, I wouldn't be shocked if they'd met.'

'Is there any evidence of that?'

'Kind of. The courtship progresses. The chats become sexual. Henry has to pay for explicit shots, but she offers him a more personal service.'

Barton's ears perked up. 'Go on.'

'If he pays more, he can ask for whatever he desires. She'll dress up how he wants. Pose how he wishes. Do what he asks. Henry requests naked washing up. Photographs with a variety of sex toys.'

Robert tapped various keys on the touchpad for a moment.

'Do we need to see them?' said Barton.

'I'll save you the most graphic images, although I will say most of it is more titillating than smutty. More *Playboy* than *Razzle*. Here's an example I found earlier.'

The video that appeared on the screen was of a naked Sweety-pie taking a snooker shot. Her head was out of the picture, but her large breasts were resting on the red balls.

'I think that's a foul,' said Hoffman.

'More than one, by the looks of it. Okay, so what are you getting at, Robert?' asked Barton.

'There are messages about her doing a private show for him. I guess like a live webcam. Henry keeps all the recordings on his PC, but, like this one, they're still on his DreamViews account. I read an exchange where she discusses giving him an extra-special performance, but there were no more comments about that until I saw ones of him thanking her. He told her the show was extraordinary. That video appears to be missing, and it's only from a few days ago.'

'So, why would he delete that? If he loved it, there's no chance he wouldn't keep a copy.'

'Yes, that's what had me thinking. And it led me to believe he met her.'

'So, the performance was live and not a recording,' said Barton.

'Yes, which would also suggest she may not live far.'

Barton sucked in a deep breath as his brain put the tumbling blocks of the conundrum into place.

'Robert. The snooker scene. Are you able to zoom in on the breast area for me, please?'

Barton felt Hoffman observing him as Robert's fingers moved over the laptop. He applied the magnification feature that the site had for obvious reasons. This time, Barton did rest his head on the table. On the woman's chest, near her left shoulder, was a birth mark. It was identical and in the same place as the one Henry's neighbour had on her body.

Sandy was Sweety-pie.

41

DCI BARTON

Barton glanced from Robert to Hoffman.

'Sweety-pie is no other than Sandy Faversham.'

'No way,' said Hoffman. 'That is so weird.'

Robert didn't seem to be able to wrap his head around the revelation. 'Sandy? From next door? It can't be.'

Barton considered whether telling Robert was a breach of any police rules, but Robert had brought the evidence to him. They'd need his testimony at court, although Barton already suspected Sandy hadn't broken any laws.

'Okay, let me think out loud,' said Barton. 'Sandy and her husband haven't been getting along. His behaviour becomes increasingly controlling the more she tries to distance herself from him, but Charles holds all the cards. It's his house, and his wealth. Sandy told us she has a plan to get away but remained ambiguous about what that meant. It had to involve money, or how would she start a new life?'

'Yes, but it feels a leap to saying this is her,' said Robert.

'When I visited the other day and found her in the pool, she was topless and spread out in the water. Hair fanning around her. I suppose she could have been relaxing, but it seemed staged. I wondered at the time if she heard us coming and did it deliberately. Then when I turned away as she put her robe on, I saw movement at Henry's window. The date fits. That was Henry enjoying the show.'

Barton waited for Robert to catch up. He was a smart chap, and it didn't take long.

'Sweety-pie lies in her pool in a provocative manner for Henry to watch,' he said. 'But that would mean she knew who he was, and vice versa.'

'Wait a minute,' said Hoffman. 'What would be the chances of them meeting on a random site like DreamViews?'

Barton paused for him to twig.

'Oh,' he said. 'Sandy must have told him. Henry was rich, and it would be a way for her to save the money to escape Charles.' Hoffman pulled a face. 'That's pretty cynical. I guess it's clever, too.'

'But why would she believe Henry would be interested in such an arrangement?' asked Robert.

'There was another clue,' said Barton. 'After I suspected someone at Henry's house was ogling Sandy in the pool, we went over. He appeared sheepish.'

'Right,' said Robert. 'Perhaps she'd spotted him spying on her before.'

'That would make sense. What unsettled me was I thought Henry hadn't seen just one naked person down there. Timothy mentioned Poppy had been nude in the garden. Henry briefly looked ashamed when I informed him that Poppy was only fourteen.'

'Christ,' said Robert. 'Are you saying Henry's a pervert?'

Hoffman coughed next to Barton, who managed not to make any sound.

'Not as such,' said Barton. 'I could tell from Henry's reaction he didn't know her age. Poppy doesn't appear fourteen.'

'That's true,' said Robert unconvincingly.

'The video with the snooker balls confirms the fact.'

Hoffman clapped his hands together.

'Timothy told us he and Jerry use the games room at the Faver-shams' property to relax and have a drink away from the main rooms in the house. I bet they have a snooker table in there. Henry keeps that show, but the private pool one wasn't recorded because he observed her performance through his window.'

Robert scratched his head. 'Gosh. It's a lot to take in.'

That, thought Barton, was an understatement.

'But is any of this criminal behaviour?' said Hoffman. 'It sounds like the actions of two consenting adults. It's different from the blackmailing woman.'

'Yes,' said Barton, staring at the ceiling, 'and it doesn't explain Henry's death, either. If you look at it from Sandy's point of view, she's probably lost her best client.'

Barton noticed Hoffman frowning. 'What is it?' he asked.

'I just recalled the attempt on Sandy's life. Who would want to hurt Sandy?'

Robert made the leap.

'It's got to be her husband. If he didn't know about Sandy's little part-time job and found out, he would be hopping mad.'

42

DCI BARTON

Barton stood for a second time and shook Robert's hand. It was a limp effort from Robert.

'Let's leave it there for the day,' said Barton. 'We have a lot to consider.'

Robert nodded but avoided eye contact. His face ashen.

'I'll take a look at the CCTV tonight,' he said. 'Perhaps you could ring me in the morning.'

'Of course. I don't suppose the cameras cover his pool area?'

'No. Henry wasn't worried about his water being stolen. The back of the property is fairly inaccessible with the river and a barbed wire fence, so his bigger concern was the front of the house.'

Barton asked Hoffman to escort Robert out of the building while he tried to run through everything in his mind. Hoffman returned and slumped in his seat.

'I'm glad you're in charge. What do we do next?'

'If we forget Sandy's DreamViews angle, we have definite crimes we're interested in. The road rage on Sandy, the missing Breitling, and Henry's demise. Mortis will give us more on the last one tomorrow. It doesn't make sense that Timothy would steal the watch, and it's even more unlikely that he would kill Henry over it, but he could be desperate. We've made no progress with the near hit-and-run, but what we also have is blackmail.'

'I was pondering that as I walked Robert out. It's more likely a foreign scam, especially with the odd bit of broken English. We'd struggle to make much headway if the people who did it are abroad.'

'Yes, that's true, but Huntingdon HQ has a department that deals with that kind of thing. Malik's dealt with them before. I'll get him on it. We've clearly got enough evidence that the extortion happened. Where's DreamViews based?'

Hoffman took out his phone. He brought up Google. Thirty seconds later, he tutted.

'Bollocks. The head office is in the Bahamas.'

'Right. A location notorious for shady shell companies. I suppose I should head over there.'

Hoffman smiled, but then he scowled.

'I've had another thought. We already mentioned that if Charles found out Sandy was working in her new creative role, he might want to scare her or worse.'

'Yes?'

'What do you reckon he'd do to Henry if he discovered he was perving on his wife?'

43

DCI BARTON

Barton blinked rapidly as Hoffman's words hit home.

'Drown him in his pool?'

Hoffman smiled. 'Exactly.'

'I know love can drive people to distraction, but, in my experience, creeps like Charles tend to take it out on their wives. I'm not sure how to play this, but I reckon a visit to the Favershams' is our first port of call. Let's spring this DreamViews thing on Sandy and see how she reacts.'

'What if Charles, our potential murderer, is there?'

Barton weighed up his options.

'Charles has CCTV in the house. Sandy believes it isn't operational. Perhaps he saw her making her content on the snooker table. No, wait. He might have seen her doing that, but there's no way of him knowing Henry was involved. The worst Charles would suspect is that Sandy is having an affair, and he wouldn't consider seventy-five-year-old Henry as the potential suitor.'

'Right, and she'd be unlucky if he checked the footage for the games room. If he's got cameras in every room, there'd be thousands of hours for him to trawl through each week.'

'He probably follows her from room to room. Okay, let's visit Sandy now and find out what she has to say for herself. We'll update the team in the morning when we have a clearer idea of what's been going on. Sandy can't deny it, because we've seen everything.'

'Literally everything. What about Robert wanting to keep all this quiet?'

'I promised nothing. Besides, I doubt Sandy will be running to the newspapers.'

'That's true.'

Hoffman booked out a car, and they returned to Castor. On the way, they discussed what to say to Sandy. As they approached the house, they noticed the gate was open. Just before they turned in, out drove Timothy's white Ford Transit, then Jerry left in his black pickup. Hoffman stopped at the side of the road. Timothy cruised past and stared at them as if they were strangers. Jerry braked to a stop, clambered out, and marched to the gate. He pulled it shut, then jumped back in his truck. He spotted their stationary vehicle and waved. Barton lip-read him saying to use the small door.

Hoffman parked and they got out. The little entrance was unlocked. They stepped through and walked towards the building. It was quiet. Nobody else appeared to be around, but lights were on inside.

Barton paused at the front door. He sometimes had a sense when something untoward had happened before he came across it, but the place felt peaceful. Hoffman rang the doorbell. After a long wait, the door swung open. It was Sandy. Dressed to kill in a tight black dress and strappy high heels, she'd finished the look with a gold choker and matching earrings.

'Evening, officers,' she said. 'If you're here for Charles, he's gone out for the night.'

'Didn't you fancy going with him?'

'That's none of your business,' she replied. 'How can I help?'

'You're the person we want to have a chat with,' said Barton.

'Oh, yes. What for?'

'It's about a little bird called Sweety-pie.'

44

DCI BARTON

Sandy's expression didn't change, but she crossed her arms. Her gaze shifted from Barton to Hoffman, then fixed on somewhere behind them.

'I suppose you'd better come in,' she said, finally.

They followed her inside and she led them to a fantastic lounge. It had a vaulted ceiling, thick carpet, and a large fireplace. The log burner crackled, and candle flames danced above it. A bottle of champagne was in a silver cooler. Two glasses rested on coasters.

'So, Charles is out for the evening,' said Hoffman.

Barton watched a scowl form on Sandy's face. 'Yep,' she said.

Barton guessed she wasn't expecting visitors, though, at least not in person. Sure enough, he spotted a tripod that was almost hidden by one of the armchairs. Barton looked back at Sandy, who had followed his gaze.

'I assume you came across DreamViews when you were looking into Henry's death,' she said. 'Or Robert told you.'

Barton frowned, while Sandy smirked.

'Yes,' she hissed. 'Henry said he'd informed Robert about our little dalliance. You'd be surprised at what men tell me. I wear many hats. Agony aunt is one of them.'

Barton changed tack. Sandy was bordering on hostile.

'Look, Sandy, I'm sorry to bother you. You understand we have to investigate Henry's demise. He seemed like a pleasant guy.'

Sandy's face was a mask, but then it slipped. She perched on the edge of the sofa.

'He was, and, trust me, most of them aren't. How did you realise it was me?'

Barton pointed at his left collarbone.

'Ah, excellent. I bet you consider it all rather sordid, don't you, Inspector?'

Barton smiled at her.

'I did at first. I've met a lot of sex workers in my time. They're generally exploited. It's a tough life, and a dangerous one. I understand this DreamViews thing a bit more now, although you must admit it is unusual to be doing peep shows for your next-door neighbour.'

A smile crept onto Sandy's face. 'I'll give you that. Now, seeing as I have work to do, ask your questions. Surely you don't think I had anything to do with Henry's passing.'

'No, but an unexplained death, next to a house where you reported a dangerous driver, and where an underage missing schoolgirl spent the summer, has to concern us. There's something not right here.'

'I've known that for a long time.'

Barton remembered the CCTV in the property. If Charles saw this little set-up, he would erupt. The chances of him checking the footage would be much higher if he was suspicious already, seeing as he was away for the evening. Sandy was calmly observing Barton. She'd caught his gaze wandering around the architraves. Explaining the cameras were functional could cause all manner of problems if she confronted Charles over it, but not telling her could put her life at risk. It was a grey area. Charles could say he didn't think she'd mind, but ultimately Sandy had a right to privacy in her own home.

'Don't worry,' said Sandy. 'The CCTV doesn't work.'

'How do you know he hasn't fixed it?'

'The lights used to flash on them.'

Barton reckoned if he had a close inspection, he'd find tape or paint over those lights. Still, he didn't want to get into that then.

'What would Charles do if he found out?'

Sandy studied her nails for a moment.

'I'm not sure. He doesn't like confrontation, although he is protective of me. He likes to keep me safe.' Sandy's nostrils flared. 'In my gilded cage.' She then chuckled. 'Ah, I see. You're wondering if Charles knocked off Henry because he discovered our tête-à-tête. If I say yes, he did, would Charles go to jail?'

Barton grinned back at her. 'We tend to need a little more proof than that. I suppose I want to hear a bit of background, and then we'll get out of your way. I'm concerned I'm not seeing the full picture.'

Sandy huffed out a big breath.

'Right. I caught Henry staring at me out of his window years back. At first, I was shocked, but I later found it erotic. My husband stopped paying me that kind of attention long ago. It's funny, we used to be very much in sync in the bedroom. As I mentioned, I don't know where it went wrong, but look where we've finished up. It's incredible how I've found myself trapped like this. I remember reading stories where women found themselves in my situation, and I used to believe them weak. I've been a fool.'

Barton nodded at her to continue.

'Anyway,' she said. 'I liked it, feeling desired. I started sunbathing topless when the workmen were around. Timothy is most appreciative. I thought Jerry's head was going to combust when he came across me doing yoga on the grass wearing only a thong bikini bottom. Then I read about Kerry Katona having one of these accounts. Why not me? I'm attractive, especially to men who drive white vans. Builders in particular whistle at me all the time, and most old men stare. I did some research and chose DreamViews.'

'Why not OnlyFans?'

Sandy bobbed her head. 'Looks like someone else has done their research. OnlyFans has much more competition. DreamViews will help you gain subscribers.'

'How did Henry find you?' asked Hoffman.

'I popped around and gave him the link.'

Hoffman nodded, no doubt at the audacity.

'And you've suggested you were making enough money to separate from Charles,' stated Barton. 'Won't Henry's loss of business curtail your leaving plans?'

'Not now, no. The company noticed I was picking up subscribers and got in touch. They offered to help. My fanbase has grown exponentially these last few months, hence me being ready to flee. I felt bad taking too much money off Henry, even though I knew he was rich. He was incredibly sweet.'

'We think he watched Poppy sunbathing as well,' said Hoffman. 'So not that sweet.'

Barton shot Hoffman a look. Sandy's top lip curled, but then she shrugged. 'I only ever saw Poppy in what I would describe as a sensible bikini. Certainly not a raunchy one, and never topless. How would he know what age she was? Henry wouldn't have peeked if he'd known. I really liked him. He was a father figure. Like the dad I wished I had. It's probably all bound up in that. The need for me to be wanted. Needed. Valued.'

'Do you mind telling me how much you make?'

Sandy cocked her head to one side.

'Twelve thousand pounds last month.'

Barton's eyes widened. 'Impressive.'

'I've been cultivating a whale. That's what I call the ones who have money to burn. Speedster22 is my best customer. He's fairly kinky, but nothing I haven't done before. In fact, nothing I haven't enjoyed before.'

'Is he similar to Henry?'

'In what way?'

'A lonely much older man?'

'I guess so, but I don't see their faces. In some ways, I'm providing a service. During the day, I chat with these men like any friend or girlfriend would. I help build their confidence. Many have been without intimacy for years. You wouldn't believe the number of guys who say their wives lost interest in sex when they hit the menopause. I suspect that's simply because the women don't want physical contact with their husbands, who are in the habit of throwing the dog more compliments than their partners.'

Sandy rose from her seat.

'Time's up, officers. I have an appointment.'

'Okay, one last question,' said Barton. 'There are scams with this kind of thing. Do you worry about blackmail? I noticed your face is covered or out of focus in every shot on your landing page.'

Sandy leaned forward.

'Interesting you use the correct terminology. Do you have an account?'

'I prefer real relationships.'

'These are real. You have Facebook friends. People you communicate with at a distance. Share photos with. It's not so different.'

'Apart from the sex angle.'

Sandy's flirty expression dropped away.

'Yes, there is that. I am in contact with men of all ages. There's a pattern. The young want dirty talk and porn, the middle-aged want me to be their girlfriend, and the older gents are lonely. The latter men can chat for days on all kinds of topics. As for swindles, I've had a few who threaten to out me, but they're just trying it on. I block them. Others say they know my address and they're coming to get me, but nobody's turned up.'

'How do you remember who's who, and what you've said to them?' asked Hoffman, who had been scribbling notes.

Sandy reached behind the sofa and grabbed an A4 notebook. 'This is my bible. I have each user profile listed, which I update each time we chat. Then I can tell them what they want to hear, and I'm aware of their interests.'

'Do some relationships become platonic?' asked Hoffman.

'Never. It doesn't matter who it is, men or women, it always ends in them wanting to see me naked. A lot of them insist on me doing it with that day's newspaper next to me, or the news on in the background, so they know I've done it just for them at that moment, not simply pulled the pic or vid out of my archives.'

'You wouldn't want Charles seeing that book,' said Barton.

'God, no,' she said. 'I keep it well hidden.'

Barton exchanged the briefest of glances with Hoffman.

'Don't you fear getting exposed?' asked Barton.

'I did at the start. I blocked anyone who got in touch who told me they were from Cambridgeshire. To be honest, I don't give a damn now. Put me in the newspapers. I'd only get more subscribers.'

'Okay,' he said. 'Thanks for talking to us. You've been generous with your time and most informative.'

Sandy rose from the sofa and stood in front of Barton, slightly closer than he was comfortable with.

'Don't believe that I told you out of the goodness of my heart. The moment to leave Charles has come. I'm uncertain how he's going to react when he finds out. If he goes crazy, it's better you know everything.'

Barton thought back to the car chasing her down the street.

'You are worried he might hurt you.'

Sandy picked what Barton suspected was a hair from Gizmo off the lapel of his suit. Her voice had quietened.

'Who knows what you men are capable of?'

'Ring 999 if you feel threatened in any way.'

'Or you could stay and protect me. Perhaps you could help with the camerawork.'

'Night, Sandy.'

Barton strode from the room. He was looking forward to getting out into the chilly air.

45

DCI BARTON

Barton decided he wanted to sleep on everything they'd learned. When they got back to the office, he booked a meeting room for nine the following day, checked his emails, then drove home rubbing grit out of his eyes. He staggered through the front door, hoping to be greeted by the aroma of home cooking, and dropped his coat on the back of the chair. Instead, he was met by the hostile face of his wife.

'Those two have been doing my pip in today.'

'Luke and Layla?'

'No, Mork and Mindy.'

Barton could feel eggshells breaking under his less than dainty feet. To remain silent was paramount in such situations, but he was hungry.

'What's the plan for dinner?'

The air crackled with tension. Barton's life expectancy plummeted with the temperature in the room. Holly folded her arms.

'How about you take me out for a bar snack instead?'

'Oh, honey, I'm knackered.'

His longevity dropped to seconds as Holly's eyes narrowed.

'No problem. I'll do you some jam sandwiches. Old bread. Warm marg.'

Barton put his jacket back on. 'Why are we still here?'

Five minutes later, they set off. Holly had put a bit of lippy on, but hadn't bothered changing.

'Shall we just go to the Gordon Arms?'

Barton was about to say sure, when he had an idea.

'Actually, why don't we visit The Royal Oak?'

'In Castor?'

'Yes. I fancy a mooch in the village. We've got a case there. You and I visited once before.'

Holly started to laugh and struggled to stop. 'Of course I remember.'

'Well, we don't need to hear about it again.'

'God, it must be around eighteen years ago. I said I had something important to tell you, and you sat there all po-faced thinking you were getting dumped.'

Barton smiled as he turned along Love's Hill and drove past Paddock Green and Bancroft's. Holly nudged him.

'I thought you were going to be sick when I told you I was pregnant.'

'Ah, such fond memories.'

Holly was distracted by the view.

'Wow, I forgot how steep this slope is, and look how pretty the houses are. Why don't we come here more often?'

'I suppose it's one of those things. Habit. The guy who ran the pub before was pretty grumpy. I saw a lot of him when Lawrence was doing his project.'

'There's probably loads of gossip and intrigue going on behind these antique doors.'

'There have been a few murders here.'

'Really?'

'Yes, about forty years ago a bloke got shot in the head while he was sleeping. His new beauty queen wife was responsible. She'd hired a pair of scallies from Liverpool to do the job, who weren't the brightest. They asked for directions to the house in one of the local watering holes. In another case, a guy picked a girl up in town and brought her to the woods here where her body lay undiscovered for nearly a year.'

'Did they find who did it?'

'They haven't caught me yet.'

'John!'

Barton pulled into the spacious car park at the back of The Royal Oak. A window spilled a warm glow onto the cobblestones as they walked past and went inside. Fortune favoured them as a couple were leaving from a table near the fire.

'Grab that,' said Holly. 'I'll get the drinks in. Look, they do craft beer.'

Barton made another seat creak ominously as he sat down, but the warmth from the flames and the welcoming scent of woodsmoke soon distracted him. Holly came back with a pint and a half of amber liquid, sat down and picked up the menu.

'Hand-stretched sourdough pizza. Yum. Shall we share one?'

'I must be so tired that I'm starting to hallucinate and hear crazy things.'

'You're supposed to be eating less, remember? I'll have the squashed goat one.'

'Okay, that does sound good.' He read the ingredients. 'Hey! It's vegetarian.'

They sat in silence for ten minutes and enjoyed the ambience. Every table was taken. They glanced around at the smiling faces lit by soft candlelight as the warming buzz of quiet conversation and the odd burst of laughter filled the air.

'I'll have the meat one,' said Barton, swiftly heading to the bar before Holly could comment.

While waiting, he felt eyes on him. The short, wizened old man next to him was staring.

'Evening,' said Barton.

'Are you a policeman?'

'What makes you think that?'

'Well, you aren't a ballerina.'

'No, not for a few years now.'

The fellow pulled a strange face as though he knew something, or wasn't convinced about Barton's dancing habits.

'I bet you're up here investigating that Love's Hill lot, aren't ya?'

'No, I'm just here for some goat.'

The old guy grinned. 'Ah, you can't kid a kidder.'

'Do you have something to tell me, then?'

'Charles Faversham comes in here. Did you know that?'

'I didn't.'

'He's a great man. Pushes his friend in here in his chair.'

'That's nice to hear.'

'Aye, but one to be watched. That's all I'll say.' His beady eyes stared into Barton's. 'I'll say no more.'

The old guy shuffled away, his pint swaying with his gait so not a drop was spilled. Barton smiled because he was already thinking the same way.

46

DCI BARTON

When Barton rose the next morning, his mildly stiff leg had turned into a distinct hobble, but it was still a price worth paying. He ate a bowl of porridge with something called crushed chia seeds on top of it, which he suspected a starving budgie would turn its beak up at, then left for the office. At nine, the team gathered for their briefing and Barton updated them on their DreamViews findings and his and Hoffman's conversations with Robert.

None of those present appeared fazed. Even Malik and Leicester, who were likely the more conservative, took the revelations about the online platform on board with the minimum of fuss.

'It's an easy way to get extra cash if you've got the looks for it,' said Minton. 'I knew a guy who did it.'

'For men or women?' asked Hoffman.

'Both. For all the curious guys in the room, you're not alone.'

'Okay,' said Barton. 'If we bring together everything we've heard, there are obvious concerns. Perhaps one of her clients worked out where Sandy lived and came down for a visit.'

'To run her over?' asked Minton.

'Who knows what's going on with her business?' asked Zelensky. 'It's clickbait for stalkers. She covers most of her face, but if the customer was someone techie, they might be able to use the Internet to find her. AI would probably make a good guess at what her face really looked like. Maybe they'd get a match with her photos on LinkedIn or Facebook, or using Google image search.'

'Exactly,' said Barton. 'She could also be lying about what she's been up to. Who's to say she hasn't met quite a few of her fans in person? Although Robert reckoned the relationship between her and Henry seemed normal. Let's look at this from all angles. There's too much occurring down there for this to be just careless driving.'

'Sir,' said Malik. 'I found something interesting, and potentially important, just before this meeting. I haven't had a chance to consider the impact yet, but it concerns Frannie Bone. We were more or less right about what happened in Wales. The farm was similar to Emmaus.'

'Explain to those who might not know the background, please, Malik.'

'Emmaus is a charity which offers a home, employment and personal support to a community of formerly homeless people. That includes prison leavers. Probation are happy for sex offenders to live there. There are around thirty residential sites around the country, although I think a few struggled during the pandemic. The companions, as they call the service users, often work in their shops and cafes. They sell donated furniture, clothing, homeware or sometimes coffee in a cafe. The farm had a comparable set-up. The residents gave their time to help on a working estate in exchange for bed and board.'

'I take it the farmer ran out of money,' said Barton.

'Correct. Covid lockdowns stopped the paying visitors coming. I spoke to a newsagent nearby. He told me the workers were a great asset to the community, but the owner was getting on a bit. Eventually, he couldn't keep going because they were edging further into the red. Everyone was forced to leave.'

'Poor old Frannie Bone had nowhere else to go,' said Barton. 'So he came here. He headed home.'

'Why not up north?' said Zelensky.

'Perhaps his memories of Peterborough were better.'

'I bet he still knows someone in the city.'

Malik nodded.

'That was my line of thinking, but we had no address for him. We could examine his bank accounts or benefits record, if we get authorisation, but in the meantime, I traced his family to see if that might give us anything. Both parents are dead. He has a sister, though. Married, so no longer a Bone. I didn't need to check where she lived.'

Barton could have filled a pillow with the tension in the room as Malik kept them in suspense.

'Frannie Bone's sister's name is Audrey Madden. That means he's also Poppy's uncle.'

47

SANDY FAVERSHAM

When Audrey arrived on Friday morning, Sandy was still in bed. A cool breeze blew into the house when she opened the front door to let her friend in.

'This wasn't forecast,' said Audrey, zipping up her pink tracksuit. 'I'm a bit of a fair-weather swimmer.'

'You'll soon warm up. People are jumping in mountain streams for health benefits, so I'm sure you can handle my tepid pool.'

'Okay, but I'll need a large coffee out of your lovely machine afterwards.'

'Deal. I'll put my swimsuit on and meet you down there.'

'Is the arsehole about?'

'Is his car outside?'

'Yep.'

'So, yeah. He went away on business last night, so he must have returned.'

'The hot gardener's here. Perhaps he could warm me up.'

'Timothy is not hot, and he's young enough to be your son.'

'Maybe I should pretend to struggle in the water now he has

form for pulling people out. It's been a while since I received any mouth to mouth.'

'Henry died, remember?'

Audrey frowned. 'Yes, that's sad. He seemed pleasant. Do you think he was killed?'

Sandy shrugged. 'Who knows what's going on? I can't wait to get out of here. Next time Charles says he's away for the night, I'm leaving. Shit. Sorry, I meant to ask about Poppy. How is she?'

Audrey stopped at the back door while Sandy unlocked it.

'The cheeky little mare used my login for EduLink to tell the school she was poorly.'

Sandy couldn't help a chuckle. 'She's so impudent and confident. I was never that sassy and bold at her age. I bet she's been skipping classes all the time and seeing whoever this new bloke is.'

'That's what I thought, but I checked her attendance. It's the first day she's had off this school year.'

'How come she knows your passwords?'

'The silly sod forgot her own laptop was plugged in and charging. She tried to walk off with it and dropped it on the floor, so we've been sharing mine since January. My logins and passwords are on Post-it notes stuck to a corkboard in the kitchen.'

Sandy had opened the door for Audrey but kept her arm in the way.

'What? Does that mean she can read your emails and see what you're up to?'

'We have our own icon to log in, so she should be on hers. Poppy does nearly everything on her phone, so I only saw her on it a couple of times. I didn't use it much either until all this started.'

'Well, be more careful in future.'

'Yeah, I know. Look, I have separate folders for DreamViews stuff. Poppy's just spreading her wings. Blagging a day off through EduLink is hardly the crime of the century.'

'But running away for over a week is serious, then not telling anyone where she was? You need to get a grip on her.'

Audrey pursed her lips and glowered. 'I didn't come here to be nagged at.'

Sandy smiled and stepped out of the way. 'I'll see you at the pool in a few minutes.'

While Sandy was getting changed, she thought about her friendship with Audrey, who was a complicated individual. Sandy would have been more protective if it had been her own daughter, and frantic if her child were missing, but Poppy had always been a strong, dominant character. She'd even scared Sandy once when she'd trudged mud across the carpet at Audrey's place and Sandy had made a comment. Poppy had been only twelve, but she'd been the same height. She'd walked over, got up close in her face, and snarled, 'Not your house.'

Sandy shivered. There'd been numerous flashes of belligerence over the summer. Audrey and Poppy often swore at each other. Charles wasn't the only relationship from which Sandy needed to extricate herself. Audrey might be the angriest of them all to be left behind. Still, that wasn't a problem for today.

Sandy slipped flip-flops on her feet, threw a towel over her shoulder and strolled from the house. She trotted down the lawn with the grass splashing her feet with dew. It was strange weather. Out of the breeze it was mild, close even, but the wind had a sharp edge. When she reached the exposed pool area, she shivered after dropping her towel on a recliner. Audrey was staring at a clump of brown leaves that had collected and was floating in the corner of the pool. She peered across at Sandy and cracked up.

'Is that really necessary this early in the morning?'

Sandy glanced down at her gold bikini, which left little to the imagination. Her look was tempered by the goosebumps all over her body, but she didn't care.

'If you've got it,' she said with a grin, although her mind had slipped to the last time she'd worn this outfit. Well, the bottoms. It had been for Henry.

She turned around and looked up at his window. Odd to think he would never be there again. She missed him. Other punters would take his place financially, but she'd connected with the kindly fellow. He had never asked for highly sexualised images of her, but, seeing as he was a bloke, he'd taken them when offered.

She suspected he'd been after only a connection and would have carried on chatting even if no more raunchy material had been forthcoming. Sandy understood, too late, that she'd been getting as much from the relationship as he had. She should have sent him some of the videos he'd wanted for free.

'Yuck, it's a rat,' shrieked Audrey.

Sandy turned back to her friend, who had one hand over her mouth, and the other pointing at the furry wet thing that had floated to the centre of the pool. Sandy walked to the water's edge.

'No, it's a squirrel.'

'That's still gross.'

Sandy grabbed the long plastic skimmer and scooped the critter out of the water in a smooth move. She tipped the small body out under a rose bush.

'There. Timothy will bury it later.'

Audrey's nose wrinkled.

'I don't fancy splashing around in there if Rocky's been gently stewing like he's been dropped in a slow cooker. I thought squirrels could swim.'

'Pigeons can float, but I'm often fishing them out.'

Audrey waved a finger at her. 'Not helping!'

'The chlorine kills most bacteria in under a minute.'

'Oh, great. That's not reassuring, either.'

'Well, I'm going in. You go and make the coffee.'

When Audrey had gone, Sandy prepared to dive in. She wasn't keen herself if she was honest, and wasn't sure why she'd argued with Audrey over it. The breeze died and a strange fishy aroma assaulted her nostrils.

The branches behind her in the paddock rustled. Was it the wind, or more likely Timothy or Jerry going about their work? She nervously licked her lips when the sound drifted across to her again. Just the creepy noise was unsettling, never mind the floating rodent and the strange smell.

Sandy stared at the crystalline blue water, which shimmered ominously. Nothing else seemed to be floating on the top or had sunk to the bottom. There was no way a dead fish could be in the water without her being able to see it.

Usually the pool appeared welcoming, embracing, almost womb-like, but not today. Another squirrel dropped out of a tree to Sandy's right, startling her. It glared over in an adversarial way, then chittered and fled through the undergrowth.

Sandy swore to herself and dived in. She held her breath and surfaced. The water still felt refreshing because it was so cold, but it didn't feel as cleansing as usual after Audrey's slow-cooker comment. Sandy decided to do a few lengths of breaststroke. Then she'd head in for a cappuccino.

48

DCI BARTON

Barton had risen from his seat upon hearing what Malik had to say about Frannie and Audrey being siblings, but he dropped back down as he tried to get his head around the implications. Hoffman was the first to comment.

'Perhaps Poppy's been hiding out at Uncle Frannie's.'

'That's possible,' replied Barton, 'but Frannie Bone is likely still dysfunctional. Away from the security and routine of the farm, he's liable to be chaotic, and maybe not taking his meds. It's highly unlikely he found a place to rent on his own, which means he'll be in a house-share, bedsit, or hostel. I believe there's enough evidence pointing to him now to justify us requesting access to his benefits records, and we can see if they have a current address.'

'Perhaps he's homeless,' said Minton.

'No, I don't think so,' said Barton with a sigh. 'I doubt he'd be able to look after himself properly. We'd be aware of him by now. The man who's been approaching kids has been called dapper as well. If it's Frannie, someone's helping him. Whether that's the council or his sister, we'll soon find out.'

'It would explain why Poppy had no trauma from her absence,' said Leicester. 'She was at her uncle's place, so no bother.'

Barton wrung his hands together while he recalled Frannie from all those years ago. 'I'm not sure about that either. I agree she might not have felt threatened being with him, but she'd have been bored out of her brains. If I know anything about young girls, it's that they don't want to hang around with uncool old blokes in grotty environments, even if they are related.'

Barton couldn't shake off the sensation of having missed something. Then it came to him. Often when he experienced this it was because there were two strands or more to the investigation he was focusing on. There were several people up to no good in Castor, but he didn't believe Frannie Bone was among them. These approaches by the dapper young man in Bretton were likely to be him though, so he needed picking up asap. They hadn't got to the bottom of what happened with Poppy, but it seemed her mother had some questions to answer.

He cleared his throat.

'We need to locate Frannie Bone and bring him in. Next on our most wanted list is Audrey Madden. I find it hard to believe she hasn't heard about the strange approaches to youngsters that have been occurring in the city, especially in light of the fact her daughter was missing. Does anyone care to extrapolate?'

'I'm not sure what that means,' said Hoffman casually looking around the room, 'but I'll take your comments to a conclusion.'

Cocky so-and-so, thought Barton. 'Get to it.'

'The chances of Frannie being back in Peterborough and Audrey Madden not having had a visit are slim. So, Audrey knew he was here, and she would also be fully aware of what he was like. She would have to suspect her brother of being the guy the police want to question.'

'Excellent. There's one last thing. Most of you haven't seen all the photos or images of Sandy, but I studied them and realised something.'

Hoffman grinned but kept quiet.

'Hoffman,' said Barton. 'You saw the camera tripod at Sandy's house when she was creating her latest show, but quite a few of the other pictures were taken from a distance.'

'Timer delay,' said Hoffman.

'Is that what you do?' asked Zelensky.

Hoffman gave Zelensky the finger.

Barton couldn't help remembering Ginger, an officer who'd lost his life in the line of duty. He had loved to take the mickey out of the other officers, and often went too far, but those days were ending. People took extreme offence. He decided to let that one ride, but would have a quiet word with both of them later.

'Yes,' he said. 'A timer would work, but we all know from having used them, they aren't simple. Out of focus. People moving. That's not ideal if you're flogging this kind of end product. I expect image clarity of the rest of the body is a minimum requirement if the face is out of view or fuzzy.'

'So, you're saying someone else has been taking the shots?' said Minton.

'Yes, and it isn't Charles. Who better to help than your best friend?'

49

DCI BARTON

Barton looked at his watch. It was ten thirty.

'Right, Leicester. Get the ball rolling on requesting the address Frannie Bone uses for his benefits. As soon as you have it, head there with Malik and bring him in.'

'Malik, while he's doing that, find out where Frannie Bone and Audrey Madden grew up.'

'I already know those details,' said Malik. 'Audrey still lives on the same street. Plenty of social housing. Families sometimes don't move far.'

'I bet the people around there know each other's business, then. If Frannie returned and visited his old address, I expect someone would point him in the direction of Audrey's new one.'

'I agree, sir.'

'Try to get some background on Audrey. Take a look at her social media. Maybe her brother's on it.' Barton smiled. 'Actually, the Social Service file for Poppy will have the address and contact details for the person who knows Audrey the best, and who's also the one most likely to dish the dirt on her.'

'Her ex-husband?' said Malik.

'Exactly. Shirley should have Glenn's details.'

'On it.'

Barton sensed the energy in the room. 'We checked if Charles Faversham had a criminal record, but what about Audrey Madden, Jerry Cann, Timothy Steele or Glenn?'

'I'll get on those, too, sir, but I checked Poppy's father's slate. He's been clean since 2005.'

'What was he convicted of last?'

'Affray.'

The offence of affray came under the Public Order Act and referred to the threat of unlawful violence where a person at the scene had reasonable concern to fear for their safety. Football hooligans were often charged with it.

Barton frowned. It was a worrying offence, but it was nearly twenty years ago.

'Leicester, you look into that. Zelensky and Hoffman, you head down to Audrey's house and pick her up. If she isn't there, I'll bet she's at Sandy's place. We should have Frannie here later today. If we interview him and Audrey under caution, we'll discover if their stories match up.'

Barton leaned his knuckles on the table, head bowed. Was the siblings' relationship the connection to the incidents at Paddock Green? Frannie wasn't a criminal partner to rely on, and neither of them would have cause to hurt Henry, unless Audrey had somehow blackmailed Henry in a way Robert hadn't discovered.

Or had Audrey sent her easily influenced brother around to Henry's with simple instructions? No, it still didn't make sense to cook one of the golden geese, unless it was going to sing, Barton thought, mixing up his idioms. His team had almost left the meeting room, when he recalled Mortis saying he would have the PM report back in the morning.

'Wait in the office for a minute, guys,' said Barton.

He checked his phone. There was an email from Dr Simon Menteith. Barton concentrated on the medical jargon as he scanned the details. The findings were inconclusive, but with the mesh impression on the victim's head and no evidence of a blood clot for myocardial infarction or brain damage indicating a stroke, Mortis would lean towards an unlawful killing. The skin and the mesh of the net were being analysed to see if they matched, and CSI had taken samples of the water at the scene in case of excessive chlorine, which could cause death in extreme amounts, or any other contaminating substances.

At the bottom of the email, Mortis had written an extra line.

Thanks for having a chat with me the other day. I appreciated it.

Barton left the room and marched to the office with purpose. The team had gathered together in the centre of the room.

'Okay,' said Barton as he strode over. 'Mortis and CSI have made progress. Henry's death is likely suspicious.'

Barton noticed they were all distracted.

'What is it?'

Zelensky stepped forward.

'Control received a call five minutes ago. It was a panicked request for an immediate ambulance at Paddock Green.'

'Who was it for?'

'They didn't say. The caller was male, but they heard a shriek in the background before any other details were given. That voice sounded female. Then the line went dead.'

Barton rushed to his office and grabbed his coat. He hoped Mortis wouldn't be receiving a call about overtime.

50

DCI BARTON

Barton took a moment. There was no point in everyone racing down there. Uniform would control the scene and allow the paramedics to do their job, but Barton wanted to hear and observe first-hand what had occurred. He'd been the person most involved with this unfolding drama at the Favershams' and it would be him who would need to make the call about whether more lives were at risk.

'Continue with the tasks I set you,' said Barton. 'Minton and I will head to Castor. We'll report back as soon as possible. I suspect this case is ready to crack, so let's focus.'

Barton and Minton booked out a Ford Puma with a radio and headed off to Castor. Minton was quiet. The voice from Control sounded tinny.

'All units. Situation is stable at Paddock Green. Ambulance technicians are working on one patient. Transfer to PCH imminent.'

PCH was Peterborough City Hospital. Minton's jaw clenched as they turned into Love's Hill. She stopped their car much further up from where they usually parked due to the plethora of emergency vehicles and response cars. It must have been a quiet day in the city.

An officer Barton recognised stood at the open gate. 'Morning, Matilda.'

She wrote his name down.

'Nice to see you again, sir. If you can stay back for a minute, they're bringing the stretcher out now.'

Barton could see over her head where two paramedics were pushing a stretcher towards them with what appeared to be a small adult lying on it. The feet were at the front, so Barton couldn't identify the injured party. Another paramedic held an Ambu bag above the patient. Their faces were stern. Their pace urgent.

'We'll stop the traffic,' said Barton.

'Thank you,' replied Matilda.

Minton jogged in the direction of Castor village and raised her hand to an oncoming vehicle. Barton walked the opposite way and stood in the middle of the road. Behind him, one of the ambulances reversed up to the gate. The rear doors opened. In a smooth manoeuvre, the paramedics shoved the stretcher up the drive and swiftly into the back of the ambulance. With a side-on view, Barton could finally make out the identity of the injured individual. Flashing lights and sirens came on and the ambulance left at speed. Two PCs left the property a few seconds later, got in their marked car, and accelerated after it.

Barton strode to the front gate with his mind whirring. Things didn't look promising for Sandy.

51

DCI BARTON

Barton turned back to Matilda.

'Who's in charge?'

'Sergeant Coehlo.'

'Inform him we're coming in.'

Barton marched around the rear of the property where a bitter burning smell hung in the air. Coehlo and three other uniformed officers were standing together on the other side of the pool. Charles scowled at one side of them, Audrey on the other. Both had flushed faces, but Charles had a cut on his forehead. Timothy slumped in a recliner to their right. He was wiping his eyes so he could see the screen of his phone.

'Calm down, please, sir,' a female PC was telling Charles. She had her hand raised in front of her, which kept her directly between him and Audrey. Two PCs had their gaze fixed on Audrey. Her eyes were narrowed, fists clenched.

Barton halted on the other side of the pool to let Coehlo walk over. Barton noticed a large box covered in powder next to the pool and a red fire extinguisher with a blue label lying near it.

'What do you know?'

'This is a peculiar one, John. I'm not sure what's gone on. It appears the heat pump could have malfunctioned, which has caused an electrical short circuit. Timothy found Sandy Faversham, the lady who lives here, at the bottom of the pool. If you recall, he's her gardener. His account was garbled but it sounds as though he was about to dive in when black smoke poured from the pool's heater. Electric sparks leapt out of it. He guessed the current was in the water and had electrocuted Sandy.'

'So, he didn't jump in?'

'No. There's usually an extinguisher there, but it was gone. He knew the garage had another one, so he sprinted there, grabbed it, and rang 999 on the way back. When he returned, the woman over there had come from the kitchen. She screamed and tried to get in the pool, but he stopped her. He put the fire out with the powder extinguisher but didn't want to risk touching the water.'

'I take it he didn't fancy pulling the plug of the pump out, either?'

Coehlo shook his head. 'He raced into the house to the circuit breakers, but they'd finally tripped, so he knew it was safe. When he returned, he and Audrey managed to get Sandy out. The woman, Audrey, had a go at CPR, but wasn't confident with how to do it.'

Barton cursed under his breath. A lot of time had passed with Sandy underwater.

'What's happened with those two?' he said, pointing over at Charles and Audrey.

'Charles heard the sirens from his office and rushed out. He thought Audrey was attacking Sandy. Audrey blamed him for the faulty equipment. They came to blows just as we arrived.'

'Who started it?'

'Charles, possibly, but he came off worse.'

Barton stared at the blue water and imagined an electrical

current zigzagging through it. He looked at the injury on Charles's face, but was he the aggressor?

'Right, I need all of them back at the station. We'll have a doctor check them over there. Treat this as a multiple crime scene and get CSI down here right away. This could be a complex and serious incident, especially if she was underwater too long.'

'I've got two patrol vehicles. Luckily, we're close, so if I escort the warring factions, will you be able to take the gardener?'

'Yes.' Barton looked over at Timothy, who was sobbing.

Barton paused while he thought of the bigger picture. A husband might have lost a wife. Audrey would be frantic about her closest friend. Timothy had witnessed another drowning. Barton turned back to Coehlo. 'Have you seen anyone else here?'

'Like who?'

'There's an older guy, although he doesn't usually work in the mornings, Jerry who does the maintenance.'

Coelho's gaze shifted from Barton to the pump. He shook his head.

52

DCI BARTON

Barton and Minton stood with Timothy while Coelho's officers escorted first Charles to the front of the property, then Audrey. The fighters had calmed down as the reality of the situation dawned on them. Barton had expected one or both to insist on going to the hospital to be with Sandy, but neither complained when they were told they were heading to the police station.

Barton opened the door for Timothy when they reached their Ford Puma. To his surprise, Timothy held his gaze as he got in.

'You won't be pinning that on me.'

Barton shut the door and exchanged a glance with Minton. They both got in the front, and she pulled away.

'How are you feeling, Timothy?' asked Barton looking over his shoulder.

'A little stunned. Will she be all right?'

Barton doubted it. 'She's in the best hands.'

'My heartbeat has only just returned to normal.'

'We'll have a GP check you over.'

'No, that's okay. I understand you'll want to hear what happened as soon as possible.'

Barton looked over at Timothy and gave him a reassuring nod, despite being surprised by his matter-of-fact manner, particularly given how emotional he'd been when Barton had arrived.

Barton escorted Timothy into an interview room when they got to the station.

'There will be an investigation into the incident,' said Barton. 'It's important we take your statement while your memory is fresh. There's also the chance of a coroner's inquest.'

'What's that?' asked Timothy, cringing. 'Would I have to go to court?'

'Coroner's inquests are slightly more informal than that, and they only occur after an unexplained death,' replied Barton. 'The purpose is not to sentence anyone, but to find a reason for the person dying. The coroner might find it a suicide or an accident, or something else. But let's hope an inquest isn't needed and Sandy pulls through.'

Barton didn't mention the verdict could be referred to the Crown Prosecution Service to press charges if the coroner decided it was an unlawful killing. He nodded at Minton, who had explained they were recording the conversation.

'Please tell us what happened today.'

Timothy ran a hand through his hair, then took a deep breath.

'I was working in the paddock. Cutting back a tree. I heard Sandy talking to another woman. I guessed it was Audrey, but they were out of sight. A little while later, I caught the sound of a splash and someone swimming. There was a bit of a squeal. I assumed they were larking around.'

'Do they often do that?'

For the first time since they'd been back, Timothy cleared his throat.

'I suppose.'

Barton had a thought.

'Or did Poppy shriek a lot when she came over?'

Timothy swallowed deeply.

'Sometimes. I don't know. Women.'

Barton smiled. 'So, you rushed over.'

A blush crept up Timothy's neck. 'No, why would I?'

'But you went to the pool.'

'Yes, maybe a minute later. It had gone quiet. Too quiet. I just had a feeling.'

'You like Sandy, don't you?'

'Yes, she's great. A tremendous boss.'

'A pretty woman, too. She told us she sometimes bathes topless.'

Barton expected flames to come out of Timothy's face, but he just nodded.

'Yeah, that's right.'

'What happened when you reached the pool?'

'I couldn't see anyone. There was a strange smell, kind of fishy. Then I noticed Sandy had sunk to the bottom.'

'How did you know it was her?'

'Her blonde hair was fanning out.'

'And you jumped in.'

Timothy stretched his neck as though his T-shirt collar was stifling him.

'I almost did, but I've heard burning electrics can have a fishy smell and I also spotted smoke coming out of the heat pump. It had been playing up, so I went to pull the plug. When I got close, the box snapped and fizzed, and I didn't want to touch it. Maybe Sandy received a shock in the pool. I think electricity travels through water, doesn't it?'

'Then what did you do?'

'I looked for the extinguisher. It was gone, but I knew we had another blue one in the garage.'

Barton couldn't remember the different extinguishers for each fire.

'Would blue have worked on an electrical blaze?'

'Yes, Charles has them specifically because they work on most types. I sprinted to the garage and grabbed it. Audrey was at the kitchen door with two mugs when I raced past on the way back. I shouted that Sandy was drowning, then legged it to the pool. I remembered I should ring for an ambulance, so I did. When I was on the call, Audrey had caught up. She attempted to leap in, but I prevented her, and my phone got knocked out of my hand. The pump was on fire by then, so I doused it, but I think I saw sparks still and wasn't certain if I'd stopped the water being electrified.'

'Keep going.'

'I remembered the mains and raced inside to the circuit board in the utility room. It had already tripped so I ran back out and jumped in. I managed to pull Sandy from the bottom of the pool and Audrey helped as I lifted her out. She started CPR. That bit was terrible. She didn't have a clue what she was doing, but I don't either. Then we heard sirens.'

Barton pursed his lips as he estimated Sandy had spent at least five minutes submerged, but likely much more.

'You mentioned the pump was faulty. Did you try to fix it?'

'No, I don't know enough about that sort of thing.'

'So, who repaired it?'

'Jerry.'

'I see. Sounds like he did a bad job. Is he accredited?'

Timothy finally lifted his gaze up from the table. His eyes shifted left. His fingers flexed. 'No idea.'

'Was Jerry around today?'

'I thought I heard a man's voice near the pool area this morning. And someone whistling.'

Barton wasn't sure if you could tell someone's sex from a whistle, but he needed to clarify if Jerry had been present.

'But you didn't see him.'

'No. If Jerry had been around, he'd have come over when all the sirens and police turned up, so perhaps it wasn't him.'

'Unless he understood he might have been at fault.'

Timothy shrugged, seemingly with something else on his mind. He glanced at Minton, then to Barton.

'When can I have my phone from the water?'

Barton raised an eyebrow at the heartless comment, especially seeing as it wasn't likely to work. Timothy's face flushed once more. Something was definitely off with this guy. What was on that phone? Barton recalled Mortis's thoughts on the damage to Henry's skin and his suspicions around the net being pressed on Henry's head.

Barton needed to offer Timothy legal advice before he probed that.

'Timothy, we've had a couple of confusing points come from the post-mortem on Henry. I've got a few questions for you concerning that, but I'd advise you to talk with a solicitor first.'

Timothy's face crumpled up.

'Why? I tried to save him. I fished him out.'

Barton tensed. 'What do you mean, fished him out?'

'He was floating about a metre from the edge. I couldn't see the point of leaping in. I wouldn't have been able to push him out of the water on my own.' Timothy licked his lips. 'I used the net thing to hook him to the side.'

Barton leaned back.

'You didn't mention that at the time.'

'You never asked. I thought about what I did afterwards. Pulling him out like that doesn't sound great, but it was practical.'

Barton crossed his arms. Was Timothy a hero? That didn't sit right. He wasn't necessarily lying to Barton, but he was definitely hiding something. Barton was tempted to delve deeper, but he would wait.

When the time came, he wanted every opportunity to catch Timothy out.

53

DCI BARTON

Barton thanked Timothy for talking to them and asked if he'd stay while they checked the others' stories because they might want another word with him. After he'd agreed, Barton advised him to have a meeting with the duty solicitor while he waited. Timothy didn't appear overjoyed at that suggestion but followed Minton to a waiting room without complaining. Barton strode back to the office where the rest of the team were present and chatting in a huddle.

'Well?' asked Barton.

Zelensky was finishing a call. She put the phone down with a small smile. 'Sandy's in the ICU, so there's hope.'

'Excellent,' replied Barton. He pictured Sandy, who had seemed so full of optimism for the future. 'I've just spoken to Timothy Steele, the gardener, about what happened. You can watch a recording of the interview, but his story fits with events. It appears the maintenance guy, Jerry, fixed the heat pump but didn't do a great job. Timothy isn't acting naturally, though, but I don't think it's to do with the pool incident this morning. He seemed extremely concerned about his phone, but I don't have cause to look at it. What else have you come up with?'

'We've picked up Frannie Bone from his shared house,' said Leicester. 'It was as easy as that. Another tenant let us in. He was lying on his bed listening to music. He kept quiet. The duty solicitor is with him.'

'Brilliant. We're making genuine progress now. I'll talk to Sandy's husband, Charles, next. Then I'll need someone to take him to the hospital. I thought he'd have asked to head there already, but he hasn't, which is odd in itself. Charles should have an address for Jerry.'

'Jerry will probably get sent down if this accident is due to his incompetence,' said Hoffman.

'If she dies it will be a case of involuntary manslaughter by gross negligence, and he'd be looking at a long stretch, but let's hear what Charles has to say first. He was arguing with Audrey in front of the police after Sandy was taken away. I'll talk to Audrey straight afterwards. She'll also need the duty if I'm going to ask her about aiding and abetting a known criminal, her brother. Did you go to her house?'

'Yes,' said Zelensky. 'Nobody answered. We suspected she'd be at Sandy's, so we came back here, seeing as you were already there.'

'What about those criminal record checks?'

'All clean so far,' said Malik. 'Audrey's husband only had that affray, which appears to be a pub fight. There's a file on the database for a home visit to Audrey's house over ten years ago. A domestic reported. No further action. I even checked Robert's history. He's here, by the way.'

'Is he? I was expecting him to ring me first.'

'Reception just rang to say he'd arrived. They warned me he was extremely agitated.'

'I don't like the sound of that. Malik and Leicester, have a word with him.'

'There is one minor hiccup,' said Malik.

Barton groaned. 'Hit me with it.'

'It's Jerry Cann. He doesn't exist.'

54

DCI BARTON

Barton inwardly cringed. Jerry Cann. He should have known. 'So, there's nobody of that name on the local electoral roll or any of the other records you've checked?'

'I found a few scattered over the country, but they're all under fifty-five. Unsurprisingly, it's not a popular combination.'

'Well, Charles must know his address. Jerry's been employed by him for a while. I'll get it off him now, then you can bring Jerry in.'

Minton had reappeared.

'Let's grill Charles,' said Barton. 'Afterwards, I want you to drive him to the hospital. Stay there and find out the latest on Sandy. I suspect Charles is going to be cagey with me. He might open up more away from the station.'

Charles had been waiting in a separate area from both Audrey and Timothy. He appeared relaxed for a man who had potentially lost his wife that morning. There was a small plaster on the side of his head. Barton took him to an interview room and explained that the conversation would be recorded.

'Charles, have you had an update about Sandy?' asked Barton.

'My phone's in the house, and nobody has said anything to me. Sandy will be all right. She's made of solid stuff.'

'We've heard she's in the ICU, but that doesn't mean she's out of the woods. I'll have you taken there as soon as you've answered a few questions about today.'

'Okay, thank you.'

'Could you give me your version of this morning's events?' asked Minton.

'My version? I can tell you what happened. The truth.'

Minton gave Charles the smile Barton knew she had in her armoury. 'Sorry, that's what I meant.'

Charles's shoulders dropped a little. He placed his hands flat on the table.

'I was on the phone in my office taking a call from abroad. I heard the sirens, then saw the flashing lights when I looked out of the window. It was a shock when an ambulance came through the gates.'

'Did you have to open them first?'

'No, they were already open.'

'That's not usual, is it?'

'No, although idiot Audrey occasionally leaves them ajar, and her car was parked up.'

'What happened next?'

'I was concerned, so I raced to the front door. The paramedics asked me about the emergency but of course I didn't understand what they meant. They said a 999 call had requested an ambulance. I assumed someone had played a practical joke until I heard shouting coming from the rear of the house. So I rushed round to the pool and the paramedics followed me. That's when we found Sandy laid out beside the pool. Audrey was kneeling next to her. At first, I thought they were fighting. Timothy stood nearby with his hand over his mouth.'

Charles rapidly blinked. He frowned as he relived the moment.

'I demanded to know what was going on. Timothy said Sandy had been submerged at the bottom. It didn't seem real. I asked for how long and he thought a few minutes.'

Barton suspected Timothy had said five minutes.

'I understand this must be hard for you,' said Barton.

'She'll pull through. They did CPR on her. It looked like the paramedics got her back.'

'You had an argument with Audrey after Sandy had been taken to hospital. Why was that? She'd been trying to help her.'

Charles stared at the ceiling and Barton noted that his eye contact had been good up until now.

'Audrey should have been looking out for her friend. I suppose I wanted someone to blame.'

'You received a cut. How did that happen?'

Charles moved a hand to his face. 'A tree. It's just a scratch.'

'Okay. We'll need to talk to you again, but first we want a word with Jerry Cann.'

Charles's gaze dropped back to Barton. 'Do you mean Jerry McCann?'

Barton let out a deep breath.

'Yes. Where does he live?'

Charles held out his hands, palms up. 'I don't know.'

'I thought he'd been working for you for ages.'

'He has. I pay him by BACS transfer at the end of each month. I've probably got a letter or something at home.'

'No contract?'

'He's self-employed. Jerry did a few one-off jobs at the start. He's a man of many talents. Fixes most things. Is that what hurt Sandy? I saw the smoking heat pump. That thing was supposed to be turned off.'

'Timothy thought the pump had been fixed.'

'No, Jerry said he hoped it was fixed, but the power appeared to be surging every now and again. He said not to use it until he'd double-checked with an approved electrician and made it one hundred per cent safe. It needed a part. I can't remember the initials. RCD maybe. It's a safety device. He was going to have one fitted. Until it was in place, using the pump was risky. He was firm about that. His name is Gerald with a G McCann, by the way, but he prefers Jerry.'

Barton could feel a headache coming on. He suspected if Sandy died, he would need to bring up the issue of her side business. It was possible Charles had found out about the DreamViews angle, anyway, or at least had seen worrying footage. Maybe after Jerry had told him the pump was dangerous, deliberately leaving the pump on was his response and it could therefore follow that he was involved in Henry's demise.

'Did you tell Sandy the in-house CCTV was working?'

'I planned to do that today. We haven't been talking much, so I was looking for an opportunity.'

'Tell me about your relationship with your neighbour Henry.'

'The chap who died in his pool?'

Barton nodded.

'I didn't have one with him. We spoke occasionally at the front of the properties when he was younger and out walking, but nothing more. Waved a few times nowadays, when I've seen him in his car. Seems a pleasant guy.'

'It's easy to slip through the fence from your property to his.'

'Yes, down at the paddock.'

'Do you ever use it?'

'Why would I want to go to Henry's garden? I spend little time in my own, never mind have any interest in his.'

'So, you have a pool and don't swim in it.'

'Nope, I got out of the habit. It's been a stressful few months. Sandy uses it to get out of my way and relax.'

'Did you explain to Sandy why she shouldn't turn on the heat pump?'

'I think so, although she's the water lover, apart from the bitch and her daughter, so I'm reasonably confident Jerry would have told her. He was forthright about waiting for the part. Weirdly insistent, now I come to think about it.'

Barton studied Charles's face. 'I must say, you're certainly very calm considering what's happened today.'

Charles's expression was unreadable.

'Are you implying something with that comment? Sandy and I have a complicated relationship, but I can assure you, Inspector, I love my wife more than you can imagine.'

55

THE VILLAGE KILLER

I can't believe what's happened. That was not part of my plan. It seems the paramedics saved the day. What would I have done otherwise? How could I have continued? It doesn't bear thinking about. Who knew you could die that way?

I bet the police are confused. They must realise by now everyone is under Sandy's spell but maybe they don't know the extent. We'd all like a piece of her, but our true desire, our real obsession, is possession.

Imagine, having her want to spend every second with you. Perhaps on holiday, where the worries of modern life don't apply. I can see us strolling into a candlelit restaurant together. The gaze of everyone there would be on her, not me, but that's okay. That's the way it should be.

Resplendent in high heels, a choreography of confidence and poise, she would glide past fawning waiters and jealous eyes. We'd laugh and joke and share our meals. Nobody else would matter. I would bask in her reflective glow.

Days at the beach. Rubbing suntan lotion into her perfect skin. Perhaps even a cheeky toe massage. Actual paradise on earth.

Heaven would become hell without her. If I ever got over the shock of her leaving, for whatever reason, I'd be looking for someone to blame.

56

DCI BARTON

Barton finished the interview with Charles and sent him off with Minton. Then he returned to the office, where he found Zelensky and Hoffman.

'Are Malik and Leicester in with Robert?' he asked.

'Yes,' said Hoffman. 'I collected Robert, and Reception was spot on. He was trembling.'

'Right, Hoffman, you lead the discussion with Audrey. Ask her exactly what she knew about the pump. Charles said Jerry specifically told them not to put it on until he made it safe.'

'You think someone turned it on deliberately, then?' asked Zelensky.

'It's possible. Can you do a quick search on a Gerald McCann? It seems Jerry gave us a wrong name, which makes me suspect you'll find something damning.'

Zelensky spun her seat around. She must have already been logged into the PNC because she simply typed in Jerry's full details. She leaned towards the computer as she read what was there. Her mouth dropped open.

'Oh, dear.'

'Brilliant.'

'He got charged with exactly what you said. Involuntary manslaughter by gross negligence.'

'Charged and then convicted?'

'Yes, sentenced to three years at Norwich Crown Court seven years ago. God knows how much he'll get for another one. What a fool. Sounds like he did his time, then left Norfolk and came here, where nobody had heard of him. Hang on a mo.'

Zelensky typed Gerald McCann, Norwich, jailed, and manslaughter into Google. She scanned an article.

'There was an issue with the electrics in a home. The owner's nineteen-year-old daughter was killed.'

'Bloody hell. Locate his address from DVLA, then arrange for Uniform to pick him up. We've got too much going on here for us to attend. Delve into the details of that death. It could have been sloppiness, but it's so similar we can't ignore it. I suppose he would naturally move to somewhere new, and if he's a handyman by trade, he'd struggle to find work doing something else.'

'Yeah, once might be a mistake. Twice probably makes him a psycho.'

Barton couldn't disagree. 'Make sure Uniform have plenty of bodies.'

Ten minutes later, Barton and Hoffman were sitting in front of Audrey. Hoffman cautioned her, then smiled.

'Okay, Audrey. At this point, you are helping us with our enquiries. There are two subjects we need to discuss.'

Audrey's eyes narrowed. 'I'm beginning to feel like a suspect here. My friend nearly died.'

'That's the first thing. Can you tell me about this morning?'

'What's to tell? I arrived. We were meant to swim together. I'm trying to lose a few pounds. We also had business to go through.'

'Are you working with Sandy, then?'

'Is that important?'

'I need all the facts to find out what occurred.'

'We've got a project.'

As Barton suspected, Audrey was the photographer, but it sounded as though she might be more heavily involved.

'Okay,' said Barton. 'So, Sandy dived in the water, but you didn't.'

'Right. It was a miserable day, and we found a dead squirrel in the pool.'

'But Sandy leapt in anyway?' asked Hoffman.

'Yes. She said the chlorine killed all the germs.'

'Did you know the heat pump wasn't supposed to be on?'

'Why would I know that?'

Hoffman shrugged. 'Where were you when Sandy found herself in trouble?'

'I wandered inside to make a coffee before she got in. Sandy has a posh machine. Next thing, Timothy ran past the kitchen in a panic. I followed him to the pool and saw her at the bottom. He stopped me from jumping in. I'd have been electrocuted as well if he hadn't. How is Sandy?'

'She's in ICU.'

'What does that mean?'

'It's the intensive care unit.'

'I'm aware of that, you cretin. I meant, has she regained consciousness? Will she be okay?'

Hoffman looked over at Barton, who could see Audrey's insult had annoyed him. To his credit, Hoffman didn't respond. Audrey's reaction was at least more natural than Charles's.

'That's the latest update we have,' said Barton. 'We'll keep you informed. Carry on with what happened when you discovered Sandy under the water.'

'Timothy used the extinguisher, but there were still sparks, so he ran to the fuse box to make sure we wouldn't get shocked. Once he was sure it was safe, he jumped into the pool and we lifted her out. I tried to pump her chest. I saw Vinnie Jones do it on a TV ad. Then the ambulance turned up.'

'How long would you say she was under the surface from when you became aware?' asked Hoffman.

Audrey scratched her head.

'Five minutes perhaps. The paramedics arrived really quickly.'

'Okay,' said Hoffman. 'The other person we'd like a chat to you about is your brother.'

Audrey's head swivelled towards him. Her chin jutted forward.

'What about Frannie?'

'When did you last see him?'

'A week ago.'

'Where was that?'

'At my place. He comes once a week. I feed him. He has a bath. I wash his clothes.'

Hoffman looked as confused as Barton felt.

'Where does he live?' asked Barton.

'A shared house on Lincoln Road. It's foul, but that was all the council had for him.'

'Couldn't he stay with you?' asked Hoffman, with what Barton suspected was a mischievous expression.

Audrey abruptly leaned forward. 'With your condescending grin, I suspect you know all about Frannie. I have a beautiful fourteen-year-old daughter who walks about in just her knickers, so the answer to that is no. What's he done now?'

'He may have been approaching young children again.'

Audrey shook her head. 'Poor old Frannie.'

'Not poor kids?'

'He's bloody harmless.'

'He did prison time for exposure, amongst other things.'

'Frannie's different from other people.'

'How so?'

'He doesn't understand the rules. I reckon he has some sort of Asperger's. He likes spending time with smaller kids because he never grew up himself. My parents split up. Frannie kept getting into trouble with the police for being weird, so Dad moved up north and took Frannie with him. Frannie got into more serious bother because he wouldn't stop talking to younger children. It was like a compulsion. He wanted to be friends with everyone.'

'That doesn't explain the exposure charge.'

'Frannie reckoned a kid told him to pull his trousers down, and he would take his off. Frannie did *The Full Monty*. All caught on CCTV. He was in the papers. Bricks flew through my dad's window. Paedo was painted on his door. He had a fatal heart attack the day after Frannie got sent to prison for six months.'

'I'm sorry to hear that,' said Barton.

'He was a shit father, so don't be, and jail was the best thing for Frannie. They assessed him, prescribed the right drugs, made sure he took his meds, and put him on a wing with a load of other odd bods. I visited him once. He had friends. When it reached the time for him to leave, they got him a placement on this farm. Some type of charity where they get to live on site. I hadn't heard from him for years. Knowing how he was, I doubt he'd have got on with mobile phones, and he struggled to write. I just hoped he was happy.'

'When did he come back?'

'About a year ago.' Audrey's face fell. 'If I'm honest, I kind of expected him to return to his old ways.'

'You should have told us about him earlier,' said Hoffman.

Audrey rolled her eyes at him. 'I'm not grassing up my own brother. I assume he'll go down again, but that's fine. Prison's the safest place for him.'

Barton had to admit Audrey was a convincing interviewee.

She'd also described Frannie Bone as he remembered him. Someone like that couldn't cope with a character as dominant as Poppy, but she wouldn't be hanging around in his grubby bedsit, either.

'The courts are more sympathetic to neurodivergent conditions nowadays,' said Barton. 'If you spoke on his behalf, they'd probably sentence him to a community order with the opportunity to work with probation. It's been a long time since he offended.'

'They tried that before. He needs to be kept away from children.'

'You said he was harmless.'

'He is, far from temptation.'

'Can you give me a minute? I'm going to nip out of the room to have a word with a colleague.'

Hoffman suspended the interview, and Barton raced back to the office to pass on Audrey's comments regarding her brother. Zelensky was the only one there. Barton cursed.

'Are the others still talking to Robert?'

'Yeah, they've been in there a while. Malik popped out, though. He said for you to see him the moment you finished your interview with Audrey.'

Barton was about to head off to find Malik and Leicester when Minton wandered in.

'Didn't I ask you to stay at the hospital?' he barked, then realised she appeared deep in thought.

'You did, but Charles insisted on being alone. Sandy died a few minutes before we arrived.'

57

DCI BARTON

Barton considered passing the investigation of Frannie Bone back to CID. It wasn't serious enough for Major Crimes, but keeping it linked with the other suspicious deaths and the missing girl probably made sense, even though the links remained tenuous.

The Barton belly was also telling him there'd be more surprises for the team.

'Apologies for snapping, Minton. Are you okay?'

'I can handle a few harsh comments.'

Barton smiled. 'I meant with Sandy's passing.'

'Oh, sorry. I didn't go to the ICU. Charles demanded I leave immediately.' Minton puffed out her cheeks. 'I'm fine.'

'Did he appear devastated? I think it's fair to say his behaviour towards his wife's welfare has been inconsistent.'

'Yes, the colour drained from his face. Luckily, the nurse sat him down first. She had to stop Charles falling off the chair as it was.'

Barton again thought of Sandy and her hopes for the future. He knew her image would be one of many that came back to haunt him, but the investigation had accelerated. They had to push on.

'Right, we'll arrest Mr Bone for harassment when he's finished speaking to the duty and see if he talks. I reckon he'll admit to everything he's done. Make sure Frannie's vulnerabilities are recorded. What he needs is a proper assessment for any personality disorders and a judgement on his overall capacity to stand trial. His solicitor should be able to refer him to the LADs team at the magistrates' court tomorrow morning.'

LADs stood for Liaison and Diversion Team. They assisted in cases like Frannie's to ensure sentencing was fair.

'What do you think is most likely to happen to him?' asked Minton.

'It will depend on what LADs says but I hope the magistrates ask for a full mental health assessment. They can remand Frannie in the meantime. It's still possible they'll decline jurisdiction and pass to Crown because their sentencing powers are limited if the report comes back saying he's a serious risk to the public. They tend to be careful when they don't have all the details, the guilty party is a convicted sex offender, and he's been repeatedly pestering children. Frannie should start praying for a sympathetic judge when they decide what to do with him.'

'Are you going to find out what Robert was so bothered by?' asked Zelensky. 'Malik asked you to see him immediately.'

'Yes, where are they?'

'Interview room six.'

Barton returned to where he'd left Hoffman and Audrey and asked them to take a break. He knocked on the door of number six and entered. Henry's MacBook sat open on the table with a list of files on the screen. Robert had aged overnight. Leicester and Malik's faces were set like stone.

'What is it?' asked Barton.

'Robert searched Henry's computer again,' said Malik. 'He found a section named obsolete, where Henry had kept communication and photographs from the two other profiles who he'd been in contact with. It was more of the same for the Eastern-European gymnast, but the other account grabbed his attention.'

Barton readied himself for a shock. Leicester cleared his throat.

'There are photos of a girl in heavy make-up, but a couple of pictures were sent au naturelle,' said Leicester. 'In those, she looks noticeably young. In fact, she appears underage.'

Barton took a seat. He could see where they were going. 'Is all of her face in view?'

'Yes.'

'Are there any close-ups?'

'A few. It's definitely Poppy Madden.'

58

DCI BARTON

Barton steepled his fingers. Now, this was a case for Major Crimes.

'Are you sure?'

'Yeah. Her username is Popsicle16.'

'Bloody hell. Are the pictures bad?'

'They're nothing like the extreme material the blackmailing account sent, but they are still full nudity with little left for the imagination.'

Barton rose and opened the door.

'Robert, we're going to step outside for a few minutes.'

Barton was the first to speak when the three officers had left the room.

'I've been speaking to Poppy's mother. She gave me a plausible explanation about her brother, who is unlikely to be involved in this. Audrey also told us she had a business arrangement with Sandy. That has to be the DreamViews thing, but would she set up her own daughter on the site?'

Malik shrugged. 'When I passed the details of the blackmail case to the cyber-crimes team, I had a chat with one of their guys.

He said it's relatively easy to open an account as long as you have ID, but even the shady offshore companies are careful with who's on their platforms. All of them shut profiles down if they suspect any extortion or underage activity, but the less reputable set-ups, places like Panama, don't tend to report any crimes to the authorities.'

'How are accounts opened?'

'It varies, but for most, the person fills in an online form, then emails a photograph with their passport photo page next to their faces.'

Barton absorbed the information. 'Which means Poppy's been helped or coerced by an older person using either their ID or that of someone else overage.'

'Seems that way. Her application to join could have slipped through. Who knows how stringent their controls are? Fake IDs can be bought. You wouldn't get through Border Control with them, but they might pass muster in a photograph.'

'Poppy's fourteen. She's unlikely to know of a reputable counterfeiter. I reckon she used someone else's account.'

'They'd need to be above the minimum age and look similar,' said Leicester, 'but we've got nobody like that on our radar.'

'Obviously, we need to tell Audrey,' said Barton. 'Her immediate response will be the best indicator of whether she knew.'

'It's probable that Poppy's hiding place when she vanished is where the pictures were taken,' said Malik.

'Good point. See if the images contain any clues. Perhaps there's something in the background that could help us. Take as much detail as possible from Robert. We'll need to send the laptop off to a specialist now.'

Barton stood up. He grinned at them before he left the room. 'And keep up the outstanding work.'

He located Hoffman, and they went to collect Audrey, but she wasn't in the family room where she'd been taken to wait. The PC who had been sitting with her was checking her phone.

'Where is she?' asked Minton.

'Gone for a vape.'

Barton imagined Audrey sprinting down Thorpe Road with an expression of murderous intent, but then she trudged into the room with an officer.

Barton escorted her back to the interview room. Audrey was about to experience a terrible few minutes. There was no easy way to break a sudden death to anyone. Interviewing her afterwards about her daughter being on the DreamViews site would be brutal, but he didn't have the luxury of time. Not when a girl was being exploited.

Barton waited until Audrey took her seat.

'I'm sorry to tell you Sandy has died of her injuries in hospital just a few minutes ago.'

Audrey gawped at him. Seconds ticked by. 'What?'

'I'm sorry for your loss.'

Audrey stared at Barton, then glared at Hoffman, as though he were complicit in a sick joke. Her mouth twisted open as if to scream but, instead, she covered her mouth.

'No, no, no. I should have been with her,' she whispered.

Audrey's forehead lowered to her hands, which were crossed on the table. She buried both hands in her hair. Her face was bright red when she looked back up.

'No!'

Her fingers turned into claws which scraped at her scalp. Hoffman reached over and rested his hand on Audrey's arm.

'Try to stay calm,' he said. 'I know it's terrible news. Charles is with her at the hospital.'

'I can't believe it.'

'I'm afraid we need to ask you a couple of questions.'

'What the hell do you want to talk to me about now?'

'This could be a case of manslaughter.'

Audrey roared her reply. 'Fucking Jerry. He killed her. Could have killed me!' Her face twisted up. 'I don't believe it! He should rot in jail, useless bastard!'

'We've heard he told other people not to use the pump, but they didn't pass the message on in time.'

'Charles?'

'It might be a tragic accident.'

Audrey shook her head. Her voice lowered. 'I wouldn't be surprised if he did it deliberately.'

'Why do you say that?'

'I suppose he guessed she was getting ready to leave him. She'd been looking for the opportunity. Goading him into arguments so she could storm off. I told her to come to mine, but she reckoned that was the first place he'd look.'

'Did Charles scare her?' asked Hoffman.

Audrey cocked her head to one side. 'A bit. He's a strong man, but Sandy never said that he'd hit her, although her leaving him would up the ante, wouldn't it? Jeez, I can't wrap my mind around her dying.'

'Are you still okay to carry on?' asked Barton.

'Yes, but can we get on with it?'

'The reason I mentioned Charles was to do with your little project.'

Audrey crossed her arms. 'Yeah?'

'What do you think he'd do if he found out about it?'

Audrey shrugged. 'I've no idea. What would you do if you discovered your wife was flashing her tushy for a fiver?'

'I'd up her housekeeping money.'

Audrey sneered. 'It wasn't just about the money.'

'Could you explain that to me, please?' said Barton. 'I'm not sure if it has anything to do with what's been going on, but you could argue this morning was the second attempt on her life in a short space of time.'

Audrey fixed her gaze on the table for a moment, then locked eyes with Barton.

'I guess it doesn't matter with her gone. It was Sandy's idea. She looked fairly plain as a child, so I think she felt this was her time to shine. She got off on the attention as well as the cash. The control appealed to her.'

'What was your role?'

'She was so successful, it became difficult to cope. Sandy had a real showgirl's flair. At Halloween, she dressed as a vampire nurse, blood oozing from her fangs and dripping onto her heaving cleavage. The punters came crawling. DreamViews could see she was bringing in the subscribers, so they helped out and pushed her profile. Making the content took ages on her own, so she suggested I film her and take photos.'

'Did that make you feel uncomfortable?' asked Hoffman.

'We grew up together. I'd seen it all before. I enjoyed it if truth be known. She kept in incredible shape for her age. It was fun. Like being in the movies.'

Barton didn't mention it was more like the pornography industry. Audrey gazed into the distance.

'It was exciting. That's how Sandy made you feel. She brought enjoyment to life. In her company, I felt alive.'

'Did she pay you for your time?' asked Hoffman.

'Yes. She couldn't keep up with the volume of interest because it was hard to do it when Charles was there. He'd insist on eating together. She had chores.'

'If he affords a gardener and a handyman, why doesn't he hire a housekeeper or a cleaner?'

'It was part of his shitty behaviour. Charles forced her to do those menial tasks. He considered that her job. So, I took over Sandy's admin. I dealt with the new customers. The ones who only asked to see the videos and pictures. When they started chatting and were looking to build a relationship, I passed them to Sandy.'

'So, it's not just seeing her naked. Many of them wanted to talk.'

'Yep. The messages always ended with "have you got a picture of" and then insert their particular taste. If someone blatantly came across as creepy, I usually blocked them, but there weren't loads of them. You blokes are unoriginal. Topless in dungarees, the office in suspenders, naked in the woods, vibrators on the bed, splashing in the pool. I sometimes sent the same photograph out ten times a day. There was a common theme to nearly all the clients, though.'

'What was that?' asked Barton.

'They were lonely. Loads of the guys were married. They'd invariably mention their wives had gone off sex. It's the menopause. I consider DreamViews a service. Men have needs. This kept their marriages intact, and you don't get the clap from DreamViews.'

'We heard some people meet their clients,' said Hoffman.

'Sandy never did. Or at least she never told me she had.'

'Is it possible she may have done?'

'Nah. I can read all the messages.'

'Can't you delete them?'

'I suppose, but why would she lie to me?'

'You two were close, then.'

'Like sisters. Funnily enough, Sandy used to sit on the sofa chatting to them via the messenger on DreamViews, while Charles watched TV on an armchair beside her, completely unaware. She got a kick out of that.'

'Right,' said Barton. 'There's another point I should mention.

You know Charles told Sandy the CCTV was broken inside and outside.'

Audrey frowned. Barton nodded.

'Only the outside cameras stopped working.'

Audrey gritted her teeth and snarled through them. 'No fucking way.'

59

DCI BARTON

Audrey swiftly recovered from the surprise.

'He will have seen a few sights.' Then her face dropped as she realised the implications. 'What are you saying? That Charles didn't tell Sandy about the pump on purpose to get back at her because of what he'd seen?'

'We're checking all the angles,' said Barton.

'Charles would consider it stripping at best, prostitution at worst.' Audrey fanned her face with a hand. 'Shit, I've come over all peculiar. To know he's been watching me and Sandy doing things together.'

Hoffman coughed. 'I didn't think you were quite that involved.'

'Well, kind of. Blokes love that sort of thing. They reckon we're all lesbians deep down. You do get a lot of late life gay women, but that's generally after they've finally understood men aren't worth the hassle. We're sick of cleaning up after ungrateful dickheads. Mostly Sandy and I posed in photos. It wasn't like we were hard at it. Just me holding her boobs, poking my tongue near other places. They were a brilliant money spinner. I'd be on DreamViews myself if I was more of a looker and hadn't eaten so many mince pies over the years.'

'Charles might have recognised you in the videos. That's perhaps why your relationship with him was fraught.'

'We hated each other on sight long ago.'

Barton thought back to the electrocution.

'You, Sandy, or Poppy could have jumped into that pool first,' said Barton.

'Too right, but Sandy was always the most likely.'

'Is it possible someone else wanted to hurt her?'

Audrey shook her head.

'I can't see it. Everyone loved Sandy. Her death robs all of us of her company, especially Charles. He was mean to her, but Sandy told me he occasionally tried to be kind. Charles often said he wished for life to be back the way it was. He missed the good times.'

'So, he isn't all bad,' said Hoffman.

'Bollocks. He's a fucking disgrace. Charles booked a two-week cruise for them to Barbados. Sandy was nervous about spending so much time together, but she eventually got in the mood. Used some of the early DreamViews money to buy new outfits, then the shitbag cancelled the holiday at the last minute.'

'Marriage can be complicated,' said Barton. 'We need to hear all that you know, Audrey. Sandy's case will be passed to the coroner's office, who'll investigate, which is why we need you to answer a few tough questions now, when everything is still clear in your mind.'

'I suppose it might be one of her clients. A couple of them are pretty nutty. But how would they be aware of the faulty pump? How would they get her address?'

'They're the issues we're having. It would help if we looked at her personal DreamViews account. I assume you still have the logins. You could hand over your computer.'

Audrey's gaze dropped.

'I don't know about that. Do I have to give it to you?'

She would have to hand it over, but Barton wanted her to hand it over willingly.

'Surely, you'd prefer us to investigate this thoroughly. If there was anything underhand, it'd be justice for Sandy.'

'Can I think about it? Maybe I should get lawyered up.'

Barton stared at her. Was this sudden cagey behaviour because Audrey had something on Sandy's account she didn't want him to see, or perhaps it concerned the one Poppy opened? Barton suspected Audrey would be searching the web for how to erase hard drives if she got to her laptop first.

'We have a duty solicitor here who you have access to so we can organise that for you but first there's one final subject I must bring up.'

'Okay,' said Audrey, eyes darting from Barton to Hoffman.

'You don't need to answer or comment at this point, but this interview is being recorded. Anything you do say could be used as evidence against you.'

'It sounds like you're going to accuse me of something.'

'Audrey, we have reason to believe your daughter, Poppy, has also set up a profile on DreamViews.'

Audrey's eyes became saucers. 'Bullshit. Who told you that?'

'I've seen it.'

'What? You've been looking at photos of my fourteen-year-old daughter, naked!'

'The photographs I saw were evocative not gratuitous, but ones like that are available to view.'

'What the hell are you doing on DreamViews? How did you even know Sandy was on there?'

Barton's mind churned as he considered how much he could or should tell Audrey. She used colourful language, but he suspected Audrey was nobody's fool. She made the leap.

'Henry,' she said. 'Like Sandy, you had to investigate his death. The devious, dirty old bastard.' Audrey slammed her hand on the table. 'Wait a fucking minute. Are you offering me legal advice because you reckon I facilitated Poppy getting an account? You're out of your mind. That's my little girl!'

'I'm sorry to ask for confirmation, but, for the benefit of the tape, you know nothing about it?' asked Hoffman.

'Of course, I bloody don't. Why would you think I did?'

'Well, it is a coincidence that she has an account on the same site Sandy's registered on.'

Audrey's eyes roamed their faces, then the ceiling, as the horror ricocheted around her mind. Her hands opened and closed. Barton was pleased Hoffman knew to stay quiet.

'You're right. She couldn't have done it on her own. Someone must have helped her.'

'The question I have to ask is, where did she get the inspiration to do it?' asked Barton.

'Maybe she saw me using the site. We share a computer at home, but I was careful to close the pages down. It can't have been Sandy. She wouldn't have said anything to Poppy about it. Poppy did ask why we had a bit more money lately. Perhaps one of her friends knew about it.'

'Another fourteen-year-old girl?'

'I've told you. She's no ordinary teenager and her pals aren't much better. When she started infant school, I started to call her Pops. It suited her, all full of beans. She came home one day and said, "Mummy, my name is Poppy. Nothing else". I sometimes wonder if that was her last moment of innocence. She's so calculating. It's a terrible thing to say about your own child, but she scares me a little.'

Barton wasn't sure how to reply to that.

'Yeah, yeah,' said Audrey. 'I know how it looks. You assume I'm chaotic and neglecting her, so she's growing up too fast. That's crap. That's just who she is. I tried to raise her proper. Teach her right from wrong. It's the bloody Internet, fucking the kids up. You ought to see her around my boyfriends. They're putty in her hands, and I find it hard to watch.'

'Could it be one of them?'

'What? I don't hang about with paedos, and I haven't had a date for six months. I've been too busy with DreamViews. It'll be a man, though. A pervert who's probably shitting himself now. They should be disgusted with themselves.'

Barton coughed. He suspected the person *was* scared, and they were disgusted, but he also reckoned the man responsible was in the police station right at that moment.

60

DCI BARTON

Barton knew there was a long road ahead for both Audrey and Poppy. He tried to think about what Holly would do if something like this happened with Layla. She would have been clamouring to get out of the station and be with her for a start. Poppy was clearly a different type of girl, yet she was still just that.

The fight had drained from Audrey. Her head drooped and her eyes had become glassy.

'I'm sure you understand we are obligated to inform Social Services,' said Barton. 'Poppy's safety is our priority.'

'What happens then?'

'Social Services will take over. They'll collect Poppy from school.'

'Bringing her to a police station would upset her.'

'She won't come here today. You'll be collected to go with her. The council has a special office for this type of thing.'

'Will they separate her from me?'

'To be truthful, I'm not sure. Probably not, if you weren't directly responsible for the situation Poppy has found herself in.'

'Directly?'

'Audrey, she must have got the idea from you or something you did. The sooner you accept your role in this, and take steps to ensure it never happens again, the happier the council will be about not breaking up the family unit.'

'She's not going to a children's home.'

'She could stay at her father's house.'

'No way. I won't get her back. Maybe Glenn, he's my ex, was into DreamViews. I wouldn't put it past him.'

Barton didn't think so. He was fairly sure he had his man. Barton stood and walked to the door and Audrey's eyes followed him.

'You know who it is, don't you?'

Barton gestured for her to leave.

'Tell me. I have the right to know.'

'Everything will be explained to you when we're certain.'

'Who was it? Jerry? Nah, his phone was older than Poppy.' Audrey's brows knitted together. She jabbed out a finger. 'Timothy. That's who it was. The bloody gardener. You string that mother-fucker up by the balls for me.'

'We'll be interviewing everyone with links to your daughter. Did Poppy speak to Jerry or Timothy much?'

'Yeah, both. All the time. She's like a lot of kids. She gets easily bored, especially without Wi-Fi. Poppy manipulates people. She had Timothy getting her cold drinks.'

Barton smiled at Audrey. 'Do you realise you're contradicting yourself?'

'What do you mean?'

'One minute Poppy's been exploited, the next, she's always in control. Do you think there's a possibility she was a willing partici-pant in all this?'

'She is a child!'

Barton was losing patience with Audrey.

'Yes, and that's why you'll stay here at the station until someone from Social Services arrives.'

'I'm hardly likely to run away.'

'A social worker will talk to Poppy. They'll decide whether she is fit for interview. The earlier we take the details of what has been happening, the quicker she can put it behind her.'

'Will she have to give evidence?'

'It's possible. If we conduct an excellent recorded interview, it may be admissible and save her from being in court.'

'Can I be present during the interview?'

'You can be in a room nearby. If this goes to trial, it's likely you will be called as a witness.'

'What for?'

'You mentioned she spoke to Timothy a lot. He got her drinks. You used the DreamViews website at home.'

'Sandy could be a witness.'

Barton gave her a commiserating smile as Audrey realised what she'd said. 'You could be an important asset for the prosecution, so it's better you aren't in the room, or it weakens the evidence.'

Audrey closed her eyes. 'God, what a mess.'

'We'll get you a cup of tea and something to eat. I'm going to speak to the Crown Prosecution Service.'

'Who are they?'

'The CPS are the people who decide if there is enough evidence to have a strong chance of a win at trial. They're the experts in seeking justice. I need to keep them up to speed on how this situation is developing.'

Audrey finally got up but outside the room, she stopped.

'What's happened to my brother?'

'I don't know. I can find out for you.'

Hoffman took Audrey to get a coffee while Barton nipped to the custody suite. He found out about Frannie, rang the CPS, then returned to the interview room as Hoffman and Audrey were returning. Audrey raised her gaze to look at him. Barton directed her into the room and closed the door.

'Frannie admitted to speaking to lots of kids, asking them if they wanted to go to his place, and using inappropriate language. His solicitor put in an early guilty plea while citing mitigating factors. In light of his previous offending, he was sent to prison.'

'What will happen to him?'

'The court asked for a PSR. Sorry, a pre-sentence report. He'll be remanded in jail until that's done. In effect, Frannie will have a visit at the prison from Probation, and they'll make a recommendation as to what kind of punishment and rehabilitation would be best for Frannie. If Probation think they can work with him, they'll recommend a community order.'

'So, it's possible he'll only have to do unpaid work, yet he's still gone to jail while they get around to deciding whether to throw the key away or not.'

Barton recalled Audrey earlier saying prison was the best place for her brother. He kept his face straight.

'That's more or less it. Remember, Frannie admitted his guilt, so there won't be a trial. The healthcare team and Probation will conduct lengthy meetings with Frannie, where he'll need to be aware of what he's done and show a willingness to change. There are kids involved in his case as well. Until it's understood if there is any danger to other children, it's safer to keep him locked away.'

Audrey rolled up her sleeves. She kept her gaze on Barton, but her face was blank.

'Perfect.'

61

DCI BARTON

Audrey was taken back to the waiting room, and Barton returned to the office with Hoffman. Minton and Zelensky prepared for the interview with Timothy for an hour, then left to get started. Barton went to the room next door to observe via video link. He figured Timothy might relax more if he was interviewed by people who were closer in age to him, although whether them being female would help was up for debate.

The duty solicitor entered first. He leaned forward, fingers linked on the table, head dipped. That didn't bode well. Timothy shuffled, sat beside him and slumped low in his seat. Barton turned up the sound as Zelensky cautioned Timothy. She confirmed his date of birth, full name and address. Barton could only just make out the replies, even with the volume on max.

'Timothy, you work for Sandy and Charles Faversham as their gardener. Is that correct?' asked Zelensky.

'Yes.'

'How long for?'

'Five years.'

'You must be on good terms with your bosses, especially with them being at home a lot.'

Timothy nodded.

'For the record, could you please speak up.'

'Yes.'

'Do you know Audrey Madden?'

'Yes, she's a friend of Sandy's.'

'Do you speak to her?'

'Occasionally.'

'She spent plenty of time at Paddock Green this summer, didn't she?'

Timothy's head bobbed slightly.

'Is that a yes, Mr Steele?'

'Yes,' he croaked.

'Sometimes she came with her daughter. Have you met her?'

'Yes.'

'What's her name?'

Timothy shook his head. He placed his hands over his eyes, then shook his head more vigorously.

'You do know her name?'

Barton observed Timothy's shoulders heaving. 'Poppy,' he spluttered.

'Can you tell me about your relationship with Poppy?' asked Minton.

Barton easily heard Timothy sobbing. The solicitor leaned over and whispered in his client's ear. Timothy nodded again.

'Mr Steele won't be answering any questions about Poppy. He has a right to silence.'

'Silence isn't a defence,' said Zelensky. 'He clearly knows what we're talking about. It'd be helpful if he put his version of events forward. The victim in all of this is a child. She needs to be protected.'

The solicitor looked over at Timothy, who now had an arm across his eyes. Zelensky rubbed her hands together for a moment.

'I hear you enjoy trading cryptocurrencies.'

Timothy's arm dropped down and he shouted, 'I'll never touch them ever again. They've ruined my life!'

'Care to explain how?'

The solicitor leaned across the table.

'My client has nothing further to say.'

'Mr Timothy Steele,' said Zelensky. 'I'm arresting you on suspicion of producing indecent images of a child. You do not have to say anything, but it may harm your defence if you do not mention, when questioned, something which you later rely on in court. Anything you do say may be given in evidence. Do you understand?'

Barton watched Timothy, who remained frozen. The production of indecent images was much more serious than the offence of making indecent images, which was more to do with the viewing and downloading of photographs and videos. Zelensky continued.

'A thorough investigation of your possessions will be carried out by law enforcement officers after obtaining a warrant. These searches will include your computer, smartphone, tablet, and any hard drives, as well as your home. Your emails and social media will also be examined for evidence. Is that clear?'

Timothy moved his arm but avoided eye contact. He nodded once.

'For the record, Mr Steele, do you understand?'

'Yes,' he mumbled.

'Do you wish to make any further comment?' asked Minton.

'No,' he whispered.

Barton stared at the young man on the screen. Did Timothy leave the pump on, knowing it could kill either Audrey or Sandy? Maybe he didn't care which. He had money troubles, so it was possible he stole Henry's gold watch, then took out the owner, and had now exploited Poppy for financial gain.

Zelensky picked up the phone in the interview room. A minute later, two custody PCs arrived. Timothy's solicitor had to help him up. Police interviews crushed many offenders. The seriousness of their actions often became apparent only at that moment. Weeping and denial were commonplace with the realisation of the long and painful road that they were facing.

Timothy Steele was heading to the cells. His world was about to implode.

62

DCI BARTON

By the time Zelensky and Minton returned to the office, the whole team was present. Barton called a meeting and told them about the discussions he'd had with Charles, Timothy, and Audrey.

'It sounds like Santa should give Timothy's place a miss this year,' said Hoffman.

'I don't think HMP Peterborough has a chimney anyway,' said Barton. 'Zelensky, can you organise the searches? Custody will have taken whatever he brought with him. We need his home sealed up. His laptop is the most pertinent item to locate, but we must enter without compromising the scene. Poppy's DNA is likely to be all over his house if she stayed there for a week.'

'Ask them to use mobile digital fingerprint scanners so we know asap,' said Minton.

'That's a great call,' replied Barton. 'I'll grill Timothy tomorrow first thing after a night in the cells. Then we'll see if we can get him in front of Saturday's remand court or he'll be forced to stay here until Monday. It'll help focus my questioning if I have concrete proof Poppy has been in his house. We'll then speak to the neighbours after I've spoken to Timothy, and we've heard what Poppy has to say about all of this.'

Hoffman picked up on what Barton was implying. 'You don't believe Poppy is going to give him up.'

'No, not right away.'

'Because she loves him?'

'I'm beginning to suspect Poppy is too ambitious for love. Let's see what happens when the social workers talk to her. But I'm hopeful there should be too much damning evidence for either Poppy or Timothy to attempt to wriggle out of it.' Barton tapped his hand on the table twice. 'Stay focused. We've got a hell of a lot of paperwork to plough through with everything that's been revealed today, so get to it. This isn't over. By early evening, we'll have more of an idea what tomorrow looks like. Any other news?'

'Audrey's ex-husband, Glenn Madden, called in after we left a message,' said Leicester. 'I explained we need to discuss something with him, but the topic is a sensitive matter. He's away on business but will make it back to chat with us tomorrow at eleven.'

'Excellent, although there goes our Saturday. The background he can give us will be important.'

'I double-checked the photographs of Poppy to see if they helped with a location,' said Malik. 'They aren't great compared to the levels of professionalism Sandy reached. Not as creative, either. Most photos are set inside what looks a little like Sandy's house. There's space in the rooms. Timothy lives in a two-bed terrace in Oxclose, Bretton. Those are cosy, to say the least. Also, a few images are outside. It's the same type of foliage and shrubbery as at Sandy's. Perhaps they were taken when Poppy was at Paddock Green.'

'Are you saying the pictures on Poppy's page were shot in Sandy's house or garden?'

'Maybe.'

Barton blanched at the thought of Charles watching with interest when he was playing back his CCTV.

'Okay, we'll cross that bridge if and when we come to it. Have we had an update from the cyber guys who are dealing with DreamViews?'

'They rang in twenty minutes ago. The lady I spoke to said they were a typical international Internet company,' said Leicester. 'There's no telephone number, just a spiderweb of "contact us" and "fill in this form" crap. She implied we shouldn't rely on any help from them.'

'Understood. Okay, guys, let's crack on.'

By 7 p.m., Barton was a spent force. He had stayed in sight of the team as opposed to sitting in his office. They were beavering away behind monitors and occasionally shouting out to the others in the room. Hoffman hollered over at him.

'CSI found footprints at the back of Henry's property. They'll look again in better light, but it seems someone has climbed over recently.'

'Good. We'll get onto ANPR in the morning and find out where all those connected with this case have been driving to and from.'

'Audrey and Timothy live in Bretton, which is walkable without being under CCTV,' said Minton.

'Yes, but any of them could park elsewhere and hike to Castor. And with the ANPR report at the least we can ask people to confirm their movements, and we'll know if they're lying.'

Minton gave him a thumbs up and returned to her screen.

Barton was considering if another coffee would prove beneficial or make things worse when his phone rang.

'Hi, John. It's Shirley.'

'Hey, how are you?'

'Busy! You understand what it's like with these multi-agency cases, so I offered to be the link to you lot at Major Crimes regarding Poppy. We had a quick chat with her and our specialist services after school. Obviously, we're still worried about her disappearing again. Poppy stuck to her guns. She was staying with a friend. Denied having another mobile phone. She even mentioned wanting to be free of the burden of social media. Cheeky little cow laughed as she said it.'

'Great. We don't think that'll be a long-term problem once we've piled up the evidence. Timothy will crack. Sex offenders usually panic and try to minimise their role.'

'Yes. It's an unsavoury business, but our world is becoming a more unsavoury place. This DreamViews thing concerns me greatly around exploited children.'

'I know what you mean. People argue prostitutes are taken off the street, but I expect all of that work will remain the same. This new type of business will be lucrative for some and legally done, but a few will use it as a gateway to exploit women and kids. Others will pay for that content.'

'Exactly. Will you be interviewing Poppy tomorrow?'

'I was waiting to hear how you got on. Poppy's going to need more pressure to talk.'

'John, she's hard as nails but bright with it. I've not met a girl like her, but one of my team comes from London and she'd encountered similar kids a few times. Perhaps not as fervent as Poppy, but these young girls want fame and fortune. Nothing's getting in their way.'

'Where's Poppy going tonight?'

'They've done a risk assessment. Her house with mum is a safe place for her while Timothy is in custody. An officer arrived and took the laptop Audrey and Poppy have been using. Do you have enough for Timothy to be remanded straight to prison from magistrates' court?'

'It's touch and go at the moment, but hopefully I will have

tomorrow. I'll decide then about talking to Poppy. Her father's coming in too. I'll have grilled Timothy again by then. I'm confident he'll crack under my weight.'

Shirley chuckled. 'I almost feel sorry for him.'

'What's Poppy's father like?'

'Glenn seems a decent guy. A man who's learned from his mistakes.'

Barton paused as Leicester came over.

'Jerry McCann went on holiday this morning for two weeks. Neighbour confirmed that. He was asked to take in parcels if any came. Left a number in case of emergency but there's no answer.'

Barton finished the call with Shirley and took a deep breath. Barton recalled Timothy using his mobile after Sandy drowned. Was Jerry cunning enough to own more than one phone? He'd put money on Timothy having told Jerry what had happened. That could mean they were working as a team.

It would be handy to find out if Jerry's holiday was pre-booked, or if he was fleeing the scene of his crimes.

63

DCI BARTON

Barton could barely function by 8 p.m. He drove home with the radio volume on loud to keep him awake. The news of Sandy's demise was announced with the hourly bulletin. He staggered through his front door, wondering if he would have the energy to eat anything. His daughter steamed out of the kitchen, shot him a glare that risked freezing his blood, then spat something that started with, 'It's my life', but the latter end of the statement passed through the sound barrier and was indecipherable to mortal men.

Barton peeked around the kitchen door and found Holly frying chicken in the wok. He kissed her on the cheek.

'What was that about?'

'Are you referring to the Queen of Doom who recently vacated these parts?'

'Our daughter, yes.'

'Something to do with Kai going to the cinema with a friend and two girls.'

'Ooh, what a ratbag.' Barton grinned. 'It might be just a mates thing.'

'He was seen holding one girl's hand.'

'Maybe she had high heels and was unsteady on her feet.'

'I don't think we need the professional insight of the major crimes team to explain this.'

Holly sprinkled a variety of spices onto the meat, then continued to stir. Barton's nose flared like two windsocks. Perhaps he could eat.

'Why was she shouting at you?' he asked.

'Because I popped around Kelly and Shawn's house. I took a few loads of washing yesterday to give them a break from it. I knew I'd be a while, so I left the kids a note saying they should have a sandwich for tea. Layla was too upset to do her own, so now she feels ill, and that's my fault.'

Barton frowned. 'That doesn't make any sense.'

'I know! Apparently, I always shout at her. I don't care, and I'm mean. Her life isn't important to me, and I'll be sorry.'

'Is this curry for me?'

'You're all heart, John, but no. It was to freeze for Shawn and Kelly.'

Barton cast an eye over the sizzling pan. 'Seems a lot for two people.'

'Okay, you may have a small bowl. I did do extra.'

Barton beamed. Then he remembered the case.

'I've got disappointing news about tomorrow night's babysitting.'

'Let me guess, the investigation has cracked, and you'll need to stay late.'

'Spot on.'

'Well, I've spent twenty years dealing with an eighteen-stone toddler on my own, so two little ones shouldn't be hard.'

Barton frowned at her. 'You are mean.'

They heard a clump from upstairs, then silence.

'Aren't you worried about Layla?' he asked.

'The reason I did extra is because she'll struggle to smell this and remain in a sulk. I've won our argument without even raising my voice. She just doesn't realise it yet.'

'Sneaky and underhand. Impressive. Although wasn't she upset because you hadn't cooked for her and now you have?'

Holly gave him a sneer. 'Damn.'

'Can I have a sandwich while I wait?'

'No, you cannot. Willpower. Find some. Make us a cup of tea. I'm only doing couscous, so it won't take long.'

Luke wandered in. 'What's that yummy stink? I'm starving.'

'When were you last not hungry?' asked Barton.

His son gazed into the distance and spoke slowly. 'I am not sure.'

'I'm so hungry, I could eat a whale spread on toast,' said Barton.

Luke waggled a finger at him. 'Whales are protected. You'll have to choose something else.'

'Dolphin.'

'No, I love dolphins.'

'Which animals don't you like?'

'Hyenas. They're vicious.'

Barton smiled at Holly, who waved a wooden spoon at him in a threatening manner.

'Got any hyenas in the fridge, honey?'

'Nothing fresh. If I find an old one rattling around at the back of the freezer, I'll defrost it for you.'

'How's that, Luke?'

'Okay, but it better not be a baby hyena.'

After Luke had gone, Holly boiled the kettle because Barton hadn't risen from his seat. He rubbed his temples.

'Tough case?' she asked.

'It is. So many angles. Odd behaviour. Untrustworthy people. A fourteen-year-old involved. We've possibly made a few mistakes. I can't see the big picture yet, and I'm absolutely cream-crackered.'

'Shall I paraphrase for you?'

'I wish you wouldn't.'

'You thought you could mosey back into Major Crimes, after three years as a pencil-twiddling desk jockey doing nine-to-five, and carry on as if you'd never been away. And now you're struggling to sleep because you haven't solved your first case, despite this being your fifth day. Need I paraphrase more?'

'No, you need not.'

'Excellent. You prepare the couscous.'

'Can't we have rice?'

'No, couscous is healthier. We might as well have a bowl of curry each, and I'll cook another batch in the morning. There should be more chicken next to that frozen hyena.'

Ten minutes later, Barton and Holly were enjoying a medium-sized plate of curry in contented silence when Layla appeared.

'Any left over for poor, sad, unappreciated me?' she asked at the door.

'You might find it tastes a bit sour for you,' said Holly, 'with an evil old witch having made it.' She looked at Barton. 'Did I tell you she called me that?'

'Sorry, Mum! The Kai thing was such a shock, but I'm cool now. I've been chatting to one of the boys in my English class about an assignment we have to do, and he's kind of cute.'

'Cute like a baby or cute like a kitten?' asked Barton.

'Cute like a stud muffin.'

Barton almost spat his dinner out.

'But he's a total geek,' replied Layla. 'He's coming around now to chat about the project.'

Barton wrinkled his nose. 'What do you mean, he's coming around now? It's nearly midnight.'

'Dad, it's eight thirty.'

'He's probably a nice lad,' said Holly. 'I'll make you both a hot chocolate.'

Layla grabbed a plate and ladled a large helping of curry onto it with a lot more pieces of chicken than Barton had in his. She sat opposite him and tucked in. He was glaring enviously when the doorbell rang. Holly gestured at her and Layla's plates, with Barton's being empty and theirs still containing food.

'I'll get it, shall I? Seeing as I've done nothing all day,' said Barton, rising from the table. 'Layla, why is he geeky?'

'Oh, you know. His clothes are square. I think his parents are both accountants, and he's the captain of the school chess club.'

'Interesting,' said Barton, striding from the room with purpose.

He gave a thought to Poppy, whose life was so much more complicated than Layla's. Poppy's innocence had already gone, and it could never be restored.

Barton yanked open the front door and gawped down at a slim ginger boy with thick black glasses on. The bright eyes behind them cautiously took in the large creature in front of him.

'I'm here to help Layla with her homework, sir,' he said.

Barton opened the door wider. He stepped aside to allow the lad into the hallway, then rested his hand gently on the boy's narrow shoulders and guided him towards the kitchen. Barton's voice was cheery.

'Welcome to the family, son.'

64

THE VILLAGE KILLER

I turn off the TV and rest the remote on the arm of my chair. The house is quiet. I imagine the entire world is silent now Sandy has left it. How strange, seeing her death announced on the local news. Hearing the newsreader say, 'A woman has died today,' and they meant my Sandy. Will I ever be happy again?

Although, saying that, I don't feel that terrible. No real anger or sadness, which is a little odd. I am empty and listless, but there's also an emotion present that I never anticipated feeling, and that is relief.

Thoughts of Sandy have dominated my life for so long, I kind of lost myself as a person. The need for her to want me has been all-consuming. The pleasure of simply being around her made everything else pale into insignificance.

I knew she was leaving me behind, leaving us all behind, I suppose. The aftermath would have been terrible. The thought of her elsewhere, chatting with other people, laughing with new friends. That would have crushed me.

With her gone, I can't claim her for my own, whatever I do, but neither can anybody else. The pursuit is over. I can draw a line under it and move on. The sadness will come, I'm sure of it. A tidal wave of grief will no doubt swamp me, but at least when I'm pining for her, I know where she'll be. In the ground. Nearby.

I'll be able to visit her and chat.

The police must be confused whether her demise was a deliberate thing or just an accident, which has given me a brilliant idea. It'll be a big win for a few lucky souls, me included. A bitter blow for others, but there will be a tragic end for the one who deserves it.

65

DCI BARTON

Barton breakfasted alone the following morning and had reached his desk by seven thirty. The time to tackle Timothy was first thing. Barton had received an email regarding the search of Timothy's home, which he read twice. The next word out of his mouth was a curse.

Zelensky arrived next. Barton came out of his office. 'Have you read this report?'

'Seeing as I'm yet to turn my computer on or take my coat off, that's a negative.'

'Not only is there no trace of Poppy in his house, it's not even his house. It belongs to his sister, Rachel.'

'There were no fingerprints at all?'

'Nope. There's no way Timothy and Poppy could have wiped all of them. She can't have been there.'

Zelensky put her jacket on the back of a seat. 'How old is his sister?'

Barton smiled, but he was also surprised he hadn't made the link. He reckoned Zelensky had pointed out the person who helped set up Popsicle16.

'I don't have her age, but great spot,' he said. 'Having a word with her will be an excellent little job for you first thing.'

Hoffman and Minton were next to enter the office.

'Have you seen this morning's news?' asked Hoffman.

'No,' said Barton. 'What does it say?'

'Cambridgeshire police made an arrest last night of a twenty-six-year-old in connection with two unexplained deaths in Castor.'

'What? Who the hell told them that?'

Hoffman shrugged. 'God knows. I assume we didn't charge Timothy with those crimes after I'd gone home.'

'No. We were fine to hold him on the Poppy angle. Sounds like they have the wrong end of the stick.'

'Or someone gave them that end,' said Minton.

Barton rubbed his temples.

'Timothy's definitely involved with the DreamViews thing,' said Hoffman, 'or he'd have denied it. Just for the record, having seen him in interview yesterday, his killing Henry or Sandy would appear out of character.'

'Desperate men do desperate things,' said Minton.

Zelensky spun her seat around. 'Timothy's sister is on the PNC. Possession of class A five years ago at age eighteen. Took a simple caution for a few milligrams of cocaine. It's got to be her ID that was used as proof of age.'

'Yes, but with or without her permission?' asked Barton.

'Shall I get her now?' asked Zelensky.

'No, let's talk to Timothy first. This gives me more leverage. Minton, you and I will grill him at nine. I ruminated over everything last night.'

'Sounds painful,' she said.

'It was productive. I don't believe Timothy understands how much trouble he's in. The sentencing guidelines for his offence would scare the most hardened of felons.'

'Did they find his laptop?'

'No, which is annoying. The sister had one, but she wasn't under suspicion last night, so we couldn't take it. They described his room as bare, which fits with him having no money after his crypto failings.'

'How did she react when the police arrived?' asked Hoffman.

'The report said she was annoyed with her brother, but not overly so, almost like it wasn't a huge surprise.'

'Maybe she thought we were only interested in his dodgy crypto dealings,' said Minton.

'Or perhaps she's well aware he's twisted,' said Hoffman.

'Poppy's prints weren't present,' said Zelensky.

Minton frowned. 'Oh. Then where the blazes has she been?'

Nobody had an answer to that.

At nine o'clock, Minton cautioned Timothy Steele, who trembled next to the duty solicitor. Timothy didn't comment throughout, nor did he make eye contact with the two on the other side of the table. Barton cleared his throat.

'I'm not going to ask you any questions straight away, Timothy. I'm going to explain the charges against you. The production of indecent images is an offence that is triable either in the magistrates' court or more often in Crown court. The sentencing range upon conviction is from a community order to nine years in custody.'

Timothy flinched but stayed quiet.

'The higher end of the band is obviously for the more serious offences. Those that involve penetrative sexual activity and children.'

Timothy's head lifted. He glanced at Barton. His mouth had formed a sad clown's smile. Tears poured from his bloodshot eyes.

'Other aggravating factors would be if a substantial number of photographs were produced, and if those images had been placed where there was the potential for a high volume of viewers. Also, any collection that includes moving images is more serious. Judges would frown upon a straightforward abuse of trust where the child depicted knew the offender, and it is worse if there was a commercial motivation. Finally, if there had been a blatant attempt to dispose of or conceal the evidence, it would also be looked upon more seriously. Is all that clear?'

Timothy merely blinked in response. Barton shifted his gaze to the solicitor, who shrugged in reply.

'Before we move on,' said Barton, 'I need to explain that your sister will be brought into this investigation. We believe her identification was used to open the DreamViews account.'

Timothy's head jerked back. He gasped a word. It might have been a no.

'Could you repeat that, please?' asked Barton.

Timothy's eyes scrunched up. His face was a mask of pain. He appeared to struggle to open his eyes as his head rotated towards his solicitor, who spoke loudly.

'Timothy, you don't have to say anything at this point. I would recommend keeping quiet.'

Timothy shook his head. 'Rachel is innocent.' He swivelled back to face Barton. 'She didn't know.'

'I'd like to believe that, Timothy, but you need to talk to me. Your solicitor is giving you his best advice, but the evidence we have is compelling. I'll go through it with you now, but these are serious crimes. If you hope for leniency, plead guilty at the first opportunity, and tell us everything. It may lessen your sentence.'

'I think we'd like to hear the evidence,' said the solicitor.

'No,' said Timothy firmly. 'I did it.'

66

DCI BARTON

The solicitor reached over and whispered into Timothy's ear. Timothy dismissively waved a hand in his face, but he turned to Barton.

'What happens if I say nothing, admit to nothing?'

'The case goes to trial. That will mean putting a fourteen-year-old girl in the witness stand.'

'They'll be able to do it by video link,' interjected the solicitor.

'Perhaps, but she'll still have to give evidence. Relive what happened. It'll be a traumatising experience.'

Timothy shook his head. 'Not for her. It was her idea. The court will see that.'

The solicitor again attempted to get Timothy to take advice away from the room, but Timothy's jaw had set.

'Poppy's not a child. She's a controlling woman.'

Barton pressed his advantage.

'You also run the risk of her turning up in the courtroom in her school uniform, hair in pigtails, placing the blame firmly on you, and possibly even saying you assaulted her.'

'I never touched her.'

'Judges and juries look harshly upon defendants who deny the seemingly obvious, especially as you've now admitted to your involvement with DreamViews.'

Timothy's pained features slackened. He took a couple of deep breaths.

'That's true. I need to explain, or I'll come across as a paedophile.'

'Perhaps if you start from the beginning.'

Timothy closed his eyes, then began to speak.

'I love working for the Favershams. Charles is grumpy, but he pays well and promptly, at least he did until recently. Sandy was a joy, though. She was incredible. I'd never met anyone as lovely as her before, not in real life. And she was always happy to chat. We'd sometimes talk for half an hour. Time flew by.'

A hint of a smile flashed onto Timothy's face, then vanished as rapidly as it had appeared.

'Things changed over the last year. Charles and Sandy weren't close, but they were civil to each other, but recently their arguments had become more public. I lost respect for him. We heard loads of shouting. It all coincided with Audrey coming around more. I'd seen her a few times over the years, but we'd rarely spoken. She started to visit a lot, especially when Charles was off on business, which he seemed to be much more lately. I'd say having time away helps him because he returns less angry.'

Barton sensed Minton was about to ask a question. He made a discreet cutting motion with his hand, and she closed her mouth. Timothy shut his eyes and continued.

'At the start of the summer, Audrey brought her daughter over to use the pool for the day. They'd sunbathe if it was warm enough and eat out there. Relax. Poppy liked to swim. They used those little disposable barbecues. Under an umbrella if it was raining. I tended to keep away because Sandy enjoyed being topless, but as the weeks passed, Poppy would hunt me down in other parts of the garden. She would even follow me through the fence to Henry's place.'

Timothy's eyes opened.

'Henry was a nice man. Anyway, Poppy and I got to chatting. She's extremely attractive and flirty with it. She asked me if I had a girlfriend. When I said no, she offered to be mine. I laughed because she was too young, but Poppy reckoned sixteen was fine.'

Timothy's eyes drilled into the faces of all those present, one by one.

'She said it was the age of consent. Why would I doubt her? After that, she often visited with full make-up on. Sandy and Audrey would leave her while they went out. Things got kind of crazy. She looked miles older than sixteen, dressed in what I can only assume were her mum's clothes. I'll admit, I did like talking to her. I pretty much told her about my whole life. She had this way of getting me to tell her everything. I explained how I lost all my money on cryptocurrencies, fell behind on my rent, and had to move into my sister's place.'

Timothy tried to smile at Barton.

'Rachel's been so kind to me, even though we've never been close. I had nowhere else to go. Around that time, Poppy sometimes came over to Paddock Green without her mum. I assumed Sandy didn't mind. She was nice like that. I think Poppy even climbed over the back fence to chat to me when nobody was there.'

Barton watched Timothy's Adam's apple bounce up and down.

'Poppy sunbathed topless, too. Honestly, she said she was sixteen. Then she mentioned she'd heard about this moneymaking idea. Me and her, we could get rich. Poppy toyed with me, kept banging on about it, but didn't give me any details. Finally, she told me about DreamViews. I'd seen similar sites on the Internet. Who hasn't?'

Timothy's eyes narrowed slightly, and Barton suspected he was going to lie for the first time.

'I confirmed with her she was sixteen. Poppy said nearly seventeen and I could hardly ask her mum to verify that. Poppy described how much money you could make. I asked how she knew. She told me a friend did it. I said no to start with, but she wore me down, and I desperately needed cash. We tried to open an account in my name, but there was an issue with me posting pictures of women, so Poppy suggested we use my sister's details. I'm ashamed to say we did it behind Rachel's back.'

Timothy shifted in his seat. He bit his lip.

'That's it. We took photographs. A few videos. Poppy did all the admin stuff. She understood how it all worked.'

Barton waited for him to continue, but it appeared he was finished. Barton decided he believed most of what he'd heard, but Timothy had stopped too soon. What about the period when Poppy was nowhere to be seen?

'Do you watch the news?' asked Barton.

'Nope.'

'Were you aware of the country's search for a missing fourteen-year-old?'

'No, I'm too busy trying to rebuild my savings.'

Barton opened his palms.

'Let me confirm a few things. You said Poppy photographed herself, but you also took some pictures.'

Timothy licked his lips, then nodded.

'We need your laptop, Timothy. Where is it?'

Timothy stared at him. His face flushed bright red. 'Why, if I've confessed to everything?'

'We still need to confirm all you've said.'

Barton guessed the laptop would be where Poppy had been hiding out.

'I don't want you to look at my computer.'

Barton had noticed Timothy's posture stiffen. He might never give up the location. So where would a man with no money hide a girl for over a week?

It was then that the Barton magic returned.

67

DCI BARTON

A bead of sweat trickled down the side of Timothy's head.

'Where did Poppy go when she ran away?' asked Barton.

'I don't know.'

Barton nodded approvingly at him.

'You've done well, Timothy. I understand this can't be easy for you, but half a confession doesn't count. I think your laptop will be at the large house next door to Paddock Green. The Bonaccorso property.'

Timothy's eyes scrunched up. He kept quiet. Barton leaned forward.

'That's why she was able to stay for so long without anyone finding her. He's out of the country. You still did work for him, so you probably had a key.'

'No, I only had access to the outbuildings.' Timothy let out a deep breath. 'Poppy took the key from Sandy's house. She'd overheard Sandy telling Audrey she occasionally popped round to water the houseplants and take in any deliveries.'

'And that's where you created the content for Poppy's webpage, which is Popsicle16.'

'Yes.'

'So, in conclusion, you're saying this was all Poppy's idea, and she fooled you into believing she was sixteen, otherwise you wouldn't have done it.'

Timothy's hand extended as if to seize the lifeline Barton offered him. 'Exactly! Even her username had sixteen in it.'

'I hate to be the bearer of bad news, but a defence of "the four-teen-year-old made me do it" isn't going to get you very far.'

Timothy snatched his hand back as if scalded. Barton leaned forward.

'Sixteen is the age of consent in the UK. Children under that age can't legally engage in sexual activities, even if they give permission.'

'We didn't have sex.'

'Is there anything else untoward on your laptop?'

Timothy bared his teeth. A smile or a grimace? It was hard to tell.

'Nothing illegal,' he whispered.

Barton doubted that, but they'd soon find out. Timothy looked away as Barton sized him up. It was a common ploy amongst almost all sex offenders. They watered down their involvement, their responsibility, and their culpability, but regardless the judge would view him as a man, and Poppy as a child, then sentence him accordingly.

'What will happen to me?' whispered Timothy.

'We have people to speak to this morning, and we'll continue our enquiries, but I think you'll be in front of the magistrates later today. They'll decide the allocation of the case, which means they could handle it themselves or pass it on to Crown court, and they'll determine whether to grant bail.'

'I don't understand.'

'They could release you until sentencing or remand you into custody.'

Timothy swallowed deeply. 'You mean I could go straight to prison?'

'That's a possibility.'

'What about my work? People need me.'

'You can deal with that if and when the time comes. Trust in our legal system. It's the fairest in the world.'

Only because most of the competition wasn't up to much, but Barton smiled reassuringly.

'I have a few more questions around the sad demise of Sandy and Henry. You found both of them.'

'That's right.'

'I assume you're responsible for cleaning both pools?'

'I am.'

'Is it possible you turned on the heat pump for the pool?'

'No way. Jerry was crystal clear. It was not safe until an electrician checked it.'

'He actually said that to you.'

'Yes, I remember now. He had a holiday planned, so he told me twice. Charles was there for one of those times. Jerry even put a white sticker on it, saying not to turn it on.'

Barton hadn't seen or heard anything about a sticker. He would get CSI to look for it. While he had chance, he wanted to revisit the marks on Henry.

'We suspect Henry had an injury to his head, which may have caused his death.'

'Are you saying someone hit him?'

'Not necessarily, but there were scratches on his crown.'

Both of Timothy's hands moved slowly to his mouth. 'I told you that might have been me.'

'Maybe that's just a clever story when actually you wanted him dead.'

Timothy swallowed. 'Honestly. When I first saw him he was face down.'

'For marks to be made, it must have been a violent gesture.'

'I panicked.'

'He could have been alive. Perhaps even just holding his breath, and you knocked him out.'

'No, I was trying to help.'

'Timothy, I need you to explain properly, please.'

'When I saw him floating, he was near the edge of the pool. I almost jumped in, but I wouldn't have been able to push him out on my own, so I used the pole and the net.'

Barton folded his arms. 'You hooked him to the side?'

'I just guided him towards me, then hauled him onto the grass.'

Again, Barton believed him, but, surely, two drownings so close together were too much of a coincidence. He decided it didn't matter at that moment. He nodded at Minton to tie up the interview and have Timothy returned to the custody unit.

Barton knew the reasons for remanding an offender until sentencing like the back of his hand, and later that day, with the weight of evidence against him, the magistrates would send Timothy to a cell at HMP Peterborough.

68

DCI BARTON

Barton returned to the office and organised an immediate meeting. When everyone was present, he told them about Timothy's confession. Barton heard a few cheers, but he shook his head.

'I still don't like this. Next step is to bring Timothy's sister to the station. We need a full statement from her. Has Mortis rung in?'

'Yes,' said Leicester. 'The PM results were inconclusive. Sandy was a healthy woman. She had no signs of heart weakness, but there were no electrical burns either. Although he did mention that a lack of them wasn't unusual in these circumstances. Water had filled her lungs. Electrocution from the mains could have caused muscle paralysis. If so, she'd have sunk in silence and drowned in short order.'

Barton nodded. That did sound like something Mortis would say.

'Okay, it's ten thirty. Zelensky, you and I will talk to Audrey's ex-husband at eleven, assuming he comes in. I thought our discussion with Poppy would be informal, but there's no getting around talking to her under caution now. Let's have her in this afternoon.

Arrange it with Social Services. Make sure someone from their team is here to give support and sit in if Poppy wants them to. Normally, we'd have Audrey in with her, but that's not appropriate in this instance.'

'It sounds like she has the maturity to understand what's going on,' said Zelensky.

'Yes, so the solicitor can advise her, even if it's just to say nothing. I doubt the CPS will press charges because the risk of trauma is too great. There's little to be gained from a conviction against her.'

Zelensky frowned.

'If Poppy has done what Timothy has suggested, she's almost as guilty as he is, whatever her age, so I'll be surprised if she backs up Timothy's version.'

The telephone rang next to her. She picked it up.

'Glenn's here,' she said after finishing the call.

Ten minutes later, Zelensky and Barton were waiting in interview room one for Poppy's father to be brought in. Barton enjoyed working with Zelensky. Her 'no bullshit' attitude reminded him of Zander's wife, DS Kelly Strange.

Zelensky was also excellent at seeing through anyone's façade. Glenn might have an axe to grind, so Barton wanted a good read of him.

When he arrived, Barton stood and shook his hand. Glenn had a cool, relaxed grip, and had dressed smartly in a suit and shiny shoes. He had receding hair, but he was still a striking man. A genuine smile revealed bright white teeth.

'Thanks for coming in,' said Zelensky. 'Sorry about the formal setting, but it's the only room free.'

'No problem. I would have rung, but I wanted to do this face to face. Will you video the conversation?'

Zelensky raised an eyebrow, but Glenn chuckled.

'No, I'm not here to confess to anything. Audrey has a way of twisting things to her own advantage, so I want a record taken. I've been considering approaching the courts about Poppy moving in with me permanently.'

'I take it Audrey wouldn't be keen on that idea,' said Barton.

'They're not getting on great, so there's hope, but I wanted to see what my chances are before I mentioned it. Poppy hates to go home when she's been at my place. She says she feels like a child with me, whereas her mum's place is full of responsibility.'

'Audrey said Poppy preferred to do her own washing and cooking.'

'Yeah, because her mother is crap at it. That's Audrey's way. If you wanted her to do something, and she didn't fancy it, she'd do a shit job to make sure you never asked again. Don't get me wrong, Poppy can be a handful, but she is only fourteen. It's just she appears to be getting worse these last few months. Even at mine, she sits in her room, or is vague and distracted at the dinner table.'

Zelensky shared a glance with Barton.

'Glenn, we think we know why that might be. We've got a social worker coming in this afternoon. The easiest thing would be for you, her and Audrey to sit down together and discuss the situation.'

'That sounds serious.'

'It's not great news, but hopefully it's been nipped in the bud.'

'Right. What else do you want to ask me?'

'We just need to get the background on Poppy and Audrey. Tell me about them. What are they like? Are there any problems?'

Glenn smiled.

'Well, Poppy's always been pretty, and she's known it. She was a serious child and our divorce didn't help. Poppy had a phone from an early age because she brought it to mine sometimes. I think she got exposed to TikTok and Instagram too soon. She had a Facebook account way before she was thirteen, and she rarely watched TV. Instead, she worshipped YouTube.'

Barton's own kids had spent years mesmerised by YouTube. 'Has she been involved in any trouble?'

'Nothing serious. A shopkeeper caught her stealing, but the police were never called, just her mum.'

'What about Audrey?'

'She and I met at school. We got married too young. I loved her so much at first. She was a right cracker. Lots of fun, perhaps too much fun, but she expected happiness to be handed to her on a plate. I lost a job through going in drunk and struggled to get another one. Then she fell pregnant and everything was really tough for a while. Audrey became bitter. Her life wasn't supposed to be that way. We had to live in temporary accommodation. With nothing to do, my boozing continued, then I moved away.'

'You left them in a hostel?'

'Yeah, we were three in a room with no cash. It was as depressing as hell. I got offered a job by a mate in Cornwall, and I went for it. It was a chance for me to get out of a rut. I'm not proud of that, but I said I'd send money. Audrey was furious with me for abandoning them.'

'Why couldn't they go with you?'

'I only had a room in a guest house with a load of other blokes. Audrey said I'd burned my bridges. Told the social I was a violent drunk. I returned six months later but Audrey had a council flat by then. She made it extremely difficult for me to get access to Poppy. That's why I came in to see you today. I don't want to lose my daughter again.'

'What do you do for work?'

'Fire and burglar alarm fitter. I can do windows, too. The recession was a crap time because people were cutting back on nonessential purchases but I run my own firm doing both now. My second wife does the admin. The business is going great guns with all this inflation. I probably don't need to tell you guys there's more stealing happening with the cost-of-living crisis.'

'No, you do not,' said Barton. 'You must know her brother, Frannie.'

'I only met him a few times, but yeah, nice guy. Kind of weird, but strangely confident too at times. Almost as though the rules are for people who need them, not for people like him.'

'While the rest of us know that the rules are there for a reason.'

'Yes, but in a way, I'm envious of him.'

'Why?'

'He lives honestly, guiltlessly, and enthusiastically. There's no malice in him.'

Barton wasn't sure whether to mention Frannie's offending.

Glenn smiled. 'Anyway, Audrey is really bright, too. She puts on the dumb act, but her exam results back then were brilliant, considering how little studying she did. I think she achieved top marks in English, but she always wanted the easy route to success, and I doubt that will ever change. I remember her in the school play. Some weird arty thing, yet she was awesome. I thought she had a future on the stage but she was always worried about money, back then and later, which I suppose is understandable. That's probably why she won't want me having Poppy. I pay her a decent amount of maintenance.'

'You must have met Sandy at school as well.'

'Yeah, of course. Now, she was a cracker. They were close, but Sandy got everything Audrey wanted. A life of leisure, with a rich guy, in a fabulous house. I can't believe she's gone. It's a damn shame. Audrey will be devastated.'

Barton had suspected Audrey wasn't telling the truth about

Sandy being fairly plain as a child. He'd prepared his last question, which he knew might be a delicate one.

'Do you reckon she could be so jealous she'd wish Sandy harm?'

Glenn barked out a laugh. 'Hell, no. Audrey wanted to *be* Sandy. If that wasn't possible, life by her side was the next best thing.'

69

DCI BARTON

Barton finished the meeting and took Hoffman to the interview room to prepare. He'd brought Hoffman because Barton was hoping, as the youngest of his team, he might connect with Poppy. There was a part of Barton that felt like a concerned father, but the law had been broken. Poppy's story was yet another example of victim and villain in a society that was getting ever more complex.

When Poppy arrived, she was given the option of speaking to her mother, and asked whether she wanted a social worker in the room when she spoke to Barton. Poppy chose not to speak with her mum, but she took the social worker, a Miss Akosua Mensah, in for her chat with the duty solicitor. Barton smiled when he heard who the council had sent. Akosua had been doing the job for a long time.

'I bet Poppy clams up,' said Hoffman after Zelensky came in to give them an update.

'Maybe. You'll note she didn't want to talk to her mother,' replied Barton.

'Yeah?'

'I reckon she's going to tell us everything.'

Hoffman's collar seemed tight for a moment at the thought of the revelations. Poppy, Akosua and the solicitor came in as they were talking so Zelensky left. Hoffman took care of the caution, while Barton took stock of Poppy. Considering she presumably hadn't been expecting to leave the house, she appeared highly groomed.

Akosua gave Barton a tight-lipped look that mirrored how he felt.

'Afternoon, Poppy,' said Barton. 'It's nice to see you again. We have serious matters to discuss today. Accusations have been made and I'd like to hear your side of the story. We also need to caution you.'

Expressionless after Hoffman cautioned her, Poppy stared from him to Barton. Her eyes narrowed.

'What will happen to Timothy?' she asked.

'I think it's more important to talk about you,' replied Barton.

'Will he go to jail?'

'Prison is one option the judge has at his or her disposal.'

'Has he admitted what he's been doing?'

Barton paused for a few seconds. He hadn't been expecting such a cool display, but he thought of Audrey. What would fourteen years of being brought up by that woman have done to an intelligent girl?

'Yes, he has.'

'Prison wouldn't be fair to Timothy. He's a nice person.'

'The big issue here, Poppy, is your age. Timothy is twenty-six. What he did would be inappropriate even if it weren't illegal, which it is.'

'Ah, I get what you're saying. You assumed I had sex with him, didn't ya?'

'Did you?'

She flicked her hair.

'Don't be daft. You only have to look at my mum to learn not to give it away, especially to a penniless loser.'

'I thought you liked him?'

'I did, still do. None of this was his fault.'

'Are you saying DreamViews was all your idea?'

'I'm not saying anything at the moment. My lawyer said the chance of me being prosecuted is slim. You'd end up with a load of copycat fourteen-year-olds trying the same thing after the newspapers reported it.'

Barton shifted his gaze to the solicitor, who was intently admiring her watch. Poppy cleared her throat and smirked.

'I'll have a think about what I tell you about Timothy. Do you want to hear how he stuck a gun in my face and forced me?'

Barton exhaled deeply.

'Poppy. This is serious. We need everyone to be upfront with us, so we can get you the necessary help. Your social worker and I, believe it or not, both want the best for you.'

'You're dying to find out how I knew what to do, aren't ya?'

'You're right, we are.'

'You know we used DreamViews and I bet you know Sandy did as well. My mum helped her. She emailed some of the men. Chatted to others. I'd heard about OnlyFans at school. One of my friends reckoned her sister does stuff on there and makes big bucks.'

Poppy coughed, then leaned back and stared at Akosua.

'My mum's a pisshead. We share the PC at home after I broke mine. I knew she was up to something funny because she didn't use it much before. She was actually drinking less during the day, but drank faster later on, so she'd fall asleep in her chair. The screen would still be on with her logged into DreamViews. The first time I saw it, I'd come down to get a bottle of cold water and spotted a photograph of Aunty Sandy on the screen in just a pair of sunglasses.'

'Aunty?'

Poppy stared back at Barton.

'My mum liked me to call her Aunty. I stopped calling her that after seeing so many naked pictures of her. I'm pretty sharp. It didn't take long to work out what was going on.'

She giggled, then scowled.

'There was a lot of creepy shit, though. I scrolled through loads of odd messages. Sandy used to dress up for all these blokes. It opened my eyes, reading about the things they wanted. I kept thinking, are men really this stupid? Then I noticed how much money they were paying for each text message, and there were hundreds of them, or for the same denim dungaree picture another bloke had just paid for. A lot of it seemed sad. Like they were lonely or depressed or something and didn't worry about the cost. It'd have been cheaper to go to church, or whatever normal old people do to pass the time.'

Barton gave Poppy a reassuring smile. Her speech was less stilted and practised as she told the truth. She sounded more like a teenager.

''So, you're saying there was never any physical relationship between you and Timothy. For want of a better phrase, no touching.'

'God, no. I've had time to think about what I did, and I get it now. There'll be no more of that from me. I need to focus on school. Can I keep the cash I made so far?'

'I'm not sure, Poppy, but I wouldn't have thought so.'

'You know, I wasn't doing it long, but I could see it was dark on there. These guys had money, which they were willing to spend, but it felt as if you were being watched. Chats started light-hearted, but they soon changed. It's enough to put you off men altogether.'

'I suppose that's because it's not right, Poppy, someone your age talking to adult males online. That's why there are rules about these things.'

'I understand, which is why I don't want to live at my mum's for a bit.'

Barton noticed Poppy's frame tense. She turned back to the social worker.

'I can't go back. When I'm at home, DreamViews is all I can think about. The computer kind of sits there. Knowing what my mum was up to on it. Knowing what I did on it. I just want to feel like a kid again. That's easy at my dad's house.'

Barton noticed Poppy's speech had returned to being stilted and he was again surprised by her manipulation. It was as if she'd considered what she wanted from the situation. Maybe that was part of the motivation for her foray on DreamViews in the first place. This was all about control. If your mother was erratic, or your home chaotic, then taking over other aspects of your life, money included, was a way of handling things. A teenager, no matter how precocious, wouldn't understand the consequences.

'Can you confirm the address you stayed at when you disappeared?' said Hoffman. 'We'd like you to describe what happened there.'

'Nice tattoos,' she said to Hoffman with a grin. 'Maybe I'll take the photos of you next.'

'That's enough, Poppy,' said Barton. 'There's nothing amusing about this. Lives have been lost. Others are about to be ruined.'

Akosua glanced across at Poppy. 'Talk to the inspector. We need to get to the bottom of all this.'

'Okay, okay. I was at the Bonaccorso place but it was my idea to stay there. I knew the house was empty from overhearing my mum and Sandy talking. I could climb over the fence. The Italian guy's place had no security cameras or anything. Sandy never came over while I stayed there. She probably thought she'd misplaced the key. I just chilled and set up my DreamViews page. Took some shots. Chatted to some mates.'

'On Timothy's laptop?' said Hoffman.

'Yeah, I bought a second-hand android phone from a shady shop in town to use instead of my own. Data's dead cheap if you bulk buy. I put it on an unregistered sim card and used a hotspot. Easy.'

'Did Timothy help you with that?'

'Nope. He worked so many hours, he seemed to struggle with keeping in touch, never mind much else. He brought food over and the odd takeaway.'

'Half the country was searching for you. The cost to the public was phenomenal with everyone being concerned for your safety. There are a lot of charges that could be put to you.'

Poppy looked from under her brow at Barton, then at Akosua, then smiled at Barton. 'Yeah, yeah. I'm so sorry. My head was gone. You know, mental health. I wasn't thinking straight because of being neglected. Honestly, I won't do it again. I promise.'

Barton barely managed to stop himself from rolling his eyes.

'Finally, how about your uncle Frannie? Do you see him much?'

Poppy smiled. 'Frannie's cool. A little crazy, well, nuts actually. He's operating on a higher plane, but not like Einstein, more like Jesus, but without the religious edge.'

Barton tried to get his head around what she'd said. Poppy chuckled.

'I'm saying he wants to be everyone's friend. He doesn't care about the rules. I understand he shouldn't be bothering kids, but he's sweet. There's no bad in him.'

'Is he often at yours?'

'Nah. He comes over when I'm at school. Mum washes his clothes, sends him off with a box of food for the week. I reckon he spends all his time reading. He goes to the libraries, then lies in his room. He likes cowboy books. That's what Mum says. It's a shame about the farm he was on. This world's too fucked up for someone like him.'

Barton didn't challenge the foul language because maybe she was right. Again, he could see the lines of culpability and accountability had been blurred in this case like no other.

'There will be conditions on your release, Poppy. You mustn't visit Castor for any reason or have contact, via any method, with Timothy Steele.'

'I'm not visiting him in jail. Chuh! It's funny if you think about it. Timothy and Frannie will end up in the same prison. Perhaps they'll be cell mates. They'd get on, actually. They're both a bit special.'

Barton hadn't considered that. He supposed it didn't matter, but it showed again that Poppy's mind was sharp. Her eyes narrowed.

'Talking of conditions. Surely, there's no way you're making me go back to Mum's. Maybe it was her who forced me at gunpoint.'

Barton glanced over at Akosua.

'We'll talk to both of your parents now and reach an agreement,' she said. 'Considering you already stay at your father's regularly, moving there for a while might be the smart call.'

Poppy smiled. Barton knew Audrey wouldn't agree with that. In fact, she'd be furious.

70

DCI BARTON

Barton pushed his front door open at just after 10 p.m. He blew out a breath and staggered into the kitchen. The lights were off, and the only sound was a contented hum from the refrigerator. Barton opened the fridge and grabbed a Heineken from inside. He stared at the can for a moment, then returned it.

There was a plastic bottle of San Pellegrino, which he drank a huge glug from instead. He chuckled. It was supposed to be sparkling and wasn't, so Holly had obviously refilled the bottle and put it back in the fridge. He could just about hear the TV, so he wandered through to the lounge.

Holly was sitting in the dark watching a period drama. The weaselly behaviour of the courtiers and royals in Tudor England endlessly fascinated her. He slumped next to his wife and stared at her face, which was covered with a peeling mask. He sang out of tune from *The Phantom of the Opera*.

"'Those who have seen your chops, draw back in fear.'"

Holly picked up the remote and paused the programme. Her voice was sweeter and higher.

'Those who have got some cheek, get beaten here.'

She snuggled into him. 'Long week?'

'The longest. How was babysitting?'

'Kelly rang at midday and asked if we'd do tomorrow instead. They fancied the cinema but couldn't find seats for the film they wanted tonight. She said to be there at five. I assume you have to go into work.'

'Actually, no. We charged the lad who'd helped a young girl set up an adult web page and put him in front of the beaks early this afternoon. They referred it to Crown court due to the complex nature of the case and his likely sentence, which means I'm free.'

'You're hot when you talk cop. If I hadn't had a relaxing bath with candles and washed my hair, it'd be a night in a million for you.'

'Rain check?'

'Deal. Why are they called beaks again?'

'To quote the Artful Dodger, "A beak's a magistrate, where have you been all your life?". I think it was to do with the time of the bubonic plague. Judges visited prisons wearing primitive gas masks, stuffed with herbs or spices thought to ward off the plague, so because it looked like a beak, it was referred to as going before the beak.'

'I've never found you more attractive.'

'Any food for the hot copper?'

'It's late and not the best time for a Barton banquet.'

'Boo.'

'So, will this lad receive a prison sentence?'

'Yeah, I reckon so. He'll need a probation report. There's a child involved, so until they know the full details and his part in them, it's safer to remand him in jail until sentencing. I suppose he has the chance it will be suspended.'

'That doesn't seem right after exploiting a schoolgirl.'

Barton didn't want to dive into the nitty-gritty, so he simply smiled. 'The man who was talking to kids outside libraries was remanded, too, but I believe he'll get a community order.'

'That's it?'

'Yep. In his defence, Your Honour, he's vulnerable, too. He said nothing too untoward. I suspect he didn't buy vapes for them, either. They probably lied because they were underage and shouldn't have had them. Frannie is what they now call neurodivergent. It is likely that he should never have been in prison.'

'What will happen to him?'

'In an ideal world, they'd allocate him a bed in a mental health hospital, but they're gold dust and reserved for the most ill people. I expect Frannie will be released with limited support. He'll commit the same offence again and again, which would lead to longer custodial sentences. Eventually, he'll lose his accommodation and end up homeless.'

Holly reached over and squeezed his hand. 'Can he come here for Christmas?'

Barton laughed. 'Everyone else appears to be, so why not? Then Layla really would have something to complain about, as opposed to her first world problems.'

'Is the girl who went missing okay?'

'It's hard to say. Most of us consider children to be innocent, but there are a few bad eggs. Not many are rotten to the core, and I don't think Poppy is, but she's certainly not blameless. She's grown up too quick, which her mother has to take some of the responsibility for, but it's hardened Poppy. She'll be offered more help than Frannie because she's a child, but teenagers don't always know what's best for them.'

Holly stood.

'Come on, let's go to bed. Maybe you do deserve a special cuddle. In fact, you could make love to me all night long. We have no need to get up for anything tomorrow. I'll try to keep it down, so we don't emotionally damage the children. Give me a few minutes to remove this face mask and slip into a satin nightdress. I'll be the one with the skin of a thirty-year-old if you struggle to recognise me.'

They were chuckling as they climbed the stairs, both knowing Barton would be asleep long before she returned from the bathroom.

71

DCI BARTON

Barton and Holly arrived at Zander's house at five to five the next evening and pressed the doorbell. Zander opened the door with a huge smile.

'Wow, Shawn,' said Holly, giving him a hug. 'You look well rested. Now, take me to those boys!'

Kelly appeared behind Zander. 'Come on through, Holly. We've had a busy day, so you shouldn't have too much bother with them.'

Barton shook hands with Zander to a backdrop of shrieks and screams and shouts of 'Aunty Holly' from the lounge.

'They sound exhausted,' said Barton.

Zander beamed. 'That's more energy being used up. It's fantastic news for you. They'll be the last hoorahs before they crash out. We took them to Safari Play today. It's probably closed for the foreseeable while they sweep up the plastic rubble my hooligans left behind. How's work been?'

'No police talk 'til tomorrow. Enjoy your final few hours of relaxation. What are you going to see?'

'Kelly's changed her mind again. She's decided she wants to go to The Bombay Brasserie in town. We went there on one of our first dates and it's been years since I've been for a quality curry. Remember that vindaloo we had there once? You left the premises looking like you'd spent two hours fully clothed in a sauna. You drank about five lagers to wash it down.'

Zander frowned at Barton's conspiratorial grin. Barton licked his lips and leaned into him.

'Take me for the curry. Let's sneak out of here now. I've known you longer than Kelly.'

'That's not a tempting proposition for what I've got planned for later.'

Barton recoiled. 'Yeah, I don't want any of that action. Any beers in for the babysitters?'

'Of course, and I bought the extended version of *Gladiator* too. Perhaps Holly can watch it while you snooze.'

'Very funny. I slept like a bambino last night, so I'm refreshed. We even enjoyed a bit of *l'amour* this morning ourselves.'

'Good to hear. We'd better get off before the kids realise what's happening.'

Half an hour later, after Holly had shouted at Kelly to just leave, the Bartons sat side by side on the sofa, watching BabyTV, each with a zonked-out child on their lap. The boys had lasted five more minutes after their parents had left. They'd taken some milk and were out for the count.

Holly stroked the top of Zane's head, then beamed over at Barton. He reciprocated with Zack. Moments like this were the reward for working in Major Crimes. You were reminded constantly of what was important. Of how fortunate you were. Barton was grateful for every single thing he had.

72

DCI BARTON

The next morning, Zander picked up his temporary new boss on the way to work in his car. He pulled away from Barton's property and glanced over.

'Tell me everything that's happened,' he said.

'It was an average week. Solved all your cases. Sorted out your team. Got your filing current. Then I cleaned the windows, polished a few desks, and did a bit of hoovering with the spare time I had.'

'Very amusing. I checked online and saw the magistrates remanded Timothy Steele. Was he an absolute wrong'un?'

Barton puffed out his cheeks. 'I suppose I should start at the beginning.'

The inspectors had reached the station, walked upstairs, made a coffee, and spent thirty minutes in Barton's office by the time he finished the update.

'Jeez, I wasn't expecting you to say all that. Do you believe that's the end of it? I can detect a few loose ends.'

'Nice to hear you think the same. It is the end of it for me, though, because it's over to you. I need to get on with the DCI tasks now you've returned. I'm waiting for a few emails to tie up my involvement in Castor. If you're free at lunch, I'll drive you down and show you around. It's been raining, so bring your wellies.'

'I haven't got any.'

'I brought a spare pair. Do you reckon you'll be able to walk, or should I carry you?'

'Just the lift there should be fine. I'll see if my team remember who I am in the meantime.'

Barton logged on to his PC and went straight to his emails. One was from a CSI called Paul, who said they were finishing up in Castor and that the last of the photographs would be on the file shortly. He suggested someone from Major Crimes should have another look at the rear of the properties. Barton messaged Paul that he'd meet him at the house at midday.

Robert had also sent an email with two attachments. One was a story from the previous week's *Investor+* magazine. It seemed Robert had sold one of his companies and would soon be considerably richer. The second, lengthier article concerned the charitable trust Henry had set up to help those who were struggling in life. Robert hoped for a quick call when Barton had a minute.

Barton rang him and Robert picked up on the third ring.

'Morning, Robert. Thanks for those articles. Are you covering your bottom?'

'Yes, I thought if you saw the cash heading my way from this deal, you'd be doubly reassured I hadn't knocked Henry off for financial gain.'

'I appreciate the info, but I was already above eighty per cent sure of your innocence.'

'You're too kind.'

'How does it feel to be that wealthy? I suppose money stops being an issue and you can do whatever you like. Must be nice.'

Robert exhaled deeply. 'True. Saying otherwise would be a lie, but this entire episode with Henry has made me think long and hard about my life. Henry wanted a protégé, and that's what he got. My life is becoming his. I have nobody special to enjoy experiences with. My son is great, but I don't see him often because he wants to be with his friends. I pretended I didn't care too much, but what's the point if you can't share good times with the people you love? Remember that Harry Chapin song?'

'"Cats in the Cradle"?'

'Yeah. I'm worried I'm going to grow up just like Henry.'

Barton absorbed that powerful statement. 'Seems to me you noticed just in time.'

'Thank you, John. For everything. You're a wise man. I wanted you to ring so I could tell you how much I appreciate how you've dealt with this case. I'm planning to do plenty of good with Henry's money. Spread it around. It's better if his memory isn't tarnished in any way. If you ever need something, anything that's in my power to help with, then ring me.'

Barton was tempted to make a joke about sending him a Porsche brochure, but it was a nice moment, and he didn't want to tarnish that, either.

Zelensky poked her head around the corner of his door after he'd ended the call.

'We've got hold of Jerry. He's on holiday somewhere weird. Kanegorms.'

'That's probably the Cairngorms, in Scotland.'

'He insisted everyone knew about the pump. His exact words were, "I'm not a madman. With what happened last time, I told Timothy, and especially Charles, not to use it". Jerry also reckoned he put a warning sticker over the on-off switch.'

'Timothy said the same thing.'

'It helps their case, although that could be part of a fabricated story.'

'True. I'm taking Zander later to give him the penny tour, so I'll check then. CSI is finishing today, so if it was there, they'd have found it. Is Jerry coming home to face the music?'

'No. He's continuing his break and will visit the station when he gets back. Jerry said if we were fitting him up for murder, he may as well enjoy his last holiday.'

Zelensky shut his door, leaving Barton wondering if that made Jerry seem more guilty or less. He cracked on with his paperwork. Zander popped in with a few questions but was obviously spending time with his team and familiarising himself with the cases. It was nearly midday when Zander returned to Barton's office and took a seat.

'I had fifteen hundred emails,' he said.

'Impressive. Any of them work-related?'

'Just yours. Come on, let's go. I'm interested to nose around these houses.'

They left the department and went in Zander's car to Castor. It was a mild grey day, spitting with rain. Barton told him about Jerry's phone call.

'He would need to be crazy to think he'd get away with it a second time,' said Zander.

'Unless he's a genius and moved the focus of blame to the others, while secretly leaving the pump on.'

The gate to Bonaccorso's was open but a CSI van blocked the entrance. Zander parked up behind it, and they got out.

'Hang on a minute,' said Barton.

He strolled over to the Faversham' gate and discovered a new CCTV camera peering down on him from up high in a tree. The console had also been fixed. Barton tried the small passenger gate, but it was locked. He pressed the intercom, which flashed red. Barton stared up at the camera, but nobody came to let him in.

'What was that about?' asked Zander.

'I reckon Charles Faversham made out he was skint, so not

fixing the CCTV was plausible. Sandy believed the system to be broken, but it functioned inside.'

'Right, so he got a recording of her performances.'

'Some of them, yes. The speed with which it's been repaired now she's dead suggests he had the parts and funds all along.'

'That's pretty high on the rat-o-meter.'

'I know. I can't help thinking he's somehow involved, but he was obsessed with Sandy. Surely he wouldn't want her dead.'

'We've seen many jealous rages lead to devastating consequences.'

'True. Grief does strange things to people as well. He might be angry and looking for someone to blame.'

'Sounds like he has concerns for his safety if he's fixed the console and put a new camera up at the entrance.'

Barton gave the camera a final look. Charles wasn't the only one with concerns.

73

DCI BARTON

Barton and Zander grabbed a pair of wellies each from the boot of the car and put them on. They trudged to the front of the Bonaccorso property, past the van and the small vehicle under the tree. Nobody came when they pressed the bell, so they strolled around the back. They heard someone talking further down the garden.

A man was chatting on his mobile near the rear fence. He finished his call as they approached.

'DCI Barton?' he asked.

'Yes, you must be Paul. Thanks for waiting. This is DI Zander. Are you all done?'

'Yes, they've taken the stepping plates away and secured the property. I was just leaving a message for you to ask if you were on your way.'

Barton remembered he'd left his phone on silent so he could focus on his paperwork.

'Sorry. It's been a busy morning. Have you had any last-minute revelations?'

'Not really. You would have heard we discovered a laptop, and a young woman's clothes and personal items, which appeared out of kilter with the rest of the contents of the house. It looked like house-proud squatters had moved in and not much more than that. We've spoken to the owner about securing the property in case the key has been copied. He said just board the doors up. He'll sort it when he returns in the new year.'

'Wasn't he worried about any valuables?'

'That's what I asked him. He told me he's ninety-two, and only dying concerned him now, and he wasn't overly bothered by that either.'

Barton chuckled. 'So, the back of the garden isn't particularly secure?'

'Correct. If you come and look over, I'll show you.'

Paul didn't comment again until they were peering over the back fence, which wasn't much higher than Barton's chin. Vicious-looking razor-wire snaked along the top, but one panel was badly damaged so a person could push through. Barton suspected Poppy had done that.

'There are a lot of footprints around here,' said Paul. 'We reckon some are of a small trainer size, say a six, so likely a woman or girl, and there are big work-boot types as well.'

'Poppy's and Timothy's footprints.'

'Yes, probably.'

'And nothing found in the field out beyond the fence?'

'I'll come to that. There's pasture next to the river, but it's boggy underfoot. You wouldn't want to be in there after heavy rain. We found deep hoof marks from the cattle down the bottom. It would be like walking through treacle, but you could make your way up to Milton Bridge if you didn't mind getting filthy.' Paul left a short silence. 'There's one other thing.'

Barton turned to him. 'Sounds interesting.'

'There are a few odd prints that lead up to and past Bonaccorso's to the Bancroft place. They're kind of foot sized, but they left no sole markings. It's harder to say the size of them. They don't sink as far as the work boots. It might be a determined rambler, or maybe the girl came one day and put something over her shoes, so as not to get what she had on dirty, or perhaps someone else did the same thing.'

Paul didn't need to comment about it being an attempt to leave no evidence. Another person being involved would be concerning, but why would Poppy cover her shoes sometimes and not others?

Barton wobbled the fence where it was damaged.

'Can I slip through?' said Barton.

'Sure, we're finished now, so tread where you like.'

Barton and Zander hauled themselves through the broken fence and squelched into the grassy clumps beyond it, which sat submerged in surface water. The officers peered around.

'Poppy could easily walk here from Bretton and not be seen by any cameras,' said Barton. 'It's just a half-hour stroll through Nene Park.'

'Or someone might have come from the Orton side.'

'It's not ideal for burglars, though. Imagine lugging a heavy bag of swag over this ground.'

Zander moved gingerly forward. A large squelch sounded as the brown liquid sucked the welly off his right foot. He grabbed Barton's arm, almost pulling him over.

'Careful, Zander. If I fall down in this, I might never be seen again.'

Zander laughed his head off when he'd righted himself. 'I can see it now. In a million years, after humankind has had their meteorite moment, whatever species that arrives here next will eventually dig up your remains. You'll be on their news. Archaeologists today found something incredibly exciting in an area which was once called Cambridgeshire. The perfectly preserved fossil of what's been named a Bartonosaurus has been unearthed.'

Zander had to stop talking as he chuckled to himself. He continued with a big smile.

'The Bartonosaurus, a large bovine-type creature, was generally known to be docile. However, incidents of snappiness were common first thing in the morning. They are believed to have eaten their entire considerable body weight in a single day. Their main source of sustenance came from the consumption of something called fast food, although this has not been confirmed. Tests on the contents of the creature's stomach, which contained a slice of cheese, lettuce, beef patty, pickle, onion, and a special sauce, showed it to be some kind of poison. Perhaps that's how this enormous beast died.'

'Finished?' asked Barton as they made their way back.

'Yep. You were right. It is just like old times. I should have been a comedian.'

'As opposed to the jester you became?'

'Come on, you've got to admit that was funny.'

Barton smiled, but his focus had slipped to the case. There was even more uncertainty in his mind. Paul was waiting for them.

'I'm going to lock up now,' he said, 'if that's okay? Did you find anything?'

Barton shook his head. 'Those extra footmarks have me thinking.'

'In a week, all the DNA work will be back from the lab. We'll know more about who's been over the fences and in and out of the houses.'

Barton nodded, but would a week be too late? He and Zander strode to the middle of the garden. Where both the Favershams and Henry had a pool, Bonaccorso had a patio area.

'Did the warning sticker that was mentioned ever turn up?' asked Barton.

'No, which is suspicious. That's a job for you guys. You have another problem. The DNA evidence is likely to be contaminated by all the coming and going between the properties here. All the movement and folk intermingling could put people at a scene where they weren't present.'

Barton knew that meant it might not stand up in court.

'Brilliant. The fingerprints will help, though. I take it Poppy's and Timothy's are all through the Bonaccorso house.'

'Yes, Sandy's too. One of our guys had a bright moment yesterday. The homeowner has been away for two months, so we assumed the car hadn't moved since then.'

'It had leaves all over it.'

'Yes, but our investigator ran his hand over the windscreen. The leaves came off easily. The glass was clear underneath.'

'Couldn't they have fallen recently?'

'Take it from a man who knows. That windscreen was cleared. I wouldn't be surprised if the leaves were put back on.'

'Which means a person other than the owner drove it. It could be the car used to scare Sandy.'

'That's what I wondered.'

'Did you check for prints?'

'We tried. The steering wheel has been wiped.'

'DNA?'

'We didn't have time. Our guys can return tomorrow. We have both sets of keys for the vehicle.'

'Okay, get it done.'

'Sure. A final thing. I watched the news this morning, and some of what they reported doesn't seem right. Seeing as the investigation is still live, the press seem to have got their hands on a lot of specific details.'

'I agree,' said Barton. 'Someone's feeding them information, and not all of it is the truth.'

74

DCI BARTON

By Friday, most of the DNA evidence had filtered into the department, but it raised nothing Barton didn't already suspect. They needed clear physical or digital evidence to give proof beyond reasonable doubt there was foul play involved in Henry's or Sandy's deaths, but neither were present. The missing warning sticker made Sandy's demise much more likely to have been caused deliberately, but they were no wiser about who might have removed it.

Barton worked most of Saturday to get ahead. He now had four detective teams to look over, so he spent most of the time behind his desk. Even so, he'd relished the week. The part he'd enjoyed most about being the DCI before was dealing with multiple investigations. As DI, you generally had one prominent case. The Castor issues were going cold, and Zander's team had moved on to what they now believed was a pair of men attempting to rape women on the outskirts of villages south of Peterborough. The offenders had been successful for the first time in Folksworth on Thursday morning.

Barton had kept Sunday free. He had a short lie-in, then headed downstairs and woke up Gizmo, who gave him the look the tortured give their jailer. They took a leisurely stroll down Bogswell Lane to the Herlington Shopping Centre. Barton often felt melancholic when he took the gravel road, after the notorious Snow Killer had more than once used it to escape after a series of brutal murders when it had snowed.

Barton bought a selection of papers to read the news from all political angles and grabbed a pack of treats for the greyhound. Gizmo perked up on the way home after hearing the crinkle of the packet. Gizmo ate his chicken twists while Barton made a filter coffee and a bacon sandwich. They both collapsed on an armchair with a contented groan afterwards, as though they'd scaled the north face of the Eiger.

Barton's groan turned into a growl when he saw the front page of *The Mail on Sunday.* He began to read and almost hurled the paper out of the lounge window. The details of both cases were there. A pictured Timothy Steele came across as a devious, manipulative and predatory paedophile who'd stalked a poor innocent schoolgirl and then brutally and publicly exploited her for sexual and financial gain. Barton knew if he read the comments section of the online version, there would be calls for the return of capital punishment.

What shocked him more were the specifics on Frannie Bone. They had his life history, both criminal and familial, and a current photograph. In fact, both Frannie's and Timothy's faces would be in the minds of millions of readers. To add fuel to the fire, the articles also gave the areas of the city they lived in.

The residents of Peterborough now knew both men might be free the following week. Potentially, either of these heinous villains could be walking their streets.

'Shit,' he said, just as Holly entered the room in her yoga gear.

'Charming,' she replied.

'Sorry, the newspapers have got wind of all the details of Frannie's and Timothy's offences.'

'Is that a crime?'

'I don't like what these types of articles do. They encourage vigilante justice.'

'They've committed serious crimes. Do they deserve anonymity?'

'It's not as simple as that.'

Holly rolled her eyes, but then nodded for him to continue. 'Go on.'

'Everyone who works anywhere in the judicial system understands the issues. One of the biggest problems for the rehabilitation of criminals is housing. If time-served criminals are set free without a safe and secure place to live, it's highly likely they'll return to their previous ways.'

'Why should they get housing, when I know of mothers and their children who've been in a single room at a guest house for a year?'

'They shouldn't come in front of families, but they still need housing, or they'll commit more offences.'

'Then you lock them up for longer.'

'Yes, but if we had rehabilitated them, then they wouldn't have broken the law. Each crime stopped is a trauma saved for the potential victim. Society also wouldn't have to pay the high cost of a prison place.'

'We've had this argument about paedophiles before.'

'Do you mean discussion?'

'I have no sympathy for perverts abusing children.'

Barton didn't want to get into the complex nature of some offending. As a police officer, he had to believe in what he did, or they might as well bring back market day hangings.

There were four tenets to sending people to jail. Locking the felons up, which protected the public. Punishment, so society could see that people paid for their crimes, and deterrence, so everyone thought twice about committing crimes. Finally, there was rehabilitation.

'Obviously, many sex offenders can't be rehabilitated, but these two men don't appear to be public enemy number one. It might be as straightforward as Frannie not understanding or being able to comprehend society's rules, and Timothy making a mistake that he'll never repeat. My point today is, both men had housing. After these articles, it'll be tough for them to live where they were before. They might be lynched.'

Holly put on her best cowboy accent.

'Yeehaw, it's been years since I had me some fine ol' lynching fun.'

It was Barton's turn to roll his eyes, when the doorbell rang.

'Saved from a shoot-out by the bell,' said Holly.

She disappeared for a minute, then brought in Zander, who wore his tennis kit. Strictly speaking it was his football kit and gym kit too, but they were off to play tennis again. Zander scoffed at Barton.

'Aren't you ready?'

'Two minutes.'

Barton returned in ten. His shorts were still tight.

'It's lucky I was early,' said Zander. 'How about double or quits on the sherry?'

'No way. I'm looking forward to having a glass of the good stuff on Christmas Day next to the tree, perhaps with you serving it to me on a silver platter.'

'Don't include me in your fantasies, please.'

'I have a better idea for a wager.'

'That makes me nervous.'

'It'll be high stakes. We'll negotiate at the court.'

Holly handed Zander *The Mail on Sunday.* He scanned the cover. She waited for him to look up.

'John's worried those two won't have somewhere warm for Christmas.'

Zander raised an eyebrow. 'Isn't it the season of goodwill to all men?'

'Holly used to like strays at Christmas,' said Barton.

Holly gave him a look. 'I can't help seeing it from a mother's point of view.'

Zander bobbed his head.

'I completely understand. The point John will be getting at is, when people's prospects are terrible, they're more inclined to commit terrible crimes.'

75

DCI BARTON

The following week flew by, with no further evidence appearing. Barton spent most of it glued to his desk, but that was just as well. His ankle resembled jelly after his close defeat of Zander.

Barton woke up on Friday morning after a troubled night with a sense of unease. He trudged into the kitchen.

'What's got into you?' asked Holly.

'Something concerning popped into my head.'

'Right. You were grumbling all night like a faulty combine harvester.'

Luke came into the room and turned on all the lights, which Barton had just turned off.

'Do you know electricity isn't free?' he asked his youngest son.

Luke grinned at him. 'It is for children.'

Barton and Holly couldn't help chuckling. When the boy had gone, Barton gave Holly a quick hug.

'How has the human race prospered?' he asked. 'I've told the kids for decades to turn the lights off, shut the door, close the fridge, and it still hasn't sunk in.'

She squeezed him back.

'That's funny. I've been asking you ever since we met to pick up your towels and not leave the cupboards and drawers open. Every time you make something to eat, there's a trail of destruction, so I know exactly what you've had and how you've made it, even if I get home six hours later. And yet, I still love you. Humans, eh?'

Barton blew a raspberry at her. 'I've got an interesting day ahead. It's D-Day for the gardener, Timothy Steele. He's at court. The defence team revealed they received a handwritten letter from Poppy confessing to being the main driver of the idea for her to go on DreamViews. She also admitted to telling him she was sixteen.'

'Which doesn't make what he did okay.'

'Agreed. What he's done is serious, and using his sister's ID is no laughing matter either, but her confession means that his culpability has been heavily watered down from where we were two weeks ago.'

'What are you saying?'

'He has a clean record, which means by definition he is of good character. I still think Timothy's offence crosses the custody threshold, so it's a tough one for the judge.'

'So, there's a possibility he'll be released. Why are you concerned, then? I thought you felt he'd been coerced somewhat.'

'Timothy has lost everything. The home he rented, his job, his money, and his reputation. People like that are unstable. If he's going to do anything drastic, it's likely to be in the next few days.'

'Can't you have him watched?'

'Are you talking about illegal surveillance?'

'Very funny. What happened to that Frannie Bone character?'

'The magistrates gave him a month in custody on Wednesday, which was fair enough. They held his previous offending for the same issues against him, but it was clever from the beaks. You only serve half the sentence inside for non-violent offences. Frannie had been remanded while waiting sentence, so that means Frannie's also free today. He'll still have work with probation for the next twelve months, but he'll be out of jail.'

Holly nodded.

'Okay, let's hope he gets the help he needs. By the way, you're on turkey duty again this year. There's another shortage, so do some illegal surveillance at Lidl.'

Barton curled his lip but took his punishment.

He headed to the office at seven thirty. There was a note on his desk saying Gerald McCann was back from holiday and would be at home all morning or he could come to the station.

Barton was sitting next to Zander at eight o'clock, with Zander's team seated around them. In light of what was occurring, they'd all got in early.

Zander tapped his pen on the table.

'Listen in. Today might seem like the finish of the Castor investigation, but it could only be the beginning of the end. Frannie Bone has served half his time and will be freed a little after nine o'clock. A judge will sentence Timothy Steele later this morning. You all saw the newspapers last week. Hoffman and Zelensky, I want you to head down to the court. They're on the ball down there in case he's released. They know not to let him out the front, but let's find out where he's planning to go.'

'Will he talk to us after we put him in jail?' asked Minton.

'Sex offenders usually do,' said Malik. 'Many of them are educated men and women, and they don't need to be geniuses to understand they're at risk from the general public. Timothy will be wary.'

'We'll have a word with his solicitor before he's brought up from the dock,' said Zelensky. 'They won't want to see their client attacked outside the court.'

'Right,' said Zander. 'It's possible there'll be a crowd waiting for the prison transport to arrive, but that won't be a problem. Timothy was escorted from the jail first thing in a plain car, so if there are protesters, they won't have the opportunity to hammer on the sides of the van. Uniform are aware and will attend to be on the safe side.'

'Perhaps Audrey is planning to be there,' said Hoffman. 'It could be a flashpoint.'

Zander grimaced. It was another unknown.

'That's true. Anything else I've missed?'

'I wouldn't be surprised if Poppy turned up,' said Barton.

'Why would she do that?' asked Minton.

'Remember, she's more or less asked for leniency for Timothy.'

'The way she behaves is a little scary,' said Hoffman. 'Are you certain we can't charge her for something?'

'I feel sorry for her,' said Minton. 'She won't realise what this is all about until she's much older.'

Barton wasn't so sure.

'Okay,' said Zander. 'We also have Frannie Bone released from HMP Peterborough today. Him returning to his shared house is a poor idea. Luckily, Audrey has agreed to let him stay at hers for a while, seeing as Poppy isn't there at the moment. Leicester, you saw Audrey this week and thought she seemed extremely down.'

'Yes, she wasn't the combative force of a few weeks ago. She spoke slowly and quietly, with marginally less swearing than usual. Even when I mentioned Poppy, there appeared to be no drive to get her back.'

'I don't trust her,' said Minton. 'Any chance she was putting it on?'

'Possibly, but she has a lot to be down about. She's lost her daughter and her best friend.'

'Is she picking Frannie up from the nick?' asked Zander.

'She said not, which may mean she plans to be at court for Timothy's sentencing.'

'Okay, Leicester, you and Malik meet Frannie outside the gatehouse. Give him a lift back to Audrey's place if you can. It's rare for people to hang around outside prison waiting for cons to leave, so I shouldn't think you'll have any trouble. Did anyone speak to his probation worker?'

'I spoke to her,' said Malik. 'She has a meeting with him planned for next week, but she admitted to having her hands full with much more serious offenders. I mentioned what you said. She's open to the idea and said to ring her when you have more.'

Barton sucked his teeth. 'Let's think about today. If Frannie or Timothy are left to their own devices, or insist on going off on their own, they will struggle. Frannie is likely to repeat his criminal behaviour. If he goes anywhere near a library or any kids, he's straight back inside. If Timothy is released, he's liable to be furious about what's happened or devastated about his future. So, who might he be cross at?'

Hoffman counted on one hand.

'Audrey, Poppy, Jerry, Charles, and us?'

Barton looked at Zander.

'I don't think Timothy would attack us,' said Zander, 'but it sounds as if he was obsessed with Sandy. Would he consider her death to be Jerry's or Charles's fault? I'm not sure he'd be angry enough to hurt either, never mind Poppy or her mother.'

Barton rose from his seat.

'This is the perfect moment to mention the worrying thought I had last night. It's been niggling me that Audrey wasn't that shocked by Poppy's account on DreamViews. At first I thought it was just a reflection on her own moral standards, but perhaps she wasn't surprised because she'd already seen the photographs.'

'How would she have done that, sir?' asked Minton.

'Poppy and Audrey shared a computer. Poppy knew what her mum was up to. What if Audrey guessed or saw what Poppy was doing too?'

'What are you getting at?' asked Zander.

'It could be more information Audrey has withheld from us. Did she know about the account and simply not care?'

Barton left them to ponder that for a moment.

'Okay, I've kept this morning free. Court doesn't start until ten. Minton and I will visit Audrey now, then we'll speak to Jerry, and finally, Charles. I'm convinced one of the three has played some part in this, but I'll use the ploy of warning them of what's happening today as a reason for my being in touch.'

'All of them are potentially at risk if Timothy comes out and decides the only thing left in his life is revenge,' said Hoffman.

'Exactly,' said Zander. 'I'll run things from here.'

Barton caught the tiniest of looks from Zander and realised that his friend was back on song, and, after this case, Barton could step away. Zander smiled at him.

'Before you go, John has some other news.'

'A quick update. You guys have two new DCs starting next week, but DS Kelly Strange has decided she will not return to Major Crimes. She wants to try something else. That means a DS opportunity has arisen.'

Barton smiled at the buzz in the team as they left the office. Zander stayed behind.

'Kelly still happy with her choice?' asked Barton.

'Yep. She's excited about the future now, even though she has no firm plans, but that proves it was the right decision for her.'

'She'll be missed.'

'Not really,' said Zander. 'I've got DCI Barton to do my house calls for me.'

'Thanks for the opportunity, sir,' said Barton, but he wasn't smiling. 'I'm struggling to let this case go, Zander. It keeps playing on my mind.'

Zander took a deep breath. The Barton belly was rarely wrong.

76

THE VILLAGE KILLER

The inside knowledge I've been feeding to the press is doing its job. I've enjoyed being the source of anonymous tip-offs. It's a heady feeling, even though I've deliberately given the journos slightly incorrect facts or outright wrong information. I'm creating confusion to draw attention away from me. My next move is dependent on what happens today, but it's only a matter of time.

Inspector Barton and his team must be unsatisfied with how all this has ended, but police operations can't continue for too long without making progress. Other serious crimes will take precedence, and their resources will be dragged elsewhere. We'll become a cold case.

Perhaps the moment for me to leave has arrived. A fresh start could be just the thing. I am free now. Maybe it's better to stay like that. They'd struggle to find the truth if I weren't around.

But it's hard to think about leaving Sandy. A special ceremony, me and her, nobody else, would be the perfect way to say goodbye. I'm sure she'd understand. It will help me to move on emotionally and I could always come back.

Perhaps I'm not completely devoid of self-awareness. All my life, I believed I was infatuated with Sandy, but I was wrong.

The truth is, I've been obsessed with myself.

The first festive songs are trickling onto the airwaves. I'll also be lonely this Christmas, without her to hold, but there's bound to be a replacement for me to worship. Someone pretty and striking. My own company isn't enough. I need a person whose presence makes me feel alive. I need someone else to feed on.

Sandy and Henry won't be lonely, though. One more will be on their way to join them.

77

DCI BARTON

Barton and Minton drove to Audrey's house where they were forced to park much further up the road than her house. It was one of those estates where they hadn't built enough parking.

'Keeping your hands dirty, sir?' asked Minton as they left the car.

'Yes. I might not get too many more chances to get out into the field now I'm up to speed with the DCI role. You wouldn't believe my diary up until Christmas. I've got more on than Santa.'

Minton laughed. 'And he is hectic this time of year.'

'I suspect the North Pole operates like most large businesses. The big guy will wave for the glossy photos, while the elves do all the donkey work.'

Minton gave him a serious look and stopped walking. 'I want to mention something.'

Barton turned to her. 'Whenever my wife says that I'm usually on a one-way trip to the doghouse.'

'No, it's a compliment. You didn't say anything, but you've quietly been calling me Minton instead of Mini, and everyone else has dropped Mini, too. It's funny, but I feel more professional, and more a part of the team now the nickname has gone.'

'Giving confidence is something I've picked up over the years. DS Kelly Strange also taught me a bit about respect. I think you're fitting in well. You have a promising career ahead of you. It's time to leave the nickname behind.'

'Thank you. That means a lot.'

Barton strode on.

'These types of house calls can be difficult.'

'Yeah, there's nothing like a mother whose baby has been taken from her.'

Barton did a double take when Audrey answered the door. She had a wonderful chestnut woollen coat on over a cream blouse and gave them a full red-lipstick smile.

'Morning, Inspector. I don't remember ringing 999.'

'We came over for a quick chat about what's going on today.'

Audrey also wore eyeshadow and long fake lashes. Barton felt an intense assessing gaze upon him.

'You've got five minutes. Then I'm off to the slammer.'

'Frannie is a topic we'd like to discuss. I thought you weren't meeting him at the gate.'

Audrey pouted her lips, then spun around on her heels and retreated a few metres down the hall. Barton and Minton stepped inside and closed the door. He glimpsed into the kitchen. If anyone had seen Audrey out and about, they'd never have expected her to live in such a pigsty at home.

He noticed Minton's nose twitch. Barton wouldn't be accepting a drink, although judging by the crossed-arms Audrey in front of them, tapping her toe on the floor, refreshment would not be offered.

'I changed my mind. Now spit it out. He's released at nine.'

Barton chose his words deliberately.

'They release the sex offenders after the mainstream prisoners have had a chance to disperse, so nine thirty at the earliest.'

'I know what he is, Inspector. That's why two weeks in prison doesn't help him. He won't have been able to access any of the support he needs.'

'It's nice of you to have him here. I'd have been concerned if he only had that shared house to return to.'

'He's my brother. He might be a little odd, but Frannie's no rapist. I just want the best for him.'

Barton suspected Audrey wanted what was best for herself. 'It's such a shame the farm closed down.'

'Yes, it was perfect for Frannie. Now what's he going to do? This world isn't set up for people like him, and he's under supervision for an entire year.'

'They will be able to work with him,' said Barton.

Audrey shook her head.

'There's no chance he won't reoffend, which means he'll spend his existence in and out of jail. That's no future. One day, they'll find him swinging.'

'Isn't there any support you can access on the outside?' asked Minton.

Barton winced. The question would be a red flag to the Audrey bull.

'No, Miss Fix-it. We can't afford to go private, and he's not chronic enough for the NHS to be interested. It's ironic. If he stripped naked and rushed into a school assembly, they'd sit up and notice. If he appeared more of a danger, they would offer courses and therapy. Perhaps even a residential stay. Crazy thing is, if he was inside for the rest of his days, at least he'd settle there. There are no children for him to get into trouble with. He could build a life of sorts.'

Barton nodded. It was a sad thought, but for some men, the truth.

'Are you heading to the courthouse later today?'

'What the hell for?'

'To see if Timothy gets his just deserts.'

'I'm not sure I give a damn about him. His life is a disaster now. Pretty young lad like him has probably got a sore arse from his cell mate, and I told you, Poppy's no innocent.'

'Are you missing her?'

'Yeah, of course.'

Barton wasn't convinced. 'Do you have the cloud?'

'What do you mean?'

'Where everything is backed up from your computer?'

'Yes.'

'When my kids went online, I always knew what they were up to. Microsoft sent me reports each week. Their photos used to get stored. It was an opportunity for my wife and me to check and make sure they weren't exposing themselves to disturbing opinions or exploitation.'

A tight smile forced its way onto Audrey's face. 'Ah, you're wondering if I had a clue about what Poppy was up to beforehand. The answer to that is yes. She was behaving oddly. We each have an icon to click when we log on, so I checked hers. Clever girl. I found nothing, but I could tell she'd been using my icon because it told me I'd been logged on when I had been at work.'

'Do you feel guilty about exposing her to DreamViews?'

Audrey barked out a laugh. 'One of Poppy's classmates is pregnant. Sexting is rampant. All kids are exposed to hardcore porn nowadays. It's probably why the world is in such a mess.'

Barton didn't have much time left. Could he provoke her into making a mistake?

'We're not happy about Henry's and Sandy's deaths. Two incidents like that make me suspicious.'

'I hope you're not trying to pin either on me. Wasn't Henry's death from natural causes? Sandy's a terrible accident?'

'Both appear inconclusive.'

'Henry was our best customer.'

'Wasn't that someone called Speedster22?'

Audrey's playful expression disappeared. 'You don't miss much, Inspector. Unless, of course, you're Speedster22.'

Barton shook his head. 'When's Sandy's funeral?'

'Next Friday. The arsehole wouldn't let me help organise it. I wanted a big affair. She was such an amazing person. I suppose I should be thankful he told me the date. Now, as much as I'm enjoying this, I should crack on to meet Frannie or you lot might as well steam down to the nearest library.'

Barton and Minton walked to the door. Barton stood in the doorway for a moment after Minton had stepped outside. Audrey hadn't thrown them out after a minute, and she'd spoken eloquently and calmly. Even her vocabulary had changed, and, apart from her calling Charles an arsehole, he couldn't remember her swearing on this occasion.

Had she been expecting their visit and perhaps already prepared in her head? Was it all part of a plan? Audrey seemed the type to have one. Maybe the bolshy chaotic woman was a deflecting tactic, an act. A way of coping with what life had thrown at her.

'Don't think about doing anything daft, Audrey. You need to be completely above board from now on, or you'll struggle to get Poppy back.'

Audrey's smile was hard. 'I won't be doing anything at all.'

78

DCI BARTON

Barton and Minton headed to Market Deeping next, a village nine miles from Peterborough. They knocked on Jerry McCann's door and he opened up a few seconds later. After glancing at them both, he stepped out of the way and beckoned them past him. Jerry trudged after them, not resembling someone who had just returned from a relaxing holiday.

He escorted them into a lounge, which was sparse but functional. A typical bachelor's pad. There were only two photos on the wall. Barton checked out a faded picture of a pretty young girl, perhaps around eighteen.

'My daughter, Lorraine,' said Jerry. 'She's thirty-three now, but that's the most recent photo I've got.'

They all sat down.

'What happened?'

'The usual, I suppose. My wife and I drifted a bit. I thought we were okay, but she sprang a divorce on me one New Year's Day. She kept the house. I had the savings, which was fair. You know what young kids are like when they grow up. Lorraine was busy with her pals. Travelling the world. Contact sank to birthday cards and eventually the odd email. When they moved, I didn't get their new address. When the judge sent me to prison, all communication stopped. After I got out, I tried to locate them, but I couldn't. I haven't heard from them since.'

'That must be tough.'

'Yeah. House prices had gone mad by the time I left jail, too. My credit rating sucked, so I struggled to find anywhere to live. I was lucky to get this. The landlady's sweet and hasn't put the rent up as much as she could.'

'So, you had to keep working.'

'I didn't have a private pension. Money was tight. I rented a two-bed in the hope Lorraine might come to stay one day.' Jerry puffed out a breath. 'It has been hard, but I made a terrible mistake. Not a day goes by where I don't think about that.'

'You obviously know why we want to talk to you. DC Minton will be taking notes.'

'Yeah, of course. I'm not crazy. There's no way I would repeat the same blunder as before. I put a great big hazard sticker on the heat pump, and it was turned off.'

'We haven't found the sticker.'

Jerry's eyebrows knitted together.

'Someone must have pulled it off, then. Maybe Sandy. Perhaps she thought she'd warm the pool up, then turn it off before she got in, but forgot.'

That didn't sound convincing to Barton.

'Sadly, she can't back you up.'

'Look, I loved that woman.' Jerry nodded. 'Not in that way. From afar. Few gave me a chance when I'd served my sentence. Sandy was the first person to make me feel like a human being again. She was so pretty and so pleasant to be around. I'd have considered working there for free.'

'But you didn't.'

Jerry chuckled. 'No, I doubt anyone's that pretty. Charles paid a fair wage. It meant I could live okay. I've lost everything now.'

'He sacked you?'

'Yep. By text. Can't say I blame him.'

'Does he blame you?'

'For Sandy? I'm not sure. I one hundred per cent asked him not to turn the pump on. He knew about the sticker. You'd have had to remove the sticker to get it to work.'

'Didn't you tell Sandy?'

'Yes, I told her. I told Timothy. Everybody knew.'

Barton believed him, but when you had previous, it could be a difficult thing to convince others. He had the feeling that neither Audrey, nor Timothy, nor Charles would be in Jerry's corner if the finger of suspicion began to point his way.

'This should prove what I'm saying's true,' said Jerry, walking out of the room. He came back with a small cardboard box. 'I ordered this for the pump. Came while I was away. It's an RCD, which is basically an extra safety device. It'll cut out the power much quicker than a fuse would do.' Jerry took his phone out and opened his email. 'Look. Here's the confirmation from the electrician I booked to check it over. This was sent the day before Sandy died. I'd never risk anything like that again, especially with kids using the pool.'

Jerry didn't appear to be repeating a well-rehearsed monologue. Barton had an attempt at unsettling him.

'Have you come across something called DreamViews?'

'No, what is it?'

'A website or app to chat to women.'

Jerry slumped back in his seat.

'That's not my kind of thing. I'd love some companionship, but I don't want to pay for it. Over the years, I lost touch with my friends in Norwich, so I'm rattling around here on my own. My job was more than just a way to earn money. It was a connection to other people. Now it's gone. I can't even bring myself to attend the funeral.'

'Do you know when it is?'

'Yeah, I rang the crematorium yesterday to check. I sent flowers. That'll be the last extravagant thing I can afford for a while.'

'You've still got the other jobs on Love's Hill, haven't you?'

'One of them has cancelled on me, too. He heard about Sandy's death on the news and spoke to Charles.' Jerry scratched his head. 'I suppose that means Charles does blame me. The guy who sacked me had always been polite, but he was dismissive and rude when he called.'

'I'm sorry to hear that. I need to tell you there'll be a coroner's inquest, which you are legally obliged to cooperate with. You've said there was no malice involved on your part, but if the coroner finds you negligent, it could still go to court.'

'Brilliant. I tell you, it's times like these when I feel like giving up and doing something stupid.'

79

DCI BARTON

Barton and Minton left Deeping and arrived at the Favershams' property just as the entrance gate swung open. Minton drove through when the gap permitted and they found Charles looking smart in a black suit. He glared at them, then pointed to the side for them to move their car out of the way.

'What are you doing here?' asked Charles when they got out.

Barton noticed he also had a black tie on. 'Are you going to a funeral?'

'Yes, I am.'

'Anyone I know?'

'It's Sandy's, of course.'

Barton gasped. Even he hadn't expected that. The sneaky, underhand sod had told Audrey the wrong date. He clearly didn't want her showing up.

'That's devious and more than a touch harsh, Charles. Missing the service will devastate Audrey.'

'So what? Don't you think she's been deceitful with this Dream-Views thing? The pair of them at it like tunnelling rats. That

Audrey is unhinged. I wouldn't be surprised if she removed the sticker and put the pump on. She killed my Sandy.'

Charles seemed to know a little more than anticipated and, like Audrey, his speech sounded prepared. He looked smug.

'The information about the sticker is in this morning's papers in an article about the paedo gardener getting sentenced today. Maybe he removed it. The newspapers love all this. Beautiful woman, shock death, underage girl, naked pictures.'

'The press seem to have the inside line on the case.'

'It wasn't me if that's what you're thinking. I bet Audrey flogged the info to them.'

Charles's gaze bounced around his garden. He licked his lips.

Barton wasn't sure if it was nerves or because he was distracted.

'Are you struggling to come to terms with Sandy's passing?'

Charles crossed his arms.

'Naturally, but I've been focusing on the property and making plans to keep my mind off the devastating grief. I must say, cash flow is improving without Sandy's spending and not having to pay Jerry and Timothy.'

'Every cloud has a silver lining.'

'No, this cloud is black through and through. I miss my wife. You won't believe this. That bitch Audrey is still offering me videos and pictures through the site, even though Sandy's deceased. How sick is that? I suppose at least she doesn't know who I am.'

Barton's mouth dropped open. 'What?'

'Yes, don't think I didn't understand exactly what was happening under my own roof. The CCTV lie was a cunning ploy, wasn't it? One of the cameras pointed at the sofa. I could see her laptop screen, which showed me all I needed to track her down. Then I joined DreamViews.'

Barton blinked rapidly. 'You stalked her on DreamViews?'

'In a way, I had my life anew. Sandy and I used to chat for hours. Anonymously, of course.'

'Oh, my,' said Minton. 'You're Speedster22.'

Charles's aloof expression slipped from his face. His gaze switched from Barton to Minton and back. He shrugged.

'It was worth every penny.'

Barton rubbed a hand over his pate. 'Weren't you more or less giving her the money to be able to afford to leave you?'

'Sandy had made up her mind to go, and it wasn't just my cash they were receiving. I saw how busy they were. I watched them perform their dirty little videos, some of which I requested myself. Since she died, I've come to realise a relationship with her like that, even after she'd left me, would probably have been enough. I fell in love again.'

Barton's mind was reeling, but it started to make sense. Charles had such an obsession with Sandy, he would take anything rather than nothing. He hated sharing her with Audrey, though, and today would be his revenge. Audrey would be incandescent when she found out.

It wouldn't just be her who would feel aggrieved. Timothy's phone and laptop had revealed some interesting secrets. He had sneakily taken hundreds of pictures of Sandy while she moved around the house and gardens. He'd be unhappy about missing the funeral, too.

Barton thought back to what Jerry had told him. He'd said he'd phoned the crem, so his flowers must have been for today. Maybe Audrey had called, too, and discovered the real date for herself. That was where she was going, all dressed up.

Barton considered that for a moment. No, he didn't think so. Although he now understood that Audrey was quite the actor, and quite the liar, too, she would have been too consumed by rage at Charles's deceit to not show it.

Barton heard the soft thrum of powerful engines driving at slow speeds. The funeral limousine and the hearse pulled into the driveway. Identical wreaths surrounded the coffin.

'I have to leave,' said Charles. 'It's time to say fare thee well to my reason for living. My only love. I've paid for a lovely spot for her ashes to be buried. It's called the sanctum. The ashes go in a granite box and there are marble seats to sit on. It'll be a place I can visit whenever I want to be with her. Life will continue somehow, even though it's hard to imagine how.'

Barton shook his head as Charles strode towards the limousine and climbed in. Even in death, he wanted to control her.

The hearse backed out of the drive onto the main road, where it pulled over to wait for the other vehicle to catch up. Barton walked out of the gates and watched the two vehicles cruise away along Love's Hill.

Charles couldn't find it within himself to share the ceremony with Audrey or the others. Admittedly, Audrey would have attempted to take over the service and have made demands, but it was still a shame.

Funerals provided an opportunity to put quarrels to one side and move on. They were the last chance to forgive. Instead, Charles wanted to land a final blow. What did that say about the grieving widower?

80

REVEREND BRIDGES

Reverend Sid Bridges turned into Peterborough Crematorium with what felt like a large hollow cavern in his chest. It had been there ever since he'd spoken to the deceased's husband about the funeral arrangements. After parking in the empty car park, he felt his stomach sink further.

Sid grabbed his briefcase and stepped from the vehicle. It was a beautiful early winter's day, the air crisp and clear. A weak sun peered over the trees in the distance. Aside from the odd chirp from a passing bird, there was silence. It was the kind of day the living seldom paused to value.

That was the beauty of a funeral and made taking them a privilege. They forced people to pause. To think and appreciate. Live your life, but enjoy it, too, because we are all a breath away from receiving our own rich welcome into the eternal kingdom of our Lord and Saviour Jesus Christ.

Sid trailed towards the building and headed to the changing room. After putting his robes on, he walked back outside to greet the mourner. As he stepped through the entrance, a cold sensation enveloped him. Six men in black jackets stood in a line with their backs to him. The sun had disappeared behind a bank of cloud, and a soft breeze blew discarded leaves in an ominous circle around their feet.

Usually, there, of all places, Sid sensed the presence of God. This morning, he felt alone.

Two shining black cars arrived with sombre-faced drivers. Charles Faversham stepped out of the second one and watched closely, possessively, as his wife's oak coffin slid from the hearse. The six pallbearers raised it with ease. Charles followed the procession as it passed Sid at the door. He stopped and shook the clergyman's hand.

'Morning, Reverend. A sad but beautiful day.'

'My condolences, Charles.'

'Shall we begin?'

Sid nodded. He stepped heavy-legged back to the chapel and walked to the front. He stood behind the lectern and swallowed repeatedly to put moisture into his mouth. Something he'd never needed to do, even at the beginning of his vocation with the church. His voice came out as a croak, but he pushed on.

'We are here today to remember and celebrate the life of Sandy Catherine Faversham. A mother and a wife. As our late Queen said, grief is the price we pay for love. I begin this service with a quote from the Song of Solomon.

'*Place me like a seal over your heart, like a seal on your arm, for love is as strong as death, its jealousy unyielding as the grave.*

'*It burns like blazing fire, like a mighty flame.*'

Sid glanced up towards where the congregation stood. He had taken other funerals where only a single person had come. In fact, he had spoken when nobody else at all had been watching to witness the final passing to God's embrace.

This was different.

Sid believed Sandy Faversham had friends and loved ones who

would have gladly attended to say their farewells. The reason for their absence was the lone, menacing person before him. Charles Faversham rose like a proud soldier in front of a firing squad. His eyes blazed with an intensity that was light years beyond religious fervour, and, for the first time in his life, the reverend questioned his calling.

81

JUDGE MUKHERJEE

His Honour, Judge Alpesh Mukherjee, glanced up from his notes at the silent courtroom. It was at times like these he usually most enjoyed his role. Forty years he'd spent behind the bench, and not a day went by when he didn't feel the weight of his responsibility.

He glanced over at the dock where the young man whose life lay in his hands sat quivering. Mukherjee was half tempted to allow him to remain seated lest he fell, but justice must be seen to be served.

At the back of the court, amongst the packed observers, stood the individual who'd written the letter. The missive that had tempered the entire case. Poppy Madden, fourteen years old, complete with a full face of make-up, looked older than the poor wretch peering through the reinforced glass of the dock.

The judge sensed the presence of the coat of arms behind him. People often thought lawyers and court officials bowed to the judge when they entered the courtroom, but they were actually paying homage to the coat of arms, to show respect for the King's justice.

Mukherjee cleared his throat.

'Timothy Steele. You have pleaded guilty to the offence of the production of indecent images, and I must now sentence you. You have said you were unaware the person in question was under sixteen, a mitigating factor the Crown has agreed upon. Regardless, you accept it is your responsibility and yours alone to have done more to ascertain whether you were exploiting an underage child in this manner.'

Mukherjee paused as Timothy Steele's weeping echoed around the courtroom. Mukherjee's gaze drew back to Poppy Madden. She stared at him with a cold focus. Mukherjee had sentenced thousands of criminals to prison, and he had released thousands, too. His conviction rate had hovered just under eighty per cent for years. He'd developed a sense of who was guilty, but also who could be considered evil. Timothy Steele was definitely not the latter. For a few seconds, Mukherjee wondered whether the right person had been charged.

'Timothy Steele, will you please stand?'

Steele rose from his seat, head hanging low. With a grimace, he forced his chin up to bravely receive judgment.

'This is a serious offence, which passes the custody threshold. Having reflected on the facts, there must in this case be a custodial sentence.'

The courtroom erupted into murmurs. There was one cheer. Mukherjee paused again for quiet.

'And that is what I impose on you. The sentence will be for two years. In light of your previous good character, the acceptance of some responsibility by the victim, the fact Probation has ascertained your risk to the public to be low, with a low chance of further offending, and the reality of your business and reputation being ruined, I am inclined to suspend that sentence for a period of two years.'

It took longer for the room to return to silence after his latest comment.

'That means if you commit any further crimes during this time, you shall be brought back before this court, and two years will be added to any punishment awarded you for the new offence. Heed my comments, Mr Steele, or you'll be behind bars for a significant stretch. You are free to go.'

82

DS ZELENSKY

Zelensky had spoken to Timothy's solicitor out in the foyer before the judge had handed his decision down. They'd agreed that, if he was released, Zelensky and Minton would meet Timothy in the custody suite afterwards. Normally, the clerk unlocked the exit to the dock, and the accused would leave with a smile and a raised fist. In Timothy's case, he would depart via the back door behind him. The same one he'd arrived through from the cells.

That meant, by the time Zelensky had battled through the crowd outside the courtroom after the verdict, Timothy was already sitting at a table next to those cells. He was slumped, head tipped back, white as a sheet.

'You've had a decent result, Timothy,' said Zelensky.

He lowered his gaze. Empty eyes found hers. It was clear he was hanging by a thread.

'Brilliant,' he whispered.

'We wanted to have a quick word with you about your plans. Are you returning to your sister's?'

'I was meant to be, even after what I did, but then someone pushed dog shit through her letter box and someone else set fire to her wheelie bin. She wrote to me inside to tell me she'd changed her mind. Said it wouldn't be safe for me or her.'

'What will you do?'

'I spoke to a connection worker in the prison. He helps advise prisoners who are leaving. He reckoned there's little help for anyone at the moment due to a housing shortage. Us convicted kiddy fiddlers are way down the list. Luckily for me, it's so cold, they'll open up one of the churches. I'll be able to kip there for the night.'

Zelensky suspected it would still be dangerous wherever Timothy went if they guessed what he was in for, but where would he go otherwise? Occasionally Barton had authorised and paid for a cheap hotel stay for people they'd dealt with, but that was a rarity.

Zelensky stepped into the stairwell and rang Barton anyway. She gave him the judge's verdict, explained Timothy's predicament, and asked if he wanted to pay for a room.

'No, I'm afraid he has to present to the council. There are places for men like him, but there'll be a waiting list. The churches are better than the street. He'd freeze to death with the weather we've got coming.'

'I have a bad feeling about him,' said Zelensky. 'In fact, this whole case has me concerned. There are too many crazed individuals running around for this to be over.'

'I'm with you on that. Pass on my best wishes to Timothy. Tell him to hang in there.'

Zelensky had half expected Barton to wave his magic wand, but there was little he could do to stop whatever happened next. A few days in a Travelodge would only be a brief delay before any reality hit. She wasn't looking forward to dealing with the aftermath.

'Okay, will do,' said Zelensky. 'I'll give him a lift to wherever he wants to go.'

'I might be able to pull a few strings, but he'll have to look after himself in the meantime.'

'Understood. See you soon, sir.'

Zelensky returned to the custody suite. Timothy stared up at her through inflamed eyes. She repeated to him what Barton had told her.

'Oh, that's great. It seems I have two options.'

Timothy didn't volunteer the choices.

'What are they?' she asked.

'Rob a city bank and return to jail, or jump off the town bridge, and go to hell.'

83

THE VILLAGE KILLER

I stop the car, turn it off, and dip the lights. Church bells fill the air, calling the loyal few to Castor's Sunday evening service, but I'm not here to worship.

It's quiet when the clanging has stopped. The engine ticks and hums for a bit, but soon that too is silent, leaving just me and my thoughts. Ones that loop round and round.

Life is a series of circles. From the beginning in nappies, to ending up back in them ninety years later, if you're lucky. Relationships start, they end, businesses begin, they die. Friends come, then go. My latest loop started when I nearly ran Sandy down. Tonight is where I complete the circle.

God, I miss her. The colour has leached from my world. A day with Sandy in it was a day lived and enjoyed. I didn't even need to speak to or see her. Knowing she was in Castor was enough. I used to wonder what she was doing. Was she happy? Was she sad? Sometimes I daydreamed and imagined her thinking of me. I hope she did.

Memories are all I have left now she's gone.

A sneeze threatens to come, but I manage to stifle it. There are no worries about my DNA being in the car, but it's better if the evidence isn't dripping off the windscreen.

No matter. He's here now. Strolling up Love's Hill. Actually, it's not a stroll. His stride is plodding, shoulders sloped, even after he reaches the top of the rise. That's how you walk when the joy in your life has departed. The beam from the streetlight closest to me hits his face as he approaches it. What are you thinking, Charles? Do you feel regret?

When he's a few metres behind the car, I wind the window down and poke my head out of it.

'Evening, wanker.'

He jolts to a stop, but his expression doesn't change. Then, the flicker of an eyelid. The twitch of his right cheek.

'What are you doing here?'

'I came to see you.'

'Bugger off. You've done enough damage.'

I can feel my face flush, hot with hatred. 'I've done enough damage? You fucking killed her!'

I expect him to deny it. He rests an elbow on the roof of my car and leans down to me.

'Yes. Yes, I did, but it wasn't my plan. I knew she was leaving, and my life wouldn't be the same, so I took off the sticker, then turned the pump on.' He brings his face down to the level of mine, so we're almost kissing. 'Just for fun.'

Blood pounds in my ears. I raise my hand, aim for his chin to shove him away, but he steps back out of the way.

He laughs. 'Pathetic.'

'You must have known it could be fatal. I might have been killed.'

'I didn't expect her to die. She was fit and healthy. I thought nothing would happen, or she'd get a little buzz. A nasty shock at the most, and I'd hear a scream.'

'Then you'd come running. Her hero.'

'Something like that. She deserved a bit of pain. It would have been fair for the agony she's put me through.'

'She put *you* through? You're off your head!'

'Of course, you getting fried would have been a bonus. God must have had his gaze elsewhere.'

'Fuck you, Charles. I could run to the police.'

'Go on, I'd just deny it. Why would they believe an alkie loser like you? You're not innocent, anyway.'

My fists clench. 'You murdered Sandy. You might as well have held her head under the water yourself.'

'And not a minute has passed when I don't regret my actions. With every fibre of my being, I feel remorse, but what can I do? She's gone. We move on. I've got our son to consider.'

I scoff my reply. 'As if you give a shit about him. I rang the crematorium on Saturday. I suspected a snake like you would tell me the wrong time. Imagine my surprise when you'd told me the wrong day.'

'Ah, such a shame. You missed a beautiful service. Sorry about that.'

'Seems you gave everyone incorrect details. Even your own son didn't come back for the funeral.'

'It's the final grape harvest. He's the assistant manager, so it wasn't possible for him to get away. He'll be back in a few weeks, I'm sure of that. We'll arrange another ceremony.'

Charles has to be deluding himself. It's an excuse if ever I heard one, and a poor one at that. The harvesting would be long finished. Charles probably doesn't care. He's an awful human being.

'It doesn't seem fair that you get to carry on regardless.'

He snarls his reply. 'I'm punished every time I wake up.'

Charles slaps his hand on the roof of my car and strides up the road towards his house. I don't have long to think. I nod because it has to be today, but, let's face it, nothing he could have said or done would have changed that.

Encouragingly, he has more of a spring in his step now. I turn on the engine, pop up the lights. A car cruises past. It's the only one around. I wait for the vehicle to be out of sight, then I pull away.

He turns as I approach him. His face is relaxed. I bet he's secretly relieved his wife has gone, too. The game is over, and he's still standing, or so he thinks. I don't suppose he knows it was me who used Bonaccorso's car to scare Sandy. He won't have suspected that I killed Henry. He underestimates me and always has.

The smile drops from his face as I approach. Oh, now he's worried. He breaks into a lurching stagger, moving like a man who hasn't sprinted in a long time.

I hope Sandy didn't know she was going to die as she sank to the bottom. Charles, on the other hand, should be in no doubt what's about to occur, because I'm right behind him.

My knuckles grip white on the steering wheel. Red flames of stolen love scorch my shattered black heart. Pure justice burns in my mind, while cruel vengeance consumes my soul.

84

DCI BARTON

The phone call Barton had been hoping wouldn't come, but half expected, arrived at 6.30 a.m. on Monday. He had been so concerned on Friday night, he'd put a marked car outside Charles's house, but resources were too stretched to keep one there indefinitely, at least without stronger evidence.

Barton pressed answer as he swung his legs out of bed, but he didn't talk until he was downstairs.

'DCI Barton.'

'Sir, this is Control. A body was found on Love's Hill fifteen minutes ago. You're tagged to be rung for any incidents in that area.'

'Has the victim been identified?'

'No, Uniform has just arrived.'

'Male or female? Any idea how recently they passed?'

'Male. All I have at the moment is from the 999 call. The location is outside a property by the name of Bancroft's.'

'I know the place.'

'The person who found him is a care home assistant on her way to work. She's seen her fair share of dead people, and she said this one had been that way for a while. There's also an obvious injury to the victim's temple.'

'Okay. DI Zander and I have discussed this scenario. I'll pick him up and head over. We'll be at the scene in ten minutes.'

After texting Zander an ETA of five minutes, Barton headed upstairs and pulled on his clothes. He brushed his teeth, grabbed a coat and his car keys, and was out of the door. Zander was yawning outside his house when Barton turned up. He jumped in, rubbing his hands.

'Chilly.'

Barton gave him the details.

'Is it Charles?'

'I reckon so.'

'Could be Timothy.'

'It's going to be another hit-and-run.'

'This one more successful.'

'I suppose it could be something like a hammer blow instead of an RTC. Once we get confirmation of the victim, we'll head straight to the most likely suspect.'

'You're thinking Timothy.'

'He seemed the most unstable, and he's only just got out of jail. I'll know when I see him.'

Barton stepped on the gas when they reached the parkway, and a few minutes later they pulled up behind the flashing lights of two police response vehicles. They left their car and walked towards a PC who was finishing a call on his radio.

'Morning. Everything in order?' asked Barton.

'Yes, sir. There'll be a fair amount of traffic along this road shortly, so we'll keep one lane open. Whatever happened occurred a while ago. The body's stiff as a board, so he was likely killed last night.'

'Can I have a look to identify the body?'

'Of course, sir. Stay on the path. There's a thick tyre skid mark further up, which I suspect is where he was hit. The initial impact could have caused the injury, or perhaps he was launched into the air and struck that tree next to him. We turned him over to check for life, but the damage to the skull was obvious.'

Barton and Zander strolled over and stared down at the ruined face of Charles. The officer had followed him and raised an eyebrow.

'That's Charles Faversham,' said Barton. 'Lives next door at Paddock Green.'

'Looks like he almost made it home.'

'Right. We have a few people we're interested in speaking to about this. Do you know which churches have the rough sleepers in?'

'I'm pretty sure St Andrew's is Sunday and Monday nights.'

'Okay, well done with the scene. We'll leave you to get on with it.'

'Thank you, sir.'

Barton and Zander returned to Barton's Land Rover and set off. St Andrew's wasn't far. Barton knew the area, with the school from The Santa Killer case being nearby. He drove around the rear to the car park. A vicar greeted them when they approached the lit-up entrance.

Barton explained who they were looking for.

'Yes, he's here. We only had two in yesterday, but we can sleep six at a push. Do you have to disturb him?'

'Yes, I'm afraid so. When did he arrive?'

'Fairly late. He appeared a few sheets to the wind. We rarely let them in if they're drunk, but we only had one older gentleman in, and Timothy didn't seem the usual type to cause trouble.'

Barton hadn't seen Timothy's gardening van outside. They strode in after the vicar and stood next to his bed. He was awake.

'What now?' he groaned.

Barton's phone rang. He passed it to Zander, who turned and stepped away to answer it.

'What were you up to last night, Timothy?' asked Barton.

'Not much. The College Arms for most of the day, drowning my sorrows, but I got a call from the council late in the afternoon, saying they might have a room in a house-share in a couple of weeks. Great, eh? They said this place was open if I was desperate. I bought a meal to sober up, then walked here. I nearly froze to death on the way.'

'Where's your van?'

'Parked up at my sister's, but it's undrivable. Someone vandalised it while I was inside. I planned to sleep in the back, but the windows were smashed. I thought Rachel might let me stay one night. She was home, but wouldn't answer her door, and my key didn't work.'

Barton studied the young man. The predominant emotion flooding from Timothy was fear. Not fear for what he'd done, but worry for the future. This lad had tried his best in life, and he'd come up wanting. His mistakes had left him with nothing.

Barton reached into his pocket and handed him a piece of paper. 'This might be a help. It's an option, at least. I've spoken to Probation, and they've okayed it.'

Timothy stared at the note with a furrowed brow. Zander tapped Barton on the shoulder.

'We need to go, John. There's been a 999 call about the incident on Love's Hill. A man has confessed to killing Charles Faversham.'

85

DCI BARTON

Barton said goodbye to Timothy and the vicar, then left the church with Zander. Barton waited until they were on the way before he asked the pertinent question.

'Who's confessed?'

'Frannie Bone.'

'After all this and he ends up as a killer.'

'Perhaps he felt settled in prison and decided that was home from now on. I'm not sure whether that counts as being institutionalised. It's probably another example of someone who's fallen through the various safety nets, which are supposed to catch those struggling with life.'

Barton nodded. Frannie wouldn't be the last person who needed help at various points in his life and didn't receive it.

'It's certainly possible he decided jail was a better alternative than what Audrey suggested he'd end up doing.'

'Suicide?'

'Yes. If Frannie ran Charles over, he'll be spending the rest of his days behind bars.'

'A lot of his troubles would be over. Does this make him the person who attempted a hit-and-run on Sandy?'

'I can perhaps understand him wanting to hurt Charles, if Audrey's been badmouthing him, but not Sandy, so it doesn't seem likely. Frannie doesn't have much of a connection to either Charles or Sandy, and he hasn't got a vehicle.'

'I don't see him being able to hire one either, so maybe he borrowed Audrey's.'

'In that case, he can't be responsible for Sandy because Audrey's car wasn't picked up on any cameras at that time. The team watched the footage on the A47 for days, which is the route she'd have had to come, and her Mini never appeared.'

Zander tutted. 'I bet Audrey put him up to it. She has her revenge, he receives three square meals and a roof over his head for the next quarter of a century, and she gets him off her hands.'

'Yes, clever. So we need him to admit the truth. People like Frannie Bone are like Labradors.'

Zander had heard the comparison from Barton many times before. 'They can be intelligent or daft, but they don't have guile.'

'Right. Are Uniform en route?'

'They didn't know Frannie was staying at his sister's, so Control sent a unit to his house-share. I've redirected them to Audrey's place in Bretton. No sirens. We'll be there before them, though.'

'Audrey will help Frannie. She'll tell him to go no comment all the way through.'

'You're right, but you could argue she's been harbouring a criminal. A known stalker and now a dangerous murderer. What she wants is irrelevant. We might be able to get him to talk on his own.'

'Even though we suspect Frannie is capable of high function, we risk his solicitor arguing he didn't understand the caution, or even any of the questions, citing his learning difficulties, but it's worth a try.'

Barton tapped the steering wheel as he thought.

'Reckon you can handle Audrey? She'll be livid if we refuse to let her come to the station with him. I know you inspectors don't do much operational stuff.'

'Very funny, John. I think I'll manage.'

Barton pulled up behind Audrey's red Mini Cooper and blocked it in. He stared at Audrey's house. There was a light on in the hall. Barton walked towards her car's window and stared inside. Holly had owned the same model before she bought her Fiat 500. Minis were fun to drive. The car was bigger and heavier than it appeared, but still extremely fast in the lower gears.

Zander pointed at a big dint on the bonnet, and the near side light was cracked. He strolled up to the door and knocked.

'Listen a minute,' said Barton. 'I've got an idea. I'm going to make it seem like she'll be shut out of the interview, then allow her to be present. We'll talk to them both in the lounge.'

Through the frosted door glass, they could see the silhouette of a swiftly approaching figure.

'Yeah, why?'

'Trust me.'

Zander didn't have time to pull a face because Audrey had yanked open the door.

86

DCI BARTON

Audrey spoke with a monotone voice. Her eyes were dull, and she shrugged half-heartedly.

'Frannie's in the lounge. I can't believe what he's done.'

'I better have a word with him,' said Barton. 'Wait here with Zander.'

'Frannie won't say anything.'

'He was talkative enough to ring 999 and confess.'

Audrey's face had the same expression as when she'd defended Frannie before. Chin forward, body tensed. 'I've told him to make no comment except for his confession.'

'That's okay. He can repeat that after I've cautioned him.'

'I don't trust you lot. I demand to be present.'

'What you want isn't a concern of mine. There's a killer in that room. I need to arrest him.'

'He's got special needs. I should be with him, or he'll be scared.'

Barton glared at her, then he stared at the floor. His face relaxed slightly. 'Okay, but no interruptions. Not a word. Agreed?'

Audrey gave him an unconvincing nod. She burst past him into the lounge.

'Remember what we said,' she snapped.

Barton and Zander followed her. They found Frannie sitting at the far end of the sofa. Audrey perched next to him with her arm around his shoulders. Barton nodded at Zander, who took out his notebook. They sat in the two armchairs to the right of the sofa.

'Francis Bone,' said Barton. 'I'm arresting you on suspicion of murder.'

Frannie blinked, but that was his only response. Audrey's shrewd eyes bored into Barton's as he finished the caution. He waited for a comment from Frannie, which failed to arrive.

'You rang 999 and confessed to killing Charles Faversham. Is that true?'

The question didn't seem to mean much to Frannie. Barton noticed Audrey squeeze Frannie's shoulders. He reminded himself she was a clever woman. Her ex-husband had commented on her intelligence. He suspected she was easy to underestimate.

Audrey would know that for Frannie's admission of guilt to be convincing, he would need to explain precisely what he'd done. She also clearly understood that the simple soul beside her wouldn't cope with being questioned on his own. Her lack of awareness of police procedure gave Barton one shot.

'Speak up, Frannie,' said Audrey.

Frannie's glazed eyes cleared. He nodded. 'Yes, I'm responsible.'

'You used Audrey's car, didn't you?'

Frannie beamed at Audrey.

'Yes, I did.'

'When did you pass your driving test?' asked Barton.

Frannie's grin slipped.

'Hey!' said Audrey.

'You agreed to no talking.' Barton jabbed a finger at Audrey, then turned to her brother with a smile. 'You can drive, though, can't you, Frannie?'

'Yes, of course. They let me use the tractors on the farm, and the owner had an old truck. It was fun.'

Audrey took her arm from her brother's shoulders. Her fists clenched as she frantically tried to understand what was going on.

Barton stared at Zander while he scribbled in his pad. He hadn't expected Frannie to say he could drive. No matter, he would adjust. Barton smiled at Audrey, then Frannie.

'So,' said Barton. 'In summary, you took Audrey's keys, put the key in the ignition, took the car out of neutral and into drive, headed to Glinton, then ran Charles over.'

Frannie opened his mouth, but before he could reply, Audrey jumped off the sofa. Her body shook. She twisted around and screamed into Frannie's face. 'Shut your mouth, no comment!'

Frannie leaned away from her. His skin was so white, Barton could see a vein pulsing at his temple.

'It's okay, Audrey,' cried Frannie, before turning to Barton. 'I did do that. It was me!'

'No!' screamed Audrey, moving to block Barton's view of Frannie. Barton rose from his chair. He towered over her and looked across at her brother.

'Frannie,' shouted Barton. 'Your sister's car has manual gears, and it's keyless. There's no drive, and there is no ignition. Charles lives in Castor, not Glinton.'

Audrey put one hand to her mouth. She spun around to Frannie and fixed her eyes on him. Her face twisted into an ugly scowl. She used her other hand to take a small knife from her pocket. Barton stepped back and Zander got out of his seat.

'Oh, Frannie,' said Audrey. 'I'm so sorry.'

Instead of lunging at her brother, Audrey turned to the two big men in front of her and pointed the blade at them. Zander was closer and he raised his hands. It was clear his long reach would mean he could easily punch Audrey in the face before she had any chance of using the knife on him.

'Protect me, Frannie!' she screamed, backing away.

Frannie leapt up. Zander twisted and lifted his hands in defence, but Frannie's fist was already flying. It flashed over Zander's guard and thudded into the side of his jaw. Zander slumped to the floor at Barton's feet. A younger Barton would have thundered a punch into Frannie's nose, breaking bones, but he was older now. He took a step over Zander, grabbed Frannie by the lapels of his jacket, and threw him so hard onto the sofa that he rolled over the back of it.

Barton looked around at the open lounge door through which Audrey had disappeared out of view.

87

DCI BARTON

Barton's first thought was to consider who was in danger. If the response vehicle had arrived, the officers might be walking towards a charging, blade-wielding Audrey. He needed to warn them, but Audrey could be in the kitchen waiting behind the door with a bigger knife.

Barton moved to the curtains and pulled them aside. There was no marked car outside. He grabbed his phone and rang Control.

'This is DCI Barton in Bretton. I believe Audrey Madden has left her house on foot. Armed with a knife, she should be considered dangerous. Advise closest units.'

'Understood. A unit is en route and should be at your location in seconds. Other response vehicles will be dispatched. Description, please.'

'ICi. Brown shoulder-length hair, approximately fifty years old, black jeans, brown coat.'

Barton explained the situation in the house was under control and finished the call. He pulled Zander to his feet.

'Glass chin?' asked Barton.

'Lucky shot. Like you at tennis.'

Barton walked around the back of the sofa and helped Frannie up.

'I'm arresting you on suspicion of wasting police time, assaulting a police officer, and perverting the course of justice.'

Frannie shook his head. 'Does that still mean I go to prison?'

'It does.'

'Brilliant, I thought I'd messed it up.'

88

DCI BARTON

Barton wrapped his coat around his fist to use as a blocker in case Audrey was lurking somewhere, but he could feel the breeze through the house from the back door. He stepped outside and walked up the passageway, where a uniformed officer approached holding a Taser. Luckily, he recognised Barton.

It took only another fifteen minutes for four more police vehicles to arrive and the search to begin in earnest. Audrey would know these streets like the back of her hand, though. The Bretton estate was full of interconnected paths and winding alleys. Locating her might take time. If Audrey had mates in the area, she could even disappear.

Barton wasn't overly concerned. Only rich people, or those with wealthy friends, escaped into the ether and kept most of their life intact. With those of limited means, it was only a matter of time until they were found. The focus was on reducing further harm until that time.

Zander brought out a smiling Frannie and put him in the rear of a police car. To keep Frannie relaxed, he hadn't cuffed him, but he warned the officers to be vigilant. Barton came to stand next to him.

'You all right, Zander?'

'Yeah, fine. I'll stay and co-ordinate here if you fancy getting back and instructing the team.'

'You're the boss.'

Zander chuckled, but he glanced over at the vehicle with Frannie in and frowned.

'What a despicable monster to set her brother up like that.'

'Talk about misplaced loyalties. Funnily enough, if she was more of a criminal, she'd have known to bring him to the station. His solicitor could have read out his confession and answered no comment for him.'

'What do you reckon the CPS will charge Frannie with?'

'I'm not sure. He's obviously broken the terms of his licence, so he'll return to prison. I suspect Frannie will tell us everything over the next few days. It depends if we put in our report that he slipped DI Zander's clumsy block and knocked him out with a stunning overhand right.'

Zander laughed. 'I think we can record it as a tussle.'

Barton grinned. 'No worries. Right, I need a coffee. I'll ring you when I'm at the office and I've spoken to your guys there.'

Barton got back in his car and was about to turn left at the roundabout when he had an idea. He doubted Audrey had many friends, and none who would hide her from the police. Sandy had been taken from her, and so had her daughter, but she could still visit her best friend.

Barton indicated right, drove through three roundabouts, and took the turning for the crematorium. He found a space and parked up. A long queue of people in mostly black attire stretched out from the entrance, waiting to say their goodbyes.

Barton wandered around the side of the building and glanced up at the big chimney. He had been in his late thirties when he'd been here on a tour. The council had wanted to raise awareness of what happened in these places, and Barton had been interested. Holly had called him morbid. She'd also joked that it was a trap, and they'd stick him in the oven, although they might have to chop him up, so he would fit.

The fact that had stuck with him was, once the cremation finished, the remains, which resembled fine sand, would weigh roughly the same as the deceased's birth weight.

Barton spotted a gardener doing some weeding.

'Can you direct me to the sanctum, please?'

The man stopped his raking and stood to face Barton. He smiled kindly.

'It's over there, past those hedges.'

Barton took a few steps, then turned back. 'Have you seen a woman around fifty in a brown coat heading in the same direction?'

'Yes, she approached me a little while ago. Asked for directions, too. She was distressed. It can be hard when the bereavement is recent, but that's a lovely area to remember loved ones.'

'Thank you.'

Barton walked to where the man had pointed and took his phone out. He stood behind a hedge and peered around it. Two rows of granite benches faced each other. In between them sat what appeared to be stone boxes, which Barton assumed were the sanctums to contain the ashes. Only one person was in view with their back to him. They wore a light brown coat.

Barton rang Control.

'DCI Barton here. I'm at Peterborough Crematorium. Right of the main building. Sanctum section. I have eyes on Audrey Madden.'

There was a brief pause.

'Confirmed, DCI Barton. ETA first response unit four minutes.'

Barton contemplated waiting for them before he approached her, but the air was still, and so was Audrey. A feeling of peace permeated the area. Perhaps even a sense of God watching. Barton already suspected what he might find.

'Control. Have an ambulance dispatched. Approaching subject now. Will update. Hold the line.'

Barton stamped noisily through the loose gravel on the path but the seated person didn't move. Her head was bowed and as he got closer, he noticed a large puddle of dark liquid pooling under the bench. When he was a few metres from her, he spotted the knife that Audrey had pulled on them. It lay on the ground a few feet away. He put his mobile back to his ear.

'That's confirmed. Ambulance required asap. Appears self-inflicted knife wound.'

Barton cut the call and edged in front of Audrey. Her eyes were closed.

'Audrey, Audrey!'

Still she didn't move. Barton stepped to the side of the pool of blood and placed his finger on her neck to check for a pulse. After a few seconds, he thought he detected a faint one. Audrey's left sleeve was dark red and wet so Barton eased her left arm out of her coat. A huge slit ran along the inside of her forearm, oozing bright red liquid. He whipped off his belt and tied it just below the elbow. He pulled it extremely tight, knowing that anything less would be a futile effort. Audrey didn't make a sound.

With one hand holding the tourniquet, he slipped Audrey's coat all the way off. He pressed the material onto the deep cut and his large hand squeezed firmly. Sirens wailed in the distance. He crouched to the side of Audrey and spoke firmly but calmly in her ear.

'Stay with me, Audrey. Hang on. Help is coming.' After a moment's consideration, he urged her again. 'Open your eyes! Your daughter will need you. Think of Poppy.'

89

TIMOTHY STEELE

Timothy Steele stepped out of the taxi and took a deep breath. A week had passed since he'd taken the call on his mobile. Even though he was probably being silly, he couldn't shake off the thought it was all a big mistake. Perhaps he'd misheard. So much had gone wrong for him lately that he'd stopped believing in good luck.

He handed over twenty pounds of his dwindling funds. 'Can you wait here for a minute, mate, while I check?'

'No problem.'

Timothy strolled over to the door and knocked. After what couldn't have been ten seconds, but felt like a year, the door swung open.

'Morning, Timothy.'

'Morning.'

'Step inside. *Mi casa, su casa*, and all that.'

'Look, Jerry, before I come in, I need to double-check it's okay for me to stay. You can change your mind. I wouldn't hold it against you.'

'Don't be daft. I want to help. I understand what it's like to have nothing and begin from scratch. It wasn't so long ago when I left prison empty-handed.'

'I won't let you down.'

'I know. Hey, I was thinking, we should start a business, combine our skills. It would be handy for the bigger jobs.'

'That's a great idea, but I don't need to live with you for that.'

'We can talk about our plans later. I've bought M&S biscuits. Jam creams. Your favourites. We'll have a cuppa in a minute. Is your stuff in the taxi still?'

'Yeah.'

'Come on, I'll give you a hand.'

'If you're sure.'

'I'm a lonely old man, and one who's looking forward to having some company. Help with the rent would be useful, too. Besides, that big inspector said he'd throw me in jail if I didn't offer.'

90

FRANNIE BONE

Officer Matley unlocked the final double door to let Frannie into the visitors' entrance area, which the prisoners passed through on release day.

'See you next time, Frannie,' said Matley with a grin.

'I'll look forward to it, sir.'

Matley shook his head, but he couldn't help liking Frannie. He had a sunny disposition, which contrasted with most of the reprobates he banged up.

'Sir?' said Frannie.

'What is it?'

'My duvet was a little thin on this visit, so I'd appreciate you looking into that.'

Matley threw his shoulders back and laughed. 'Get out of here, and don't come back, or your arse will enjoy a close-up of my size tens.'

Clutching an opaque plastic bag that contained his meagre belongings, Frannie fumbled at the exit door to freedom. A blast of frigid air blew the last vestiges of heat from his body as he stepped outside. He wore the clothes they had arrested him in, and he'd been wearing only a thin jumper.

Frannie had struggled to force any breakfast down, and now he felt faint. He glanced over at the car park with his eyes watering from the bitter wind. There was no movement there. Had they forgotten? Or had all the plans fallen through?

Frannie shivered as he trudged up the path. He almost wished he were back in the warmth of the healthcare wing where they'd put him for monitoring. They were nice in there. Even the screws seemed interested in how you were doing.

Yet he felt more level-headed than he had in decades. Whatever pills they'd given him were working.

One of the vehicles at the edge of the car park flashed its lights. Frannie swallowed and stepped towards it. He knew little about cars, having never driven any before, but it appeared big, shiny and new. Faster than the truck the farmer owned. The driver's door opened and a man with receding hair climbed out of the vehicle. He was dressed in a suit and a long moleskin coat and looked like a lawyer. Frannie's stride shortened.

'Francis Bone?'

Frannie managed a nod. He was just able to shake the proffered hand.

'My name's Robert Young. Did you receive the letter saying I would meet you here today and give you a lift?'

Frannie nodded once more.

'I hope the message was clear, but, to make it simple, I'm the executor of a charitable trust with deep pockets. A man I've come to respect over the last few weeks explained your situation to me, and you're exactly the type of person we'd love to help.'

Frannie squinted, unable to take in his words.

'So, the farm is opening up again?'

'I've purchased the buildings and obtained permission to move in and pay rent immediately while the paperwork goes through. Whether we go back to how it was run before is for us all to work out. I like the idea of a commune, where people can rest and recover, search for jobs, make friends, get started again in life.'

Frannie's eyes searched out Robert's. 'It's true, then.'

'Yes, Frannie. You're going home.'

91

DCI BARTON

Holly gave Barton a small list for the supermarket the day before Christmas. She was worried that two jars of cranberry sauce wouldn't be enough. She did most of the preparation beforehand, so the big day was mostly a case of reheating. Kelly Strange was bringing over her microwave so they could get everyone seated and dining at the same time.

Barton had forgotten his local Sainsbury's opened at ten on a Sunday, so he stood quietly with everyone else who'd made the same mistake and come to pick up a few last items. Barton beamed. He liked Sainsbury's. It was where his mum had shopped when he was growing up. He often experienced nostalgia when he walked around the store, and their crunchy white rolls were more addictive than crack cocaine. Barton steeled himself and tried not to picture the aisle from where they were calling to him. Be strong. Be in control.

He happened to glance over his shoulder and saw a familiar face and it took him a moment to place the girl. It was Poppy, free of make-up, in a pair of loose jeans and a scruffy hoodie, walking next to a friend. Her hair was loosely tied up with a scrunchie. The pair of them giggled, hips rocking, eyes half shut. It was the type of laugh that adults rarely do as they age. Barton grinned just as she looked over at him.

Poppy slowly stopped laughing. She stared at the throng around Barton, then beckoned him over. It was a strangely adult mannerism for a teenager. Barton picked his way through the crowd. By the time he reached Poppy, her friend had wandered away.

'Hello, sir. Checking up on me?'

'Picking up a few more mince pies. It seems the elves have been getting at them early this year. We're short on Brussels sprouts, too, but I've no idea why that is.'

'They're gross.'

'My thoughts entirely.'

'I was thinking about calling you.'

'Okay, what about?'

'My mum. I've not heard anything. She's rung a few times, but I was out, and she wouldn't speak to my dad.'

'It must be a lot for you to take in.'

Poppy glanced around her, as if to make sure nobody was listening in.

'I'm not particularly surprised by what she did. She always had a temper, and it was obvious she wanted Uncle Frannie to be looked after in jail for the rest of his life. He didn't mind it there. Killing that idiot, Charles, was probably the icing on the Christmas cake.'

'There's no justification for what she did.'

Poppy exhaled deeply. 'No, I guess not. What about the others who died? Did she have anything to do with them?'

'She's admitted to running Charles over, and that's enough for the moment.'

'What's going to happen to her?'

'The judge has no option but to impose a life sentence. There are aggravating factors, such as trying to pin it on Frannie, which means there was significant planning. I suppose a mitigating factor was her best friend had died. She blamed that on Charles, but I don't think you'll be seeing much of her for at least twenty-five years.'

'She'll be seventy-odd when she's released. Freaky. Frannie's okay, though, isn't he?'

Barton and Zander hadn't put Frannie's punch down in their report. They'd said Zander had got caught by a swinging arm. Zander wasn't overkeen on it being public knowledge, and they felt Frannie could do with a break, when he'd had so few.

'Yes. Robert rang me. He's the guy who runs the charity which is helping him. Frannie's like a pig in shit at the farm.'

Poppy scowled. 'Is that a good thing?'

'Pigs seem to enjoy it.'

'Thank you for coming over, but let me tell you this. I will not end up like my mum. No way. One day, I'm gonna be rich, and I'll be a star. I won't ever have to worry about money. I'll be happy.'

She held his gaze with a defiant stare. Her friend returned and, noticing the tension, linked arms with Poppy and steered her away. Poppy glanced over her shoulder after a few strides.

'Merry Christmas, sir.'

'Merry Christmas, Poppy,' said Barton, but they had gone.

The last of the queue filtered through the entrance into Sainsbury's. He trailed after them, but his smile had disappeared.

92

DCI BARTON

On Christmas Day, Barton answered his door in his snazzy jumper, newly opened that morning, which proudly said, 'I'm full of Christmas beer'. Waiting there was his old friend, Mortis.

'Ah, excellent. I wasn't sure you'd show.'

'I had a phone call from your wife, and I got the impression non-attendance would have led to me swimming with the fishes.'

Barton chuckled. 'Yes, probably safest to come, especially as you look the part.'

Mortis had grown a grey beard, which appeared smart and trimmed.

'I knew I should have shaved it off.'

'I love it.'

'It sounds like you are full of beer,' said Mortis, handing him a bottle of something in wrapping paper.

'It's the best way to cope with the noise.'

Barton had a large lounge, which contained most of his old team. Hoffman and Zelensky were deep in conversation on one sofa, and Minton and Leicester appeared to be getting friendly on another. Zander was pulling one of the twins out of Barton's

Christmas tree, which was listing badly. Some fool had bought the other twin a drum, which he was hammering with a Pokémon figure. Luke and Layla were arguing over the TV remote.

'Christ,' said Mortis. 'What idiot bought him a drum?'

Barton declined to answer.

Mortis stared at Zander. 'Is he wearing an elf outfit?'

'Yep, he lost a bet.'

'It's like a zoo in here.'

'Yes, but one full of love,' replied Barton, pointing above them at the door lintel, where a sprig of mistletoe was hanging. He gave the pathologist a wink.

'Clear off,' said Mortis, 'and get me a drink. Something strong.'

Barton left the room and came back with Holly and Kelly. The women had rosy cheeks, which they'd claimed was from basting the turkey. Barton had a tray full of small glasses. Sherry in all but two of them, which contained Coca-Cola.

'I want to try what you're having,' said Layla upon being offered the Coke.

Barton let her have a sip of his.

'Eugh!'

Barton raised his glass to all corners of the room. 'To friends, new and old!'

His toast was reciprocated, then Holly and Kelly returned to the kitchen for the turkey, and the half-drunk bottle of Chablis that Barton had spotted earlier on the worktop.

Mortis took another sip of his drink.

'This is bloody fine stuff.'

'Tastes like victory,' replied Barton.

Mortis began to frown at Barton, but Luke had wandered over to stand in front of him.

'Are you Father Christmas?' he asked him with an impish grin.

'Yes,' replied Mortis, deadpan.

'Excellent. I need to return and exchange a few things. You can take them back with you and speed everything up.'

'I don't work Christmas Day.'

Luke turned to Barton. 'Unbelievable, and Santa's breath smells funny. Talk about ruining the mystery.'

Mortis almost choked with laughing so hard.

'Can you take a picture of me and the elf, please?' asked Barton, handing Mortis his phone and beckoning Zander over.

Barton and Zander put their arms around each other and raised their little sherry glasses in their big hands.

'Lovely,' said Mortis, taking the shot. 'Although, it's not a sight you see every day. You're like a pair of giant sloths at a tea party.'

They carried on drinking and chatting for the next hour, then Zander nipped to the kitchen and brought Holly and Kelly back again. Holly came and stood next to Barton, while Zander dropped down on one knee in front of Kelly.

The adults went deadly quiet. Even the drummer paused.

'Wow,' whispered Barton to his wife. 'How much sherry has he had?'

Barton was rewarded with an elbow to the ribs. He pulled Holly close to him as Kelly made Zander wait.

'Yes!'

Barton glanced around the room, feeling a lucky man, as everyone cheered.

AUTHOR'S NOTE

When I write, I often plan one thing and another creeps in. This novel was supposed to be just about the nature of some relationships. A tale about how folk find themselves in situations that aren't healthy, but leaving feels terrible too. I wanted to include how other people can make tough lives tolerable because humans are all about connection. The book certainly headed off at a tangent. Poppy's story demanded to be told.

Her issues are called parentification, which often occurs in homes where one or both parents are absent, emotionally unavailable, or have addictions. Children who 'parentify' are liable to grow up too fast and miss out on important developmental milestones. The experience can have an extreme and enduring effect on a child's mental, physical and emotional health, which leads to a multitude of problems in adulthood.

www.parent4success.com is a useful source of information around the topic, both for parents and for children. Sometimes, through sickness, there's no other option but for the kids to help out more than is ideal. For those who've been through it, the first step in recovery is to acknowledge their childhood wasn't normal.

With regards to the DreamViews plotline, a friend of mine has a profile on one of those sites. It took me a while to get my head around it. Interestingly, like Charles, her partner doesn't know. She also messages customers while they watch TV. Her major concern is to hide how wealthy she is becoming.

As for Barton, I have one more up my sleeve for next Christmas when DCI Cox returns, but my next book will be another Ashley Knight story, beginning with an incident near Horsey Mere. There'll be some jail scenes at HMP Peterborough, too, so John's going to be in a few chapters as the National Crime Agency helps Norfolk MIT tackle the Typhon organisation. Please head to Amazon and leave a review for *The Village Killer*. If you wish, you can read the blurbs or pre-order both books while you're there!

Writing this one was a lot of fun. My publisher has told me I've sold over half a million books for them now, so thanks for being along for the ride.

ACKNOWLEDGEMENTS

It takes a village to raise a child. Sometimes a book feels the same way. A special mention to Paul Lautman for this one. Your assistance and special mind are most appreciated.

As always, a big thank you to my beta team and proofreaders. Kath Middleton, Trish Halstead, Jeanette Curran, Alex Williams, Alex Knell, Jos Knell, Diane Saxon and Richard Burke all deserve a mention, as do the team at Boldwood Books, who are growing so fast, there are too many to mention.

And of course, I appreciate the readers. You can follow or message me on social media. I love hearing your thoughts, especially when it concerns Ashley or John.

All the best,

Ross.

ABOUT THE AUTHOR

Ross Greenwood is the author of crime thrillers. Before becoming a full-time writer he was most recently a prison officer and so worked everyday with murderers, rapists and thieves for four years. He lives in Peterborough.

Sign up to Ross Greenwood's mailing list for news, competitions and updates on future books.

Follow Ross on social media:

instagram.com/rossg555

x.com/greenwoodross

facebook.com/RossGreenwoodAuthor

bookbub.com/authors/ross-greenwood

ALSO BY ROSS GREENWOOD

The DI Barton Series

The Snow Killer

The Soul Killer

The Ice Killer

The Cold Killer

The Fire Killer

The Santa Killer

The Village Killer

DS Knight Series

Death on Cromer Beach

Dear at Paradise Park

Death in Bacton Wood

Standalones

Prisoner

Jail Break

Survivor

Lifer

Chancer

Hunter

THE

Murder

LIST

**THE MURDER LIST IS A NEWSLETTER
DEDICATED TO ALL THINGS CRIME AND
THRILLER FICTION!**

**SIGN UP TO MAKE SURE YOU'RE ON OUR
HIT LIST FOR GRIPPING PAGE-TURNERS
AND HEARTSTOPPING READS.**

SIGN UP TO OUR NEWSLETTER

BIT.LY/THEMURDERLISTNEWS

Boldwood

Boldwood Books is an award-winning fiction publishing company seeking out the best stories from around the world.

Find out more at www.boldwoodbooks.com

Join our reader community for brilliant books, competitions and offers!

Follow us
@BoldwoodBooks
@TheBoldBookClub

Sign up to our weekly deals newsletter

https://bit.ly/BoldwoodBNewsletter

Printed in Great Britain
by Amazon

50113524R00218